It would be hard to find a more lucid an[c] classical theism, defending God's love an[c] his simplicity, timelessness, immutability a[.] jargon and obscurity, it is also imbued with ... chapter ending with a meditation, remindin[g] ...c dealing not merely with ideas but a living, holy God.
Jeremy Begbie, Research Professor of Theology, Duke University; Senior Member, Wolfson College, Cambridge

In a clear introduction to the central truths of our faith, Peter Sanlon opens up the wonder of our relationship with God and of his great love for us. Attentive to the needs of the modern reader, he applies Christian teaching to everyday reality and helps us draw nearer to that Presence who is our life and our joy.
Gerald Bray, Research Professor, Beeson Divinity School

Here is a clear and winsome apologia for classical theism. Peter Sanlon argues for a truly passionate God, beautiful in his 'otherness'. Few will read this without profit.
Michael Reeves, Theologian-at-Large, Wales Evangelical School of Theology

Peter Sanlon is a fine theologian with a deeply pastoral heart. Those two characteristics are combined creatively and intriguingly in this fine study of classic Christian theology.
Graham Tomlin, Dean of St Mellitus College, London

The doctrine of God is foundational for Christian faith and yet is one of those areas where the complexity of certain concepts can make important realities difficult to grasp. Thus, it is a pleasure to commend Peter Sanlon's brief book as a helpful introduction to the key aspects of this most important topic.
Carl R. Trueman, Paul Woolley Professor of Church History, Westminster Theological Seminary

SIMPLY
GOD

In memory of Anastasia Joy Sanlon

'Behold, I create new heavens
and a new earth,
and the former things shall not be remembered
or come into mind. . . .
No more shall there be in it
an infant who lives but a few days.'
(Isaiah 65:17, 20)

PETER SANLON

SIMPLY
GOD

Recovering the classical Trinity

Foreword by Paul Helm

INTER-VARSITY PRESS
Norton Street, Nottingham NG7 3HR, England
Email: ivp@ivpbooks.com
Website: www.ivpbooks.com

First published 2014

British Library Cataloguing in Publication Data
A catalogue record for this book is available from the British Library.

ISBN: 978-1-78359-104-6

Set in Monotype Garamond 11/13pt
Typeset in Great Britain by CRB Associates, Potterhanworth, Lincolnshire
Printed and bound in Great Britain by Ashford Colour Press Ltd, Gosport,
Hampshire

*Inter-Varsity Press publishes Christian books that are true to the Bible and that
communicate the gospel, develop discipleship and strengthen the church for its mission
in the world.*

*Inter-Varsity Press is closely linked with the Universities and Colleges Christian
Fellowship, a student movement connecting Christian Unions in universities and colleges
throughout Great Britain, and a member movement of the International Fellowship
of Evangelical Students. Website: www.uccf.org.uk.*

CONTENTS

FOREWORD

It would have been 1999 when I was asked by Peter Sanlon to come to speak to the Oxford evangelical student theology society about Christian theism. Unfortunately I wasn't able to accept the invitation. Little did I think then that Peter would develop his commitment to classical theism and that it would in due course lead to this book.

In it Peter is summoning the reader to a more disciplined and focused thinking about God, based upon the knowledge that he is our creator, and we are his creatures. The difference between the Creator and his creatures is fundamental, and too often forgotten. God is not simply 'more than' we are. Between us and himself there is a difference in order, not in quantity or scale. And in doing this Peter is recalling us to the faith of the church.

But to think consistently and clearly about God our creator, who is or has become our Redeemer in Christ, is unfamiliar and not easy. It calls for discipline, and also patience. Sometimes people object to the discipline of theology because it is an attempt to 'master' God, to pin him down, or to put him in a box. Peter warns us that the very reverse is the case. We have become used to thinking of God as our buddy, as a familiar friend. But this is lazy, and presumptuous. He is altogether beyond our imagination, too wonderful and strange to be fully captured in our words. This is so even though he reveals himself in our words.

The basic posture we must adopt is to think of God, who transcends our own fleeting existence in space and time, as coming down to us. He comes down to us in his revelation, adapting himself to our language, using figures and similes and questions in order to address us. And he comes down in the incarnation, which is not God's becoming man, as milk becomes cheese, or wood becomes ash. This God, immaculate and immutable in his perfection, takes on human nature, and so humbles himself to be our mediator and friend.

To begin to grasp this we must learn a new language that befits talking about the Creator who transcends us. The church has coined words like 'Trinity' and 'impute' to refer to divine realities, God is three and one, and in Christ, has reckoned our sins to himself, and his righteousness to us. In a similar way there is a language about God that the church, from the patristic period onwards, has adopted to speak – daringly, it must be said – of God as he is in himself. It is best to think of such language not as the language of science, but rather as a grammar, as Peter suggests. It is not that theologians can see further than anyone else, or provide explanations for us, like engineers do, for example. They attend to grammar, theological grammar, to help us 'stammer' (John Calvin, *Commentary on Genesis*, 35:7) about God, even though by it we cannot comprehend him as he is in himself. For how can the finite encompass the infinite? Rather we talk of him in such a way as not to confound the Creator with any of his creatures.

Peter shows this first by emphasizing the simplicity of God – not a simplicity to be pitied, but the oneness or unity that befits the creator of the ends of the earth. The Lord our God is one Lord, but a creature is composed of parts more basic than he is. In nature there seems to be divisibility all the way down. But in God, the creator of nature, there is unity, indivisibility. One way of thinking about this is that God does not consist of parts more basic than he is, as we and all other creatures do. To think that would reduce him to the level of a creature. Trinitarianism is not that God has one part who is the Father, another part the Son and another the Holy Spirit. If we are going to be faithful to the biblical witness, we must distinguish three persons in the Trinity, but these three persons are not three parts. Mysterious? Certainly. Incoherent? Certainly not, Peter affirms.

So we begin to learn to talk of God, the God of the Bible, when we construe his unity in this sense. We can talk some more about him if we consider the question of time. God is not subject to its vicissitudes: he is not bound by time. For one thing, time is a sign of change. We change by gaining and losing parts, by coming to have thoughts and beliefs, and modifying them, and we have brain cells and body muscles. We are in time. But God has created the universe, with ourselves a part in it, from a standpoint outside time. He does not change, for he alone has immortality (1 Tim. 6:16). So to talk of the age of God, or his memories and anticipations, would be to talk of him in creaturely, not in creatorly, terms.

Being atemporal, God is immutable. This does not mean that he has decided to be immutable, but that he is. To suppose his immutability rested upon his decision is confused. For on what would we base our confidence? So God is essentially or necessarily immutable. As the writer of the letter to the Hebrews shows, such immutability is one of God's great-making properties (Heb. 6:13–18). He is immutable by nature.

And closely connected with God's simplicity and his atemporality is his aseity, an unfamiliar word, as Peter notes, yet the idea behind it is a vital one. As we noted when touching on God's simplicity, he is not made from parts. He is not made from anything more basic than he is. That is the root idea behind the affirmation of the underivedness of God, that God is *a se*, 'from himself'. Aseity does not mean that God has made himself, which *would* be incoherent, but that the child's question 'God made me, but who made God?' rests upon a misunderstanding. In learning the grammar of his faith, the child has slipped up, misspoken. But the mistake is easily corrected. How could anything or anyone have made God, for he is the creator of everything except himself? He is uncreated. It makes no sense to say that God was made, for to do so once again confounds the Creator–creature distinction. It is a mistake in the grammar of God. Peter thinks the Creator–creature is fundamental to all Christian theology.

The interconnectedness of the simplicity, the timelessness, the immutability and the aseity of God lies at the heart of systematic theology. Peter makes a strong plea for the recovery of such theology. The separation of the elements of theological education, the development of separate specialisms, whether in college or seminary, or in the pew or Bible-study group, is a mixed blessing. We have the benefit of the various disciplines, Old Testament, New Testament, the ancient Near East, historical theology, biblical theology, and so on. But who or what is to put Humpty-Dumpty together again? Peter's bold answer is an appreciation of the synoptic standpoint of our creator, to whose word of creation and redemption every page of Scripture testifies. Not only is he our creator, but the very same God is our Redeemer, and wherever the Lord is spoken of in Scripture it is this Lord. He provides the hermeneutical key to every passage of Scripture.

In the second part of his book, having introduced us to God as he is in himself, Peter attends to how this God is toward us. His actions towards us are conditioned by his simplicity. God's goodness does not have to be wrung from him, nor is his justice other than fully deserved; it does not have to be 'vindicated'. God's goodness as seen in his creation, and in redemption and judgment, is powerful goodness. His justice is not to be pitted against this goodness. He does not get into a fix as a result of evil, and find himself forced to manufacture a way out. He makes his sun to shine on the just and the unjust; he comes powerfully to redeem and restore, and evil is under his sovereign will. Peter sees the willing of evil as part of a great drama in which, as Augustine puts it, 'The sum of all creation is better than the higher things alone' (*Confessions* 7.13.19). And all, superior and inferior alike, are creaturely powers under the Creator's sovereign control.

In the incarnation and in Christ's suffering we must say the immortal suffers. But how can we say this? He takes on our nature, and so identifies with us. God was in Christ, reconciling the world to himself (2 Cor. 5:18). When we consider God's love, we are not to think of his battling against the forces of evil, uncertain of the outcome. We are to see our own struggles from the perspective of this simple God, and have our faith fortified and strengthened. We are more than conquerors through him that loved us (Rom. 8:37).

Peter works this out in later chapters. The nature of God's love is contrasted with love as found in modern culture and in such a theology that is at home in that culture. He emphasizes the trinitarian character of our salvation, and helps us to grasp something of the immortal Son's experience of death. He discusses the work of several key figures in the church, all the while endeavouring to make clear the difference that God's simplicity makes to his love, mercy and justice. This is God's simple glory and goodness refracted into differing attributes by the differing situations of men and women and of his will for them. The book concludes with a discussion of the interpretation of Augustine's trinitarianism and its consistency with divine simplicity. The classical doctrine of God the Creator is not set in concrete, some fixed ideology to which we must toe the line, but is the axis around which living Christian teaching receives support.

It is tempting to some to think of God as he is in himself, as simply an object of human speculation. But then the ideas we have of God would merely 'flit in the brain' as Calvin put it (*Institutes* 3.2.36). It is a notable feature of this introduction to classical Christian theism that it emphasizes the pastoral side of things. Peter concludes each chapter with a brief meditation, and there are numerous pastoral allusions, not to mention the marvellous hymns of worship to this simple God in Trinity that Peter quotes.

I am pleased to have been asked to write these words commending Peter's book, and I hope it will enjoy the wide and influential readership it deserves.

Paul Helm

ACKNOWLEDGMENTS

Over the years I have had many conversations with friends who have in various ways nourished and stimulated this book. Conversations, prayers and debates with others have helped me immensely. I could not possibly mention them all, but, without wishing to offend any who remain unnamed, I am thankful to God for the encouragement of Ron Frost, Mike Reeves, Pete Nicolas, Jim Griffiths, Ben Dean, Stuart Creed and Ian Hamilton.

My first encounter with Augustine was at the age of seventeen, during A Level Religious Studies. I was taught Early Church History by a retired Methodist minister. He was a committed school teacher who taught us the two-year course in one year, as he realized he had motor neurone disease and would not live long enough to complete his class. The syllabus for Early Church History terminated in AD 325, so I was exposed to Augustine only as a result of that remarkable school teacher's determination not only to teach a two-year course in double time, but also to exceed the remit of his syllabus. At Oxford University I was privileged to be tutored in Patristics by Thomas Weinandy. His graciousness and warm-hearted love of the Lord greatly commended his persistent and careful explication of divine impassibility. At Cambridge University I valued the supervision at MPhil level of Catherine Pickstock, who helpfully encouraged me to read Augustine against the backdrop of Plato and Continental Philosophy. Moving on to doctoral research I benefited immensely from the generous supervision of David Ford. At our first meeting he advised me to view my doctorate as an opportunity to 'apprentice' myself to Augustine, and 'learn from him how to live and do theology wisely'. These teachers in differing ways have contributed to the production of this book, which aims to interpret classical Augustinian Christianity afresh.

I am also grateful for the helpful critical feedback on my manuscript given by Melvin Tinker and Chris Stead. I am most grateful for the vision and support for this project from my editor, Phil Duce, and for Eldo Barkhuizen's careful copy-editing. Obviously any shortcomings and errors remaining are solely mine.

Finally, I am deeply thankful to God that he has been kind enough to give me Susanna as a wife. She has been extraordinarily supportive and forbearing as I have spent long hours in my study, which could have been spent doing housework, playing board games or taking her out for dinner.

Peter Sanlon
The Feast Day of Jerome, 2013

INTRODUCTION

Taking time to acquaint ourselves with seemingly obtuse and obscure debates about technical theological words can seem a distraction – or temptation – away from the vital task of living for God in today's world. Nevertheless even the most natural and universal human experiences benefit from thoughtful study: 'Reflecting on love can never be as good, or as rewarding or as confusing than actually to love. But reflecting on love might help us better to understand what we are doing when we love or when we think that we love.'[1]

Reading this book is an exercise in theological thought about the God who is love. It guides us through the classical theological tradition with the aim of helping us think and speak more faithfully about God. Most contemporary presentations of the Christian God focus on attributes associated with either his 'oneness' or his 'threeness'. These are pitted against each other, and assumed to contradict one another. Many of the most venerable terms used to describe God's oneness are now foreign in popular Christian circles – words such as 'simplicity' and 'aseity'. Bereft of such concepts, language about God's love and relationality can do little other than settle into a comforting but ultimately shallow and unreliable gesture towards bland niceness. Learning to do justice to God's infinite power as well as his perfect relationality is more difficult than is often assumed:

---

1. W. G. Jeanrond, *A Theology of Love* (London: Bloomsbury, 2010), p. 6.

All our language and thought, limited as it is by created categories, is inadequate to speak of what God is. Through God's gracious revelation of himself, we have been given names to name God, and actions by which we might perceive God at work. However, our names suffer from the same limitations as our language and thought: they point towards the ineffable; they do not define or grasp it. The core illustration of this is their multiplicity: we know that the simple essence of God cannot be subject to composition, because composition is one of those created realities we can grasp. Given all this, what can we say of the mystery of the divine triunity? . . . The task of theology is to find a grammar that will speak of this adequately, a task completed by the Cappadocian fathers in Greek and St. Augustine in Latin, at least in the judgment of the majority witness of the Christian tradition. The question both had to answer, of course, was how to speak of the threeness of God without compromising the prior confession of simplicity.[2]

This book begins in chapter 1 with an orientation to the general issue of what it means to engage with, relate to and speak about God.

The rest of the book falls into two parts. Part 1 explores doctrines associated with God's simplicity and oneness. Chapter 2 introduces the all-important concept of 'simplicity'. This doctrine is the engine in the car of a healthy theology. Without simplicity it is impossible to affirm fully or coherently all the Bible teaches about God. Further doctrines, which fit most closely with simplicity, are explored, including timelessness (chapter 3), omnipotence (chapter 4) and impassibility (chapter 5).

Part 2 of our study focuses on teachings associated more with God's relationality and threeness. These are often assumed to be in tension or conflict with the material covered in foregoing chapters. Chapter 5 acts as a bridge between parts 1 and 2 – it begins to get us thinking about the threeness of God, as it relates the impassibility of God to the sufferings of Jesus.

Chapter 6 explores the relationality of God's love in Scripture. Chapter 7 introduces us to the way some figures from church history

---

2. Stephen Holmes, *The Holy Trinity* (Milton Keynes: Paternoster, 2012), p. 108.

have written about the threeness of God's love. An example of thinking through the relationship between God's oneness and threeness is given in chapter 8, which explores the connection between simplicity and the atonement. Chapter 9 offers some reflections on how Christians will be better equipped to engage the culture of the modern world if they remain sensitive both to God's simplicity and his relationality.

Each chapter concludes with a meditation. Some of the most warm-hearted devotional theology in the history of the church has grown out of reflection upon God's nature. We live in a pragmatic, activistic age. It is hoped that time spent meditating on God's nature will feed our souls, and return us to reading Scripture and living for God with renewed passion. When we see and understand God more clearly, we are transformed by the sight. There is much to do for God in these days, but being precedes doing for both God and us.

1. ENGAGING WITH GOD

All Christians are aware that sin is a serious and grave barrier to our relationships with God. Sin manifests itself in many ways: in individual lives, in families, cultures and institutions. It would be a sadly truncated presentation of the Christian message that did not give significant time to explaining the impossibility of sinful people relating properly to the pure, holy God.

So significant is the impact of sin on our relating to God that it is perhaps understandable that we often pay little attention to another reality that makes it tough for us to engage with our Maker. This is the fact that God is the Creator, and we are creatures. It is far from obvious that it should be easy for creatures to communicate with the Creator. Communication requires some common ground and capacity to comprehend the other. The Creator is infinite, perfect, timeless, free and omnipotent. Creatures are finite, imperfect, temporal, dependent and limited. The differences between the Creator and creature are so great that they pose significant obstacles to communication – quite apart from the sin that is more commonly realized to be a barrier.

This chapter explores the possibilities for creatures to engage with and speak about God, which take seriously the difference between God and his creatures. When the radical difference between God and creatures is accepted, we develop the humility that accepts the need to find ways of speaking about God that do justice to his unique, radical perfection.

A God unlike us

> If you understand a being, it is not God.
>
> (Augustine)[1]

Successive generations have latched on to dangers they see as pre-eminent. Past contenders have included nuclear war, communism and environmentalism. Today perhaps terrorism would top the list. Who knows what the future concerns will be? A good case can be made that behind and before all these problems lies our inadequate conception of God. As the Bible translator J. B. Phillips so aptly put it in his book title from 1961, *Your God Is Too Small.* The greatest and most pressing problem facing the world is that people think God is less glorious, loving, magnificent and impressive than he is.

The world at large will not automatically have an accurate conception of God. It is always the case that the 'God' the world ignores and rejects is an idol – something less than the real God. It is the joyful responsibility of the church to proclaim the true God. That nobody else can fulfil that duty means that the church has a solemn responsibility to do all it can to ensure it understands and preaches the God who is there, and not some miniaturized replica.

Developing faithful thoughts about God does not come naturally or easily, even to believers. Intellectual effort is required. Virtues such as patience and humility are needed. A deep, rich knowledge of the Scriptures is vital for mature Christian theology.

Planted deep in our hearts are the roots of a weed that smothers our attempts to think about God faithfully. We nurture the

---

1. Augustine, *Sermons*, tr. Edmund Hill, ed. John Rotelle, 11 vols., The Works of Saint Augustine, A Translation for the 21st Century (New York: New City, 1991), vol. 4, 117.5.

assumption that God is basically a bigger, more powerful version of us. This idea is a noxious weed, yet we try to grow it into grand thoughts about God. The belief that God is simply a bit bigger than us is fit only for the fire.

We must set aside our secular miniaturization and rejection of God. We want to think of God as he is. We want to tell the world what he is like. The trouble is that we naturally rely upon a method doomed to failure. So, for example, we wish to believe that God is sovereign and all-powerful. The Bible tells us this, and we believe it. The most obvious way to conceive of this, and the way most of us do, is to think that God is more powerful than us. I have a certain amount of power, but it is limited. God has greater power than me. This is true in so far as it goes, but it does not occur to me that if God's power is actually infinite and perfect, then the way that power will operate and exist will be radically different from my limited power. The very act of reasoning from my strength and experience of power to God's power obscures something essential about him. It elides the fact that at the most fundamental level possible God is different from me. God is distinct from his creation. Attempting to move from thoughts drawn from creation to conceptions of God implies that his greatness and power exist on a spectrum with ours. That spectrum may place us at one end and God at the other – in an attempt to honour him. Nevertheless it does not do justice to the distinction between God and his creation. The difference between God and his creation is not one of scale; it is a difference of order. Even for those of us who want to say that God is greater than us, we may need to heed J. B. Phillips when he rebukes us, 'Your God is too small.'

It is understandable that we struggle to think of God as being fundamentally other, rather than just existing further than us up the scale of power. All of our thinking and speaking about God involves words and instruments bound up in this creation. Gregory of Nazianzus thought that thinking about God in a manner that did not reduce him to a part of this creation was as difficult as catching our own shadow:

> Just as a man cannot overtake his own shadow, which recedes with every forward step and always stays the same distance ahead . . . In

the same way also we cannot outdo God in our gifts, for we do
not give anything that is not his or that surpasses his own bounty.
Recognise the source of your existence, of your breath of life,
your understanding [and] your knowledge of God (itself the
greatest of gifts).[2]

Since everything we engage with, think about and interact with
in daily life is a part of creation, we can think about God in an
appropriately different manner only with considerable self-conscious
effort. Although we may reject overtly casual ways of speaking about
God, which reduce him to the level of divine boyfriend who hangs
out with us, our earnest attempts to magnify him may do so using
inadequate assumptions.

Theologians from the past recognized that it is difficult to
conceive of God as being different from creation. Speaking about
John 1:1 Augustine preached, 'We are talking about God. So why be
surprised if you cannot grasp it? I mean, if you could understand
it, it wouldn't be God.'[3]

Although this chapter is prefatory and methodological, the book
as a whole is about God. Yet I find it necessary to talk about God
in the methodological section. That is because the very nature of
God as God is one of the most significant factors making it difficult to formulate a faithful methodology for speaking (and writing)
about him.

Two terms have been proven useful in describing this aspect of
God that creates the challenge. 'Aseity' was a term favoured by the
Puritans. It comes from Latin words that mean 'from himself'. Only
God can be described as possessing aseity. It means that God is not
dependent on anybody else for his existence. In the most crude
manner possible this means that he was never born nor created. It
means more subtly that he does not need or benefit from his
creation. God was under no compulsion to make the world. Aseity
safeguards his self-sufficiency, perfect happiness and contentedness.

---

2. Gregory Nazianzus, *Select Orations*, ed. M. Vinson (Washington:
   Catholic University of America Press, 2010), 14.22–23.

3. Augustine, *Sermons*, vol. 4, 117.5.

It suggests that God does not need or benefit from anything other than himself. D. A. Carson explains the term:

> The doctrine of aseity means that God is so much from himself that he does not need us. That is made explicit in many passages . . . He does not need us . . . he doesn't need me. Do you know what – God doesn't need our worship. In eternity past he was perfectly happy. You mustn't picture God coming to Thursday afternoon saying 'Boy I can hardly wait till Sunday. Wish they'd break out those guitars. Singing better be good this week – I'm a bit down.' He doesn't need us. He doesn't need our worship. He is the God of aseity.[4]

As God said:

> If I were hungry, I would not tell you,
>   for the world and its fullness are mine.
> Do I eat the flesh of bulls
>   or drink the blood of goats?
> (Ps. 50:12–13)

A second phrase has been helpful in clarifying the reason God's being God makes it difficult for us to think about him. This is the phrase 'Creator–creature distinction'. From this perspective it is argued that there is a fundamental, radical difference between God and all his creatures. God is uncreated and independent. His creatures are, by definition, created and dependent. The distinction is absolute – not one of graduation and scale. Even if you took a creature and scaled it up to the greatest possible extent of wisdom, it would not be wise in the way in which God is wise. Thinking and talking about God in a manner that preserves the Creator–creature distinction is one of the most laborious but important tasks of theology. As Van Til writes:

---

4. D. A. Carson, The aseity of God, from 'The Use of the Old Testament in Hebrews', http://www.youtube.com/watch?v=9B4J_An6i2I (accessed 10 Nov. 2013). Full talk at http://www.uu.edu/audio/ryancenter/wordwithintheword-0409/042409-DACarson-Plenary1.mp3 (accessed 10 Nov. 2013).

The Reformed apologist does while the Romanist-evangelical apologist does not make the Creator–creature distinction basic in all that he says about anything. His argument is that unless this distinction is made basic to all that man says about anything, then whatever man says is fundamentally untrue.[5]

In our age that (supposedly) prizes meritocracy, equality and casualness, we find it particularly difficult – perhaps even offensive – to accept that God is fundamentally different from us. We want to emphasize that God is like us; he became a human and walked this earth. That is wonderful news, but only if, before we get to that point in the story, we accept that the God who became one of us is fundamentally and radically unlike us. We realize how wonderful it is for God to become like us only if, first, we heed the rebuke he gave Job and accept solemnly that he is not like us:

> Where were you when I laid the foundation of the earth?
>   Tell me, if you have understanding.
> Who determined its measurements – surely you know!
>   Or who stretched the line upon it?
> On what were its bases sunk,
>   or who laid its cornerstone,
> when the morning stars sang together
>   and all the sons of God shouted for joy?
> (Job 38:4–7)

Amnesia

Forgetfulness damages relationships. Over the course of a day I have innumerable things to remember: visit that family about an upcoming funeral, return a student's essay grade, recharge my computer in time for the presentation, ensure my child is wearing a

---

5. E. H. Sigward (ed.), *The Articles of Cornelius Van Til* (New York: Labels Army, 1997), electronic ed. 'Defending the Faith', *Torch and Trumpet* 1.1 (1951), p. 18.

coat while playing outside. Forgetting any one of these will put varying degrees of strain upon relationships. Somebody will feel let down, resentful or disappointed. Our relationship may take one more imperceptible step from friendship to professionalism, or from valued collaborator to frustrating dependent. A lot of the matters I need to remember seem – from my perspective – trivial. However, another person thinks the issue momentous. I am busy and pre-occupied. I forget. A relationship is damaged.

Since forgetfulness chips away at the foundations of relation-ships, the Bible encourages us not to be forgetful hearers (Jas 1:25). It is concerning, then, that Christians often appear to suffer from a form of the collective amnesia that has infected postmodern culture more generally.

Where social and political debate is shaped by the pressures of a twenty-four-hour media cycle, all issues are reduced to irreconcil-able conflicted positions.[6] As each side shouts louder and polarizes around whatever issue is selected for discussion, caricatures are propagated. When it comes to church matters, the conflict is thought to be between liberals and conservatives. Liberals are said to challenge traditional beliefs, while conservatives champion them. However, it is erroneous to imagine that only so-called 'liberals' push the boundaries of orthodox belief. 'Conserva-tive Christians have also lost a sense of doctrine.'[7] Caught up in debating the issue of the day, we all forget the beliefs valued for centuries.

Most of the doctrines historically held as central to the Christian faith are offensive to the secular establishment. Many of them are peripheral to much of what goes on at our churches. A considered, informed and thoughtful learning of Christian beliefs is all too often eclipsed by pragmatic activism and indulgent excitement over issues prioritized not by Scripture, but by the present age.

The church's amnesia regarding doctrine is partly a function of wider society's loss of interest in history. 'The culture in which

---

6. A. MacIntyre, *After Virtue* (London: Bloomsbury, 2013).

7. Gerald Bray, *Creeds, Councils & Christ* (Leicester: Inter-Varsity Press, 1984), p. 9.

we live in the West exhibits powerful antihistorical tendencies.'[8] Technology, consumerism, entertainment, social fragmentation, favouring of science and a decline in reading swill into a potent anti-historical brew. Supping from that cup has done church and culture much ill. As the historian E. H. Carr warned, 'The belief that we have come from somewhere is closely linked with the belief that we are going somewhere. A society which has lost belief in its capacity to progress in the future will quickly cease to concern itself with its progress in the past.'[9]

Too many have accepted the irrational (and unbiblical) idea that doctrinal beliefs are divisive and unloving. Historically, the opposite view has been held by Christians. For example, the Thirty-Nine Articles of the Church of England were '[a]greed upon . . . for the avoiding of diversities of opinions.'[10] The doctrinal confessional statement was intended to unite and hold believers together. Innovation and deviation would not foster greater love and understanding – they would divide and corrupt. It is ludicrous to imagine that we can love God and people while avoiding doctrine. Doctrine is, after all, nothing less than essential beliefs about those we are called to love. As Augustine (354–430) warned, 'No one can love a thing that is quite unknown.'[11]

Astonishingly God himself has been forgotten by vast tracts of the church. Shocking and insulting though this observation may appear, it has been made by others. David Wells argues that God has become 'weightless' to his people.[12] More recently Fred Sanders

---

8. Carl Trueman, *Histories and Fallacies: Problems Faced in the Writing of History* (Wheaton: Crossway, 2010), p. 169.

9. E. H. Carr, *What Is History?* (London: Penguin, 2008), p. 132.

10. *The Book of Common Prayer* (Cambridge: Cambridge University Press, 2005), p. 607.

11. Augustine, *The Trinity*, tr. Edmund Hill, ed. John Rotelle, The Works of Saint Augustine, a Translation for the 21st Century (New York: New City, 1991), 10.1.1.

12. David Wells, *God in the Wasteland: The Reality of Truth in a World of Fading Dreams* (Leicester: Inter-Varsity Press; Grand Rapids: Eerdmans, 1995), p. 88.

has contended that we have forgotten the great doctrines of the Trinity that undergird evangelical religious practices. His diagnosis links spiritual anaemia with doctrinal amnesia:

> Our forgetfulness of the Trinity and our feeling of shallowness are directly related. The solutions to both problems converge in the gospel, the evangel which evangelicalism is named after, and which is always deeper than we can fathom. Our great need is to be led further in to what we already have.[13]

A collection of carefully discerned doctrines about God were cherished by Christians of the early, medieval and Reformation eras. Today they are barely remembered. If known about at all, they are dismissed as pointless eccentricities or divisive idiosyncrasies.

We may think we know the Bible – but what Christian group has ever believed itself to be unbiblical? We have developed a number of ministries and theological methodologies that previous generations would be impressed with – there is also much they would disown. If we have forgotten doctrines about God which previous generations thought essential, do we know the Bible more, or less well, than our forebears?

Our goal in restoring to Christianity forgotten doctrines about God is to enable a fresh engagement with God. This requires some preparatory reflection on how we do theology.

Reconnecting the dots

Since leaving school I have spent eight years as a full-time theological student, before going on to teach in seminaries alongside local church ministry. Various factors shaped each of those eight years' training: I had personal goals to meet, was taught by scholars with their own beliefs and was affiliated with multiple institutions. A crucial influence on my first theology degree was the curriculum.

---

13. Fred Sanders, *Embracing the Trinity: Life with God in the Gospel* (Nottingham: Inter-Varsity Press, 2010), p. 13.

Derived from the Latin word for a horse race course, a curriculum guides students in their race towards learning.

When I began that theology degree, I was – at first – proud of the degree's curriculum. It was a traditional, even old-fashioned, theology curriculum. Many alternative degrees had removed original language requirements. They had shifted their courses from a focus on Christian theology derived from the Bible to sociological studies of religions in general. The course I took permitted some study of other religions, but encouraged me to pursue a set of courses generally similar to that which had served English theological students for about five hundred years. Conscious that the liberal-arts theological degree I was undertaking would not be sympathetic to my Christian beliefs, I applied to take the degree from an evangelical college. That gave me increased say in my tutors, and supportive academics to advise me at crucial junctures. Combined with seemingly endless hours to study and read as one wished, I was very happy.

However, after a year or two I began to realize that excellent though my experience was, there were problems. I benefited greatly from a New Testament essay on divorce and remarriage; but my ethics tutor dismissed the conclusions. I suspected that my Reformation history tutor misrepresented Augustine's teaching regarding original sin. I felt that the modern doctrine tutor used idiosyncratic exegesis of the Old Testament to undermine New Testament teaching about the atonement. The Old Testament papers were resistant to any suggestions that Jesus was the true fulfilment of God's promises to Israel. My reading suggested to me that many critical tools applied in New Testament exegesis were the fruit of outdated and untenable philosophical assumptions.

The above were all challenges that had to be faced; I was grateful for the many academics and fellow-students who helped me. The list of struggles appears disparate. By the end of my degree I was starting to perceive dimly that these vexations were something to do with the curriculum itself. Several years after graduation my reading of early church theologians prompted me to realize that the various problems had a single cause – a (relatively modern) fragmentation in the theological disciplines.

Though my course had maintained more of the traditional shape of a theological degree curriculum than many universities, it still was suffering from a fragmentation of disciplines. The Reformation course did not have to fit with the patristics course. The New Testament, Old Testament and ethics departments operated with conflicting, incompatible assumptions.

This fragmentation of disciplines is a feature of Western education more widely. It is due to the increase in knowledge, the Enlightenment's separation of humanities from sciences, the bureaucratization of life and commodification of education.

This atomization of learning is pernicious for any human endeavour: literature, science, medicine and art are all distorted when dissected. It is particularly odious for theological disciplines to be atomized. Church historians find 'the dangers of overspecialisation, as in all related disciplines in the humanities, remain very real'.[14] Theology is the study of God. Since God created everything, true theology must offer a rationale for all things. Since God is Lord of all, he speaks to all areas of life. This does not mean that the answer to every question is in the Bible, nor does it mean that all we must do is study the Bible. It does, however, mean that in principle there should be a unifying theme to all of life. A golden thread should be discernible running through all theological disciplines, uniting and giving them shape.

When theological disciplines fragment and atomize, human autonomy resists God's sovereign control over all truth. Inevitably the Church of England's confession is ignored – it stipulates that we may not 'so expound one piece of scripture, that it be repugnant to another'.[15] Old Testament departments are set free to teach a different religion from New Testament departments. Ethics may be drawn from parts of any other discipline, or simply culled from secular learning. Each department is free to operate according to its own set of rules. The very idea that God has spoken and is truly Lord of all creation is challenged at every point, where a theological curriculum is fragmented and atomized. Incoherence ensures that.

---

14. James Bradley and Richard Muller, *Church History: An Introduction of Research, Reference Works, and Method* (Grand Rapids: Eerdmans, 1995), p. 2.

15. *Book of Common Prayer*, art. 20, pp. 619–620.

It always frustrated me that my original theology degree did not have a systematics course. The university did not have a systematic theology department. There was a 'Modern Doctrine' course, which surveyed some teaching from significant late-modern theologians. There was a 'Philosophical Theology' course, which used tools of logic to analyse aspects of Christian doctrines. Nevertheless there was no systematic theology. That ought to have been the clue to me that fragmentation had fatally wounded the theological curriculum.

'Systematic theology' is the discipline that, as its name suggests, draws together all theological knowledge into a system. It is not possible where fragmentation and atomization reign, for it pre-supposes that there is a unity to all knowledge and that there is indeed one God who created all things.

We may feel instinctively that systematic theology overly con-stricts and simplifies. This intuition leads to the accusation that systematic theology puts God in a box, limiting him to human conceptions. We might think that systematic theology distorts and misrepresents Scripture: the rich diversity of the Bible is made bland by one's system. We could argue that systematic theology idolizes reason: the systematic theologian appears to worship the cool logic of reason more than the passionate God of the Bible.

All of these criticisms are true of poor systematic theology. The solution is not to dismiss systematics; rather it is to develop better systematics. Good systematic theology does not put God in a box; it clarifies the implications of what he has revealed of himself. Good systematic theology does not misrepresent Scripture; it is shaped by solid exegesis and narrative analysis. Good systematic theology does not idolize reason; it depends on revelation and points out the areas of mystery.

We all have a systematic theology. It is whatever conclusions, assumptions and frameworks we use to interpret the Bible and world. Those who resist the study of systematic theology do have a systematic theology – the problem is that it is unexamined, uncon-scious and unpredictable. The latter feature is troubling in ministry. When a minister does not pay attention to systematic theology, imagining that he merely reads the Bible, church members will find themselves subjected to an unpredictable ministry. Parts of the Bible will be exalted to paradigmatic status; others will be sidelined.

Regular reading and preaching through the entire Bible will not alleviate this – the unexamined, intuitive systematic theology will shape and guide every step of exegesis and preaching. Unpredictability arises from keeping one's systematic theology a secret (from oneself and others).

Systematic theology is inevitable and essential:

> It is a God-given duty that we should take the content of scripture and bring it together into a systematic whole. It is plain that we are required to know the revelation that God has given us. Yet we would not adequately know that revelation if we knew it only in its several parts without bringing these parts into relation to each other. It is only as a part of the whole of the revelation of God to us that each part of that revelation appears as it is really meant to appear. Our minds must think systematically.[16]

Certainly the Bible in its entirety must be studied, for all parts contribute to God's revelation of himself:

> The canon of scripture consists not of one book but of a sacred library; in each portion of which we indeed have the Word of God but not the whole of it. It is only, therefore, by a collation of one part of scripture with another, and a comprehensive view of the whole, that we attain to such a measure of knowledge as we can in this life expect.[17]

The collation here spoken of is nothing less than systematic theology. All other theological disciplines will be involved in systematic theology, as all aspects of knowing God are interconnected. 'No systematic theology is complete unless ethics and ecclesiology are in some ways integral to its articulation.'[18] So far as historical and

---

16. Cornelius Van Til, *An Introduction to Systematic Theology* (Phillipsburg: P. & R., 2007), p. 21.

17. E. A. Litton, *Introduction to Dogmatic Theology: On the Basis of the 39 Articles of the Church of England* (London: James Clarke, 1960), p. 430.

18. Colin Gunton, 'Historical and Systematic Theology', in Colin Gunton (ed.), *The Cambridge Companion to Christian Doctrine* (Cambridge: Cambridge University Press, 1997), p. 12.

systematic theology go, 'Their tracks cross in many places.'[19] In so far as systematic theology interconnects all theological disciplines, it is a mediating faculty. In so far as systematic theology discerns coherence among theological disciplines, it is an integrative endeavour. In so far as systematic theology represents secure conclusions about God, it is the crowning discipline.

When the theological disciplines are integrated, the dots are rejoined. Systematics is then possible and can be given its due place in the curriculum. This not only permits it to be a subject in its own right, but enables all the other disciplines to flourish, making a coherent contribution to the whole.

Engaging with God demands that systematic theology be appropriately valued. We should seek to draw all that God has revealed of himself together into a coherent vision – only this gives meaning to the parts:

> All Christian doctrines are interdependent. Each major doctrine implies all the others and colours all of the others. A Protestant's doctrine of the atonement will, to some extent, colour his doctrine of God and vice versa. In fact, the difference with respect to all the other doctrines rests ultimately on a difference with respect to the notion one has of God.[20]

The created nature of people and God's revelation of himself demand this enterprise. My presentation of God in subsequent chapters is self-consciously systematic. Three important areas of doctrine inform and shape our systematic vision of God: our assumptions about God's revelation, ourselves and the church. I shall consider each in turn.

You have mail

A God unlike us cannot be known unless he chooses to make himself known. The more keenly we sense the glorious splendour

---

19. Ibid., p. 3.
20. Cornelius Van Til, *A Christian Theory of Knowledge* (Phillipsburg: P. & R., 1969), pp. 11–12.

of God, the more deeply we feel our need of his revelation. The necessity of revelation follows from the otherness of God. Since God is of an entirely different order of existence to us, there is no bridge or avenue of communication we could open up, unless he acted first. God is

> [s]olitary in his majesty, unique in his excellency, peerless in his perfections. He sustains all, but is himself independent of all. He gives to all, but is enriched by none. Such a God cannot be found out by searching. He can be known only as he is revealed to the heart by the Holy Spirit through the Word.[21]

We need God to reveal himself to us. Damage done to the world and our faculties by sin increases this need; but the nature of God as God is itself sufficient to make revelation necessary.

If we are to know God, we need to be clear about the uniqueness of Scripture:

> The Bible is a book truly unique. It is, in distinction from the millions of other books in the world, God's Word. It is in a class by itself. If we, in the external arrangement of the books in a library, wished to show the importance and authority of the books, we should have to place the Holy Scriptures on one side and all the other books on the other side . . . Scripture is neither a human nor a 'divine–human' report on God's Word and the 'facts of the revelation,' but is itself the Word of God. This is Luther's position as to Scripture. He says, 'You are so to deal with the Scriptures that you bear in mind that God himself is saying this.' . . . There is no real difference, but only a difference in expression, between the two terms 'Holy Scripture says' and 'God says.'[22]

When we realize that God is so far beyond his creatures that we need him to reveal himself to us, we are enthusiastic for the

---

21. Arthur Pink, *The Attributes of God* (Grand Rapids: Baker, 1975), pp. 11–12.

22. F. Pieper, *Christian Dogmatics*, 4 vols. (St. Louis: Concordia, 1957), vol. 1, p. 216.

Bible, where God has revealed himself. The necessity of revelation
is a doctrine that is felt and experienced. It leads to a Christian's
diligently reading the Bible. As one Reformed theologian observed,
the necessity of Scripture 'will enjoin on us the necessity of
retaining and attending to it'.[23] It is often bemoaned that Christians
today do not know their Bibles as previous generations did. The
solution is not simply to inculcate greater discipline and plan our
schedules better. The way forward is to rediscover the vision of
God as the incomparably perfect, infinite being. That impresses
upon us our deep need of his revelation. A heart that feels its need
of a God who is actually worthy of the title 'God' will be drawn
to the Bible's pages. As the psalmist wrote concerning God's
words:

> More to be desired are they than gold,
>   even much fine gold;
> sweeter also than honey
>   and drippings of the honeycomb.
> (Ps. 19:10)

If we – finite created beings – are to understand a communication
from the infinite Creator, there must be an accommodation to our
natural limitations. Even the seraphim before God's throne cover
their faces (Isa. 6:2) and long to look into the revelation from the
God who made them (1 Peter 1:12).

The manner in which language in the Bible is accommodated to
our limitations needs to be appreciated. Rowan Williams observes
that the Bible presents

> [a] God who gets his way by patiently struggling to make himself clear
> to human beings, to make his love real to them, especially when they
> seem not to want to know, or want to avoid him and retreat into their
> own fantasies about him. And typically, the Bible sometimes does this
> by a very bold method – by telling a certain kind of story from the

---

23. Cocceius, cited in Heinrich Heppe, *Reformed Dogmatics* (London:
    Wakeman, 2010), p. 32.

human point of view, as if God needed to be persuaded to be faithful to his people.[24]

Almost all readers of the Bible realize to a degree that some language God uses to reveal himself is not straightforwardly applied to him. So, for example, God is not actually a rock or fortress, despite being described as such:

> The LORD is my rock and my fortress and my deliverer,
>   my God, my rock, in whom I take refuge,
>   my shield, and the horn of my salvation, my stronghold.
> (Ps. 18:2)

Rock, fortress, shield – these are all words used to communicate something about God, but not in a direct, equivalent manner. John Calvin (1509–64) defended the accommodated nature of biblical language against the anthropomorphites, who took every expression literally, and so ascribed physical, human characteristics to God. Calvin wrote:

> The Anthropomorphites, who imagined a corporeal God from the fact that Scripture often ascribes to him a mouth, ears, eyes, hands, and feet, are easily refuted. For who even of slight intelligence does not understand that, as nurses commonly do with infants, God is wont in a measure to lisp in speaking to us? Thus such forms of speaking do not so much express clearly what God is like as accommodate the knowledge of him to our slight capacity. To do this he must descend far beneath his loftiness.[25]

Many words are used in the Bible metaphorically to communicate something about God. A metaphor takes a word out of its normal, literal context and uses it to suggest some kind of insight about the

---

24. Rowan Williams, *Tokens of Trust: An Introduction to Christian Belief* (London: Canterbury, 2007), pp. 16–17.

25. John Calvin, *Institutes of the Christian Religion*, tr. Ford Lewis Battles, ed. John T. McNeill, 2 vols. (Philadelphia: Westminster, 2001), 1.13.1.

subject. So the metaphor of a 'rock' suggests stability and perman-
ence. Such is the nature of metaphorical words. However, the
revelation of God in the Bible contains much that is not metaphorical. For example, when we read that God 'knows everything'
(1 John 3:20) we are not in the realm of metaphorical statement.
The verse straightforwardly affirms that God knows all things.
Nonetheless the presence of metaphor in Scripture reminds us that
language in general, not only metaphor, must be an accommodation
when used to reveal a transcendent, infinite God:

> In view of the Christian's insistence that he will not or cannot transpose
> his concept of God into supposedly imageless speech, attacks on the
> meaningfulness of his metaphorical language are, in fact, attacks on
> any of his attempts to speak of a transcendent God.[26]

That is to say, metaphor is a form of word quite obviously not
intended to be understood in a literal fashion. The way in which a
metaphorical image creates dissonance alerts us to its metaphorical
nature. However, metaphor is simply the most conspicuous case of
a wider phenomenon. When the Bible says that God 'knows'
everything, the word 'knows' is not a metaphor, but neither is it used
in a straightforward, direct manner. When we use a human word,
such as 'knows', to state something about the infinite God, language
is stretched and accommodated. When we read that God knows
everything, we ought not assume that his knowing is identical in
every respect to our knowing. If we think that the word 'know'
functions the same way when predicated of God and us, then we
have forgotten the Creator–creature distinction and begun to read
the Bible as if it tells us about a 'God' who is merely a bit bigger
than us. Such a 'God' could know more than us, but would learn
and hold his knowledge in a similar manner as his creatures.

Thomas Aquinas (1225–74) realized that careful thought about
the way words work would protect the Creator–creature distinction.
He pointed out that there are three ways words can be used:

---

26. J. Soskice, *Metaphor and Religious Language* (Oxford: Clarendon, 1987),
    p. x.

univocally, equivocally and analogically.[27] If a word is used univocally, then it has precisely the same meaning in each context. If I say, 'In my fridge I have a pint of skimmed milk and a pint of full fat milk,' the word 'pint' is used univocally. That is, the word 'pint' means exactly the same each time it is used, though it refers to two different subjects. An equivocal word has completely different meanings when used to refer to two subjects. So, I might tell you, 'I slipped in the mud by the bank of the river on my way to deposit money in the bank.' In that sentence the word 'bank' is deployed equivocally. There is no relationship or connection between the meaning of the first and second usage. It is used in an unrelated and distinct manner each time. Knowing what the first bank is in no way helps you know what the second bank is. The third way Aquinas thought words may be used is analogically. When a word is used analogically, it communicates some sense of meaning from one context to another. There is both similarity and difference. The difference allows for communication about subjects distinct from each other; the similarity permits that communication to pass between a distinct speaker and listener. Aquinas reasoned that if language were used univocally about God, then God would have to be of the same limited, created nature as us. If language were used equivocally, then God's infinite superiority would be preserved, but no communication would be possible with his creatures. That means that language used to speak of God must be analogical.[28] Analogical words make communication between God and humans possible. 'When there is complete absence of analogy, as between a man and a star, there can be no encounter.'[29] When the Bible says that God 'knows' everything, this is stated analogically. That is, God's knowing is fundamentally different from our knowing, but it is not so unrelated to our experience of knowing as to render the comment meaningless. Metaphors are particularly explicit cases of the more general situation: that if language is used

27. Thomas Aquinas, *Summa Theologica*, 5 vols. (Notre Dame: Ave Maria, 1948), 1.1.q.13.a5.

28. Ibid.

29. Helmut Thielicke, *The Evangelical Faith*, 3 vols. (Grand Rapids: Eerdmans, 1974), vol. 1, p. 24.

in a revelation from the infinite God to finite creatures, then words must be used analogically. Far from analogy being a small subset of words used in the Bible, such as metaphor, all of our knowledge about God is analogical. Otherwise God would be less than the perfect infinite God the Bible reveals:

> The system that Christians seek to obtain may . . . be said to be analogical. By this is meant that God is the original and that man is the derivative. God has absolute self-contained system within himself. What comes to pass in history happens in accord with that system or plan by which he orders the universe. But man, as God's creature, cannot have a replica of that system of God . . . he must, to be sure, think God's thoughts after him; but this means that he must, in seeking to form his own system, constantly be subject to the authority of God's system to the extent that this is revealed to him.[30]

Why is it important to think about these linguistic matters before formulating our doctrine of God? Three important reasons may be given. First, our failure to be aware of the analogical nature of language God uses to reveal himself makes it difficult for us to be open to the classical doctrine of God. If we were anthropomorphites, who believed that God literally has human hands and feet, because (metaphors) in the Bible tell us so, we would find it extraordinarily difficult to be open to the claim that God is spiritual and so has no body. We would think that such a belief flies in the face of a plain reading of texts that say God has hands and feet! A similarly intractable situation arises if we resist the analogical nature of language used more widely in God's self-revelation. If we insist that we understand what it means for God to know things, assuming it is basically the same as how we know things, we shall be resistant to the counter-intuitive and humbling claims the traditional systematic doctrine of God makes. Many of the objections to the classical doctrine of God arise from forgetting that language about God in the Bible is analogical. We misinterpret it when we assume that the God referred to is basically similar to us. 'By predicating compassion

---

30. Van Til, *Christian Theory of Knowledge*, p. 16.

of God, we realise God's compassion cannot be precisely the same as ours. For we speak of God only by analogy, denying qualities that imply imperfection and affirming in an eminent way those that do not.'[31]

Secondly, a due appreciation of the analogical nature of language about God inculcates humility. We too easily reduce God to our level, thinking that he is the same as, or perhaps slightly more powerful than, us. We should take to heart the exalted position God has above his creation:

> Who has measured the waters in the hollow of his hand
>   and marked off the heavens with a span,
> enclosed the dust of the earth in a measure
>   and weighed the mountains in scales
>   and the hills in a balance?
> Who has measured the Spirit of the LORD,
>   or what man shows him his counsel?
> Whom did he consult,
>   and who made him understand?
> Who taught him the path of justice,
>   and taught him knowledge,
>   and showed him the way of understanding?
> Behold, the nations are like a drop from a bucket,
>   and are accounted as the dust on the scales;
>   behold, he takes up the coastlands like fine dust.
> Lebanon would not suffice for fuel,
>   nor are its beasts enough for a burnt offering.
> All the nations are as nothing before him,
>   they are accounted by him as less than nothing and emptiness.
> (Isa. 40:12–17)

That language used of God is done so analogically reminds us that even when we are told something about God in the Bible, we do

---

31. Michael Dodds, *The Unchanging God of Love: Thomas Aquinas and Contemporary Theology on Divine Immutability* (New York: Catholic University of America Press, 2008), p. 219.

not understand or know it all. We truly do know things about God, but we know nothing exhaustively. 'The secret things belong to the LORD our God, but the things that are revealed belong to us and to our children for ever, that we may do all the words of this law' (Deut. 29:29).

Thirdly, the analogical nature of language about God offers us certainty. We can be reassured that despite God's being the infinite Creator, it is possible for us to learn about him and get to know him in a personal manner. Words are used analogically in the Bible; this means that although there is a radical distinction between the Creator and his creatures, God can stoop down to our menial level and, as Calvin so memorably put it, 'lisp' meaningful words to us. This is deeply reassuring. It should make us keen to read the Bible – and eager to correlate systematically all that God has so lovingly revealed of himself.

Mirror, mirror, on the wall

Part of my ministry in our local church is visiting people in their homes. Often I am reaching out to somebody who has had little previous contact with a church. More often than not the visit is to the home of a person who comes from a very different socio-economic background and culture from me. Our experience of and attitudes to work, education, money, relationships and politics are often poles apart. To engage people winsomely from a different culture to mine, I need to be aware of the assumptions I hold about myself. Many of the things I value are not absolutes; they are the vagaries of my background, personality and life experiences. Failure to be aware of myself in such an encounter increases the likelihood that I shall come across as judgmental, diffident or proud. Becoming 'all things to all people' (1 Cor. 9:22) to save others involves self-critical awareness of our assumptions about ourselves.

When a couple get married, they bring to their relationship all kinds of background assumptions. Tim and Kathy Keller describe how their assumptions – derived from their respective family back-grounds – led both to imagine that whoever asked the other to change their baby's nappy was expressing a lack of love for the other.[32] Their ability to express and receive love was improved when they became aware of the previously hidden assumptions they made about who did chores.

If in ministry and marriage, undiscerned assumptions about ourselves have significant impacts, how much more is it the case when we engage with God?

The impact our self-knowledge has on our engagement with God was the insight Calvin opened his *Institutes* with: 'Nearly all the wisdom we possess, that is to say, true and sound wisdom, consists of two parts: the knowledge of God and of ourselves. But while joined by many bonds, which one precedes and brings forth the other is not easy to discern.'[33]

These words of Calvin 'provide the orientation of Calvin's theology'.[34] They mean that as I gain true knowledge of God, I inevitably learn about myself. However, the 'many bonds' that join knowledge of God and humanity mean that it is difficult for us to know how to proceed. Error in one area will distort the other. Assumptions about myself, gleaned from my family, culture or education, can damage my ability to engage with God.

Two assumptions about ourselves are particularly entrenched in us. They make it difficult to engage with God according to the terms laid down in the Bible as understood by traditional Christian theology.

The first flawed assumption is that my self-knowledge is normative for learning about God. Unless we examine our attitudes critically, we all place a good measure of confidence in our ability to understand things. Functioning in life requires believing we can interpret our experiences and understand events we are presented with. The problem is that everything we interact with and think about in daily life is of a fundamentally different nature to God. God is the Creator; everything else is created. When this radical distinction is forgotten,

---

32. Tim Keller, *The Meaning of Marriage: Facing the Complexities of Commitment with the Wisdom of God* (London: Penguin, 2013), p. 152.

33. Calvin, *Institutes* 1.1.1.

34. Paul Helm, *Calvin: A Guide for the Perplexed* (London: T. & T. Clark, 2008), p. 25.

people assume God can be learned about in the same manner as other beings or things, by our using similar tools and methods. The problem is not merely that the tools are unsuited to the task, but such an unexamined approach assumes that we, as creatures, are normative for interpreting God: starting with what we know, using our methods for learning, and assessing conclusions against our criteria for credibility. As C. S. Lewis put it:

> For the modern man, he is the judge: God is in the Dock. He is quite a kindly judge: If God should have a reasonable defence for being the God who permits war, poverty and disease, he is ready to hear it. The trial may even end in God's acquittal. But the important thing is that man is on the Bench and God in the dock.[35]

Banishing such an attitude from our hearts is nothing less than a lifetime's spiritual exercise. It is essential for genuine engagement with God, because if we judge him according to our supposedly normative criteria, we preclude the possibility of his being greater than our human-centred assumptions and experience can cope with.

The second defective assumption is that I can objectify God as I seek to learn about him. While Augustine had moved in his reflections from his imperfect self towards a perfect God, Descartes promoted what Charles Taylor described as 'disengaged reason'. This was an approach – typical of the Enlightenment – to learning about God that had much in common with the Stoic philosophy Augustine opposed. Taylor suggests that Enlightenment reason forces people to disengage from the world: 'Descartes' ethic, just as much as his epistemology, calls for disengagement from world and body and the assumption of an instrumental stance towards them. It is of the essence of reason, both speculative and practical, that it push us to disengage.'[36]

---

35. C. S. Lewis, 'God in the Dock', in Lesley Walmsley (ed.), *Essay Collection and Other Short Pieces* (London: HarperCollins, 2000), p. 36.

36. Charles Taylor, *Sources of the Self: The Making of the Modern Identity* (Cambridge: Cambridge University Press, 1989), p. 155.

Many of the ways we seek to understand and learn about things in the world utilize this disengaged reason. Humanity seeks to develop tools of control in the realms of technology, management, economics, society, time and medicine. Despite numerous setbacks, we continue to put our faith in the Enlightenment project of a managed world, measured by the values of humanity. When people used to relying on such a disengaged reason attempt to learn about God, problems ensue. Disengaged reason will evaluate God at a distance, assuming that the human person's beliefs, attitudes and life will have no bearing on the study. The reasoned search for God actually pushes him away; disengagement is necessary for that elusive but prized Enlightenment virtue of impartiality. Even when some kind of God is accepted on the basis of disengaged reason, such a God cannot be approached on personal terms. The God constructed out of the wreckage of assumptions that elevate reason to the prime position inevitably is little more than a series of propositions. They can be understood, explained and evaluated. The God of the Bible calls us to worship, love and adore. Those who think emotional engagement dangerous or unnecessary for engaging with God would do well to heed Augustine's warning:

> If these emotions and feelings, that spring from love of the good and from holy charity, are to be called faults, then let us allow that real faults should be called virtues ... human emotion was not illusory in Jesus, who had a truly human body and a truly human mind.[37]

So a meaningful engagement with God will pay due attention to our assumptions about ourselves, and how we operate in this world. In order to know God, we must accept that we are dependent upon him. The task of coming to know God is a spiritual work, which ultimately rests on our turning away from our human-centred methods of knowing, which idolize the human knower, and use reason to control God.

---

37. Augustine, *City of God*, ed. H. Bettenson and G. R. Evans (London: Penguin, 1984), 14.9.

Helping one another

The Christian life is not a hike we are expected to venture on alone. The journey is too arduous for that. We are urged to help each other: 'Not neglecting to meet together, as is the habit of some, but encouraging one another, and all the more as you see the Day drawing near' (Heb. 10:25). 'Bear one another's burdens, and so fulfil the law of Christ' (Gal. 6:2).

The task of doing theology – seeking to love, believe, understand and articulate what God has revealed of himself – is one (important) part of the Christian life. In the work of theology, no less than other areas of Christian living, we are not expected to make progress unaided. We have the wider church to help us. Augustine was shocked that some Christians thought they could read the Bible without the help of others. He recommended instead, 'Let us not be too proud to learn what has to be learned with the help of other people, and let those of us by whom others are taught pass on what we have received without pride or jealousy.'[38] It is an act of inordinate pride to think that I can interpret the Bible without the help of others in the church who have been given by God as teachers to instruct me:

> The Lord has graciously provided us with a great cloud of witnesses throughout history who can help us to understand the Bible and to apply it to our present day. To ignore such might not be so much a sign of Biblical humility as of overbearing hubris and confidence in our own abilities and the uniqueness of our own age.[39]

During the Reformation era a powerful critique levelled at the Protestants was that they were woefully divided over many doctrinal matters. How could Protestants claim that the Bible spoke clearly, when those who held such a belief could not agree over what texts

---

38. Augustine, *Teaching Christianity*, tr. Edmund Hill, ed. John Rotelle, The Works of Saint Augustine, a Translation for the 21st Century (New York: New City, 1996), Prologue, 5.

39. Carl Trueman, *The Creedal Imperative* (Wheaton: Crossway, 2012), p. 107.

mean? Calvin pondered the problem and concluded that God permits his people to disagree so that they feel their need of each other:

> We ever find, that even those who have not been deficient in their zeal for piety, nor in reverence and sobriety in handling the mysteries of God, have by no means agreed among themselves on every point; for God hath never favoured his servants with so great a benefit, that they were all endued with a full and perfect knowledge in every thing; and no doubt, for this end – that he might keep them humble; and secondly, render them disposed to cultivate brotherly discourse.[40]

In other words, Calvin thought that disagreements over what God has revealed to us ought not to divide Christians; disagreements ought to draw us towards each other in warm, friendly discussion. We need other Christians.

God's church exists in the past, present and future. Each stage of the church's existence in time has a distinctive way of helping us learn and understand what God has told us about himself.

In the past God has blessed his church with many great theologians, whose efforts to understand, preach and defend God's Word have proven helpful and consistent with the Scripture. As we survey the great doctrinal statements of the Christian church, there is remarkable unity. There are, of course, many areas of difference – often they are what prompted the statements in the first place! However, a thoughtful survey of those statements generally reveals agreement around core doctrinal convictions, and divergence at points that most would accept are secondary matters. The writings of those in the past, and the statements of doctrinal belief affirmed as 'dogma' by the church, serve as guides to us today. They show us what issues matter. They aid us in looking at God's Word through lenses from a culture other than our own. They give us an opportunity to learn the Christian faith from people who have been unusually gifted in the area of Bible study and teaching. One recent

---

40. John Calvin, *Acts 14–28 & Romans*, Calvin's Commentaries, 22 vols. (Grand Rapids: Baker, 2005), vol. 19, p. xxvii.

plea for attention to the help offered us by church history argues, 'We cannot merely translate the language of Scripture into our own language, ignoring the intervening ages. Instead ... we will only proclaim the gospel faithfully if we make an effort to understand how it has been passed on to us.'[41]

Many preachers and Christians listen only to Christian leaders they agree with, who are alive. Surely an unwise strategy, at least for those of us living in the age that contains some of the most anodyne, ill-informed versions of Christianity the world has ever known. Wiser surely to heed advice from Aquinas, preaching in the medieval age: 'You should not be satisfied inquiring only of teachers present; but you ought to inquire also of the old ones who are not with us any more.'[42]

Church history has a particularly important role to play when we first approach the doctrines about God that have been all but forgotten by today's Christian church. These doctrines are counter-intuitive to us: they can seem irrelevant or intimidating. When we realize that these doctrines were held by Christians such as Augustine, Aquinas, Calvin and Edwards, it should restrain us from dismissing them prematurely. If we are open to learning, then in those great leaders we have brothers who are the best of teachers. We should not forget or try to escape the reality that God has created us as time-bound creatures, who are linked to our bodies, each other and the past:

> Faith is certainly my personal affair, but it is always also more than just my private affair. The faith of Christianity was there before I was born, and it will be there after my lifetime. It lives in and through a society. It is the faith of the church – even if we often cannot see it because the church has been distorted to the point of being unrecognisable. But

---

41. Stephen Holmes, *Listening to the Past: The Place of Tradition in Theology* (Carlisle: Paternoster, 2002), p. 3.

42. Thomas Aquinas, *The Academic Sermons*, ed. C. P. Mark-Robin Hoogland, The Fathers of the Church, Mediaeval Continuation (Washington: Catholic University of America Press, 2010), Sermon 8, p. 102.

despite this the church represents a continuity; it lives by remembrance and promise. It listens to the witnesses of faith and recalls them, and it hands on the promises of the community.[43]

Not just church in the past but also church in the present helps us understand God's revelation, because it is in the context of the local church that we see God work. In the local church, Christian disciples are given the opportunity to love and serve one another. Some of the things we learn about God's nature are difficult to understand in the abstract. So we learn that God is perfectly just and perfectly merciful. How those can both be expressed at the same time is difficult to imagine, unless one has seen a local church deal firmly but lovingly with a member who has sinned against another Christian. What it means for the infinitely powerful God to spend time humbly with people makes a lot more sense once we have observed high-powered business leaders take time off work to teach little children about Jesus. The local church provides examples of how God impacts people, and pictures for us many of the things that, considered abstractly, appear nonsensical.

Learning to engage with God is far from a merely intellectual exercise. Virtues such as humility must be cultivated; otherwise we will be unwilling to learn from others. Nothing is more calculated to inculcate humility than serving people in our local church. To engage with the perfectly loving God we must open our hearts in love. It is impossible to love God while our hearts are closed to other Christians. 'Whoever says he is in the light and hates his brother is still in darkness' (1 John 2:9). We cannot engage with God unless we engage with the local church. We do not know God unless we love him. We do not love God unless we love the people he loves. And God loves his church. Thus the local church plays a pivotal role in enabling us to engage with God.

The future church also plays an important role in equipping us to engage with God. God does not – as we do – exist in time. 'But do not overlook this one fact, beloved, that with the Lord one day

---

43. Dorothee Sölle, *Thinking About God: An Introduction to Theology* (London: SCM, 1990), p. 5.

is as a thousand years, and a thousand years as one day' (2 Peter 3:8).
From his perspective of timeless eternity all of time is present to
God. He experiences the church we call the 'early church' just as
much in the present as the 'Reformation church' or the church our
grandchildren's children will serve in. This aspect of God's timelessness means that if we are to love the church as God does, we must
love the past, present and future church. The future church is all
those who have not yet believed the message that in Jesus, God died
to bring them into his love. Jesus demanded his disciples care about
that future church: 'Look, I tell you, lift up your eyes, and see that
the fields are white for harvest' (John 4:35). 'When he saw the
crowds, he had compassion for them, because they were harassed
and helpless, like sheep without a shepherd' (Matt. 9:36). Jesus was
asking that his followers consider the multitudes who needed to hear
about him. The harvest of those whom he loved, but who had not
yet heard of him. Before his death Jesus prayed for the whole church
that would come after the first generation of disciples: 'I do not ask
for these only, but also for those who will believe in me through
their word, that they may all be one, just as you, Father, are in me,
and I in you, that they also may be in us, so that the world may believe
that you have sent me' (John 17:20–21). Healthy engagement with
God will issue in a deep concern that future generations will come
to know God. A love for the future church demands that our
doctrine of God be evangelistic. A vision of God that does not
press us on to spread the good news of Christ crucified is an idol.

    The ultimate future of the church lies the other side of Christ's
return. In that future new creation all God's people will together see
God. Our bodies will be renewed to increase our capacity vastly for
enjoying God, and all the sinful inclinations that blur our sight of
him now will be gone for ever. God will reward us for the gifts he
gave us in life: 'The reward of virtue will be God himself, who gave
the virtue.'[44] In that future world we shall engage God with a depth
of passion now only hinted at, often shrouded in suffering and sin.
The final future of the church serves as a reminder that, despite all
our failures, we shall one day engage with God as we long to. There

---

44. Augustine, *City of God* 22.30.

is much we can learn about God in this mortal existence. No matter how much we learn, humility must be our instinctive posture. 'For now we see in a mirror dimly, but then face to face. Now I know in part; then I shall know fully, even as I have been fully known' (1 Cor. 13:12). God is humble, and so must his people be as they engage with him. We learn to do this only as members of the church – present, past and future.

Meditation: humility

> Take my yoke upon you, and learn from me, for I am gentle and lowly in heart, and you will find rest for your souls.
>
> (Matt. 11:29)

> Humility is not so much a grace or virtue along with others; it is the root of all, because it alone takes the right attitude before God, and allows Him as God to do all.
>
> (Andrew Murray)[45]

O God, how often have I acted as if you were made in my likeness? I imagine you are afflicted by similar weaknesses – peevishness, envy, selfishness and resentment.

When I deign to 'learn' from you, I too often reserve the right to criticize. I sift your words to find ones I can accept (then, of course, I treasure them).

O God, grant me the gift of a humble heart. Set me free from the pride that drives me to justify myself; set me on the path of following Christ, who justified sinners. Make me willing to admit – indeed happy to rejoice – that you are greater than I can conceive.

I want to tell others of your all-surpassing glory. May my confidence flow from you, rather than from my abilities. Let my proclamation be a placarding before the world of you, not of my limited assumptions and misrepresentations.

---

45. A. Murray, *Humility and Absolute Surrender* (Peabody: Hendrickson, 2005), p. 7.

O God, you are the Master Sculptor. My heart, with all its desires, secrets and longings is within your power to mould. Use your favoured tools of time and suffering to chisel away my pride. Leave a heart humble enough to engage with the infinite God, who 'being found in human form, humbled himself by becoming obedient to the point of death, even death on a cross' (Phil. 2:8).

Amen.

PART I

THE SIMPLE GOD

2. SIMPLY PERFECTION

> We believe you to be something than which nothing greater can be thought.
>
> (Anselm)[1]

> When God made a promise to Abraham, since he had no one greater by whom to swear, he swore by himself.
>
> (Heb. 6:13)

In the eleventh century Anselm of Canterbury wrote the contemplative meditation *Proslogion*. In this he reflected on the perfection of God. Anselm realized that since (as the Bible teaches) God is perfect, nothing can be imagined that is greater than him. We are so used to engaging with fallen created things and ideas that thinking and talking about the perfect God requires disciplined effort, and the aid of those who have theologized about the issue before us. We need to be humble enough to learn new terms and manners of speech that have proven necessary for guarding the perfection of God.

The perfection of God is, according to Hebrews 6:13, the grounds upon which we are invited to rest our confidence in the gospel promise given to Abraham (Gal. 3:8). This means that learning how to explain the perfection of God is a crucial aspect of defending and promoting the gospel. Reflecting upon the perfection of God

---

1. Anselm, *Monologion and Proslogion, with the Replies of Gaunilo and Anselm,* ed. T. Williams (Indianapolis: Hackett, 1996), Proslogion, 2.

is not therefore a merely abstract philosophical exercise – it fosters
heartfelt awe and worship of the perfect God, who gave himself in
the death of Christ for his people. Admiration is due to God. So,
in the tradition of Anselm's reflections, Richard of St Victor
observed that God's perfection included perfect beauty: 'No one
believes that that which is more beautiful may be absent in the
supreme beauty, and that conversely one could find in it that which
is less beautiful.'[2]

God, in other words, is the most beautiful being that can be
imagined. Down through the ages Christian theologians have found
that reflection on the perfection of God led them to make the
claim that God is 'simple'. The simplicity of God is the most fundamental doctrinal grammar of divinity. It makes claims about God
that are profound, counter-intuitive, difficult to articulate – and
essential to a biblical vision of God's perfection. As Muller observed
of Calvin:

> Calvin could state without elaboration that 'under the name of God
> is understood a single and simple essence' (*Inst.* 1.13.20). Although he
> indicates no interest whatsoever in speculating about the doctrine of
> divine simplicity, Calvin clearly could confess it when necessary as an
> underpinning of the Christian understanding of God, and the related
> concept of divine aseity was of considerable importance to him,
> particularly in his trinitarian theology. For Calvin, divine simplicity
> functions not as a philosophical ground for discussion of the divine
> essence and attributes, but as a Biblically revealed divine attribute and
> as a basic rule of God language.[3]

If simplicity is the biblically revealed grammar by which we speak
about God, it is vital Christians understand it. God's simplicity
undergirds and recasts everything we believe and say about God.
As has been observed of one Puritan, 'Charnock affirmed that

---

2. R. Angelici, *Richard of Saint Victor, On the Trinity: English Translation and
   Commentary* (Eugene: Cascade, 2011), 5.2.
3. Richard Muller, *Post-Reformation Reformed Dogmatics*, 4 vols. (Grand
   Rapids: Baker, 2006), vol. 3, pp. 273–274.

divine simplicity is absolutely essential for understanding the other divine attributes; indeed, all other divine attributes depend upon this concept.[4]

What do we claim when we state that God is simple? We are saying that

> God is an absolutely simple being, completely devoid of any metaphysical complexity. On the standard understanding of this doctrine – as epitomised in the work of Augustine, Anselm and Aquinas – there are no distinctions to be drawn between God and his nature, goodness, power, or wisdom. On the contrary, God is identical with each of these things, along with anything else that can be predicated of him intrinsically.[5]

Another modern theologian, James Dolezal, states:

> The doctrine of divine simplicity teaches that (1) God is identical with his existence and his essence and (2) that each of his attributes is ontologically identical with his existence and with every other one of his attributes. There is nothing in God that is not God.[6]

Dolezal goes on to quote Stephen Charnock's sermon on God's simplicity:

> God is the most simple being; for that which is first in nature, having nothing beyond it, cannot by any means be thought to be compounded; for whatsoever is so, depends upon the parts whereof it is compounded, and so is not the first being: now God being infinitely simple, hath nothing in himself which is not himself,

---

4. Joel Beeke and Mark Jones, *A Puritan Theology: Doctrine for Life* (Grand Rapids: Reformation Heritage, 2012), Kindle ed.

5. Jeffrey Brower, 'Simplicity and Aseity', in T. P. Flint and M. Rea (eds.), *The Oxford Handbook of Philosophical Theology* (Oxford: Oxford University Press, 2009), p. 105.

6. James Dolezal, *God Without Parts: Divine Simplicity and the Metaphysics of God's Absoluteness* (Eugene: Wipf & Stock, 2011), p. 1.

and therefore cannot will any change in himself, he being his own essence and existence.[7]

Anglican bishop James Ussher taught of God's simplicity, 'It is an essential property in God, whereby everything that is in God is God himself; therefore without parts, mixture or composition, invisible, impassible, all essence; whence he is not called only holy, but holiness, not only just, but justice; see Ex. 33:19, 20.'[8]

The above definitions of simplicity may appear to us obscure and convoluted. However, as Carl Trueman points out, we should remember that Charnock's observations, given in 1680, came from a sermon series:

> The context of Charnock's discourse is emphatically not that of
> the university classroom, the great medieval *summe*, or even of an
> elementary textbook of theology. What Charnock is doing in his
> famous work is preaching the doctrine of God to his congregation –
> and that a non-conformist and thus socially marginalised congregation.
> The context, while pedagogical in a sense, is thus predominately
> homiletical.[9]

God's simplicity means there are no divisions or parts to him. So, God's attributes and his existence are identical. This leads us to say that, strictly speaking, God does not possess an attribute – he is his attributes. As Stephen Holmes puts it:

> God's love is not something that God could still be himself without;
> that would make it an accident. Nor is it one part of his nature; that
> would make God composite. Nor, finally, is it a way God happens to

---

7. Stephen Charnock, *Existence and Attributes of God* 1.333. Cited in Dolezal, *God Without Parts*, p. 1.

8. James Ussher, *A Body of Divinity* (London: Church Society, 2007), p. 64.

9. Carl Trueman, 'Reason and Rhetoric: Stephen Charnock on the Existence of God', in *Faith, History and Philosophy: Philosophical Essays for Paul Helm* (Aldershot: Ashgate, 2008), p. 39.

be which could be different; that would mean that his essence and existence would be separate. Rather, God is his love.[10]

To take another attribute as an example, consider wisdom. God does not *have* a certain amount of wisdom; he does not even have an infinite amount of wisdom. Rather, God *is* perfect wisdom. Were it not so, God would in some way be dependent upon wisdom – he could be conceived as not having it. Lurking behind the wisdom such a 'God' might possess would be a hidden, sub-perfect 'God'. If God is not his wisdom, then any wisdom he does have is something other than God, mingled through or adjoined to his being. The doctrine of simplicity is counter-intuitive and difficult to grasp; but without it our attempts to describe God's attributes become idolatrous. They would necessarily posit a 'God' less perfect than we can imagine or the Bible describes.

Simplicity is mysterious but coherent

Simplicity may appear to be incoherent or self-contradictory. Were this true it would be a serious problem. The Creator–creature distinction reminds us that we should expect God to be profoundly different from us, and at a fundamental level beyond our comprehension. However, recognizing that there are depths to God's nature that are unrevealed to us is not the same as saying that something he has revealed of himself is incoherent. That offends not just God's ordered nature, but his ability to communicate clearly. Simplicity means that God is identical with his attributes and, consequently, each attribute is identical with each other attribute. This troubles many theologians, as it seems incoherent to say that God's love is identical with his wrath, or his wisdom with his eternity. Clearly we can understand something intelligible from the statement that God's love and holiness are distinct aspects of his being. Still, it may be

---

10. Stephen Holmes, '"Something Much Too Plain to Say": Towards a Defence of the Doctrine of Divine Simplicity', in *Listening to the Past: The Place of Tradition in Theology* (Carlisle: Paternoster, 2002), p. 56.

truer at a deeper theological level to say with Jonathan Edwards that 'the holiness of God himself consists in infinite love to himself'.[11] If, as Edwards argued, God's holiness is his love, simplicity would be the doctrine that enables this mysterious insight to be coherent.

Nevertheless many maintain that divine simplicity contradicts logical reason and our usual expectations of words. Simplicity appears to render meaningless anything we claim about an attribute of God. If God is simple, then he is his attributes. Each attribute is identical with his essence. So God does not have love, wisdom, knowledge or power – he is perfect, infinite love, wisdom, knowledge and power. The problem is that if this is true, it would also seem that the attributes must also be identical with each other. If love is identical with God's essence, and power is identical with God's essence, then surely love and power must also be identical with each other? Such incoherence undermines our ability to describe different aspects of God. What do we mean by saying that God is love, if we mean the same thing by stating that God is wisdom or power?

One attempt to defend simplicity is particularly associated with Jeffrey Bower.[12] He argues that the problem I have described can be resolved by thinking of attributes such as power, love and wisdom not as properties, but rather as *truthmakers*. This is a term used in philosophy to refer to that which makes a statement true. I own a cat called Dyson – he is named after the vacuum cleaner! In the statement 'Dyson is a cat' Dyson is a truthmaker. That is to say, Dyson is the reality or condition that ensures the statement 'Dyson is a cat' is true. The truthmaker approach to the classical doctrine of God argues that God is simple, in that he has no parts, and his essence is identical with his attributes. Crucial significance is however given to the idea that God is his own truthmaker. So when it is claimed that God is wisdom, what is being stated is that God is

---

11. Jonathan Edwards, *Writings on the Trinity, Grace, and Faith*, Works of Jonathan Edwards, 26 vols. (New Haven: Yale University Press, 2003), vol. 21, p. 123.

12. See his article in T. P. Flint and M. Rea (eds.), *The Oxford Handbook of Philosophical Theology* (Oxford: Oxford University Press, 2009).

the truthmaker of the statement that God is wisdom. He is also the truthmaker for the observation that God is love, God is power and so forth. This arrangement of the doctrinal claims is ingenious, as it does not entail the logically incoherent conclusion that wisdom, love and power are themselves identical. All that is being said about each attribute is that whatever is being described, the same God guarantees the truthfulness of the statement. God is his own truthmaker.

That the truthmaker vision of God is a circular argument is not at all a problem – circular reasoning is inevitable when one asks what the justification for the truthfulness of a statement about God is. God must be his own truthmaker; otherwise he would be dependent upon something other than himself. The question is whether the truthmaker approach is the best way to explain the apparent incoherence which seems to suggest that simplicity entails making all God's attributes identical with each other.

In my view the charge of incoherence is better rebutted by further reflection on the implications of the Creator–creature distinction and analogical language. These insights enable us to see that simplicity can be maintained in the traditional sense, without lapsing into confusion.

Attributes seem incoherently interchangeable if they are assumed to be unrelational, static properties. It is indeed meaningless to say that a marble has both the properties of being spherical and cubical. The Creator–creature distinction reminds us that the God we are describing is the creator of creatures such as us: we are personal, relational creatures made in the image of the infinitely personal God. Personalness permits a depth of description that can embrace a wide range of characteristics and attributes. On first glance these may appear contradictory or mutually exclusive; with reference to a static, unrelational object they would indeed be so. When we consider a personal being, we are used to accepting that the depth of a person's heart may contain attributes that are apparently contradictory. Tears may be flowing – at the same time – from a sense of both joy and grief. We are used to making allowances for this when speaking about people; how much more do we have to be willing to do this when thinking about the perfect, infinite Creator? Although God's wrath and mercy appear incoherently opposed to each other, might they

not reflect a depth of personal relationality that is glimpsed in our
creaturely encounters, and is perfectly, simply, experienced in the
depths of God's beautiful being?

The Creator–creature distinction also helps us by reminding us
that the fundamental grammar of our speech about God is creaturely
humility. We should be willing to consider the possibility that the
statements 'God is love' and 'God is wisdom' are not incoherent;
God in his infinite perfection and glory is so beyond us that it might
well be that in his unique position of unsurpassed freedom and
plenitude, perfect wisdom is indeed perfect love. Similarly we assume
that omniscience and omnipresence are very different things, one
referring to knowledge, and the other to place. When referring to
creatures, this is indeed the case, but the God who is infinite, perfect
and personal experiences and holds his knowledge and locatedness
in very different ways to his creatures. From God's perspective, the
two attributes may well be identical, with no incoherence, division
or contradiction implied.

Simplicity is a necessary entailment and aspect of God's infinite
perfection. When we say that God's essence is identical with his
attributes, and each attribute is identical with another, we must
remember that we are attempting to describe the uniquely perfect,
infinite, personal Creator. The humility of creatures before their
creator demands that we ponder the possibility that what is displayed
by God's revelation of himself is not incoherence, but a profound
glimpse of the perfect, infinite unity that is uniquely his.

Does accepting the claims of simplicity then render our speech
about God's attributes meaningless? Not at all. All language about
God is analogical. This means that the attributes we describe God
as having reveal something genuine about him to us, in ways we can
understand. As the Anglican theologian E. A. Litton wrote:

> We advance . . . to the utmost limits of analogical reasoning; but we
> are conscious of something beyond, fathomless and immeasurable,
> in the nature of God. 'We know', says Pascal, 'that there is an Infinite,
> though we are ignorant of its nature.' And this something does not, in
> transcending the conceptions of understanding, become to us a mere
> blank, a yawning chasm, 'without form and void'; the created perfections
> which have been our prompters and our guides all along, project their

shadows on the bosom of the Infinite. We still anthropomorphise, we must do if we are to reason about Deity at all.[13]

God's perfect knowledge is identical with his perfect power. I can use the language of these attributes to speak of God, because the Bible does so. Genuine meaning is communicated; that the language is analogical is merely a reminder that I should occasionally recall that God knows things and exerts his power in ways that are radically different from his creatures. To explain all this every time we read the Bible would be tiresome. To dismiss the claim and never give it due consideration would be to treat God as if he is perhaps a bit grander than his creatures, but to lose the thrilling wonder that sweeps over us when we realize that God is genuinely other than us, and yet communicates something of his nature to us in ways we can understand.

Simplicity is a biblical doctrine

For a number of reasons (often combined) many wrongly assume that divine simplicity lacks biblical warrant.

In the first place, rejection of simplicity as unscriptural is often a specific instance of a general, uninformed rejection of systematic theology. A commendable desire to be biblical can lead Christians to feel uncomfortable with terms not explicitly used in the Bible. Calvin had to face this attitude over terms such as 'person' and 'Trinity':

> It is most uncandid to attack the terms which do nothing more than explain what the Scriptures declare and sanction. 'It were better,' they

---

13. E. A. Litton, *Introduction to Dogmatic Theology: On the Basis of the 39 Articles of the Church of England* (London: James Clarke, 1960), p. 60. Litton proceeds to show how the attributes God reveals of himself in Scripture enable us to trust in God as personal, rather than just as a conceptual Infinite: 'There is no food for faith in the abstract ideas of the Infinite and the Absolute . . . a God of attributes alone can be the object of worship' (p. 63).

say, 'to confine not only our meanings but our words within the bounds of
Scripture, and not scatter about foreign terms to become the future seed-
beds of brawls and dissensions. In this way, men grow tired of quarrels
about words; the truth is lost in altercation, and charity melts away amid
hateful strife.' If they call it a foreign term, because it cannot be pointed
out in Scripture in so many syllables, they certainly impose an unjust law –
a law which would condemn every interpretation of Scripture that is not
composed of other words of Scripture . . . The unerring standard both
of thinking and speaking must be derived from the Scriptures: by it all the
thoughts of our minds, and the words of our mouths, should be tested.
But in regard to those parts of Scripture which, to our capacities, are dark
and intricate, what forbids us to explain them in clearer terms – terms,
however, kept in reverent and faithful subordination to Scripture truth,
used sparingly and modestly, and not without occasion?[14]

If we accept Calvin's defence of terms such as 'Trinity' and recognize
that reflection on, and teaching of, the Bible, requires more than
mere repetition of Bible passages, we ought at least to be open to
the possibility of using a term such as 'simplicity'.

The general discomfort about systematic theology ought to be
laid to rest once and for all. There is an important sense in which
all theology is systematic:

Systematicity – the fact of being systematic, of expressing connections
between doctrines – is of the essence of theology. If systematic theology
is concerned with the web that is the entire fabric of Christian profession
and belief, then it subsists in its connections, its relations. Equally,
however, if theology is necessarily concerned with these connections and
relations, it is also necessarily systematic. The term 'systematic theology'
could therefore be considered a tautology. That the exposition of any one
doctrine will always entail either discussion of another or supposition
about some other is a point I take to need no justifying argument.[15]

---

14. John Calvin, *Institutes of the Christian Religion*, tr. Ford Lewis Battles,
     ed. John T. McNeill, 2 vols. (Philadelphia: Westminster, 2001), 1.13.3.
15. Anna Williams, 'What Is Systematic Theology?', *International Journal
     of Systematic Theology* 11.1 (2009), pp. 47–48.

On this view, all theology is in fact systematic. The only question is whether a theologian, preacher or reader is conscious of the systematic assumptions, connections and conclusions being drawn. Those who articulate a case against the value or need of systematic theology are certainly unaware of their assumed systematic theology. Since the assumed systematic theology cannot be critiqued and improved, those who wish to be faithful to Scripture have the greatest of motivations to consider and weigh the claims of systematic theologians. Systematic theologies may be more or less faithful to Scripture; denying the inevitability and importance of systematic theology is the fastest route towards making it unfaithful to Scripture. Openness to engaging in systematic theological reflection will mean that we do not dismiss terms and concepts such as 'simplicity' upon our first encounter. Particularly when it comes to the nature of God himself, we should have the humility to accept that creaturely expressions of truths about God will require the use of terms that are not in common usage, and at first appear counter-intuitive. God is, after all, not just very powerful; he is the perfect, infinite Creator.

A second reason Christians tend to feel that simplicity is unbiblical often marries with the previous instinct. Usually the person who encounters the doctrine of simplicity has had many years of faithful church attendance and Bible reading. There is a natural human tendency to be suspicious of that which is new. As the Nobel Prize winner Daniel Kahneman observes, 'You build the best possible story from the information available to you, and if it is a good story you believe it.'[16] This gives us a bias against taking on board new, unsettling insights. We long to make sense of our intellectual and spiritual lives. Becoming a Christian and becoming part of a church are usually the most radical, transformative steps into making sense of life that a person experiences. Once undertaken, they tend to make us less open to further upheavals. We feel we have arrived. Life makes sense. We know God. The proper sense of relief and satisfaction Augustine articulated with his famous

---

16. D. Kahneman, *Thinking, Fast and Slow* (London: Penguin, 2012), p. 201.

prayer 'Our hearts are restless till they take their rest in You' so
often subsides into a banal self-ease that would tame God. No
more surprises, no further mystery – the journey of discovery has
ended. Such an attitude will inevitably chafe at the introduction of
simplicity's unsettling claims. They challenge the God we have
tamed and rebuke us that the God we 'know' is all too often little
more than a steroid-pumped version of ourselves. The implications
of simplicity are profound and seismic in their capacity to disturb
our assumptions about a tame God. Are our hearts not still restless?
Having come to know God, do we not realize that he is both ever
with and ever beyond us? There is yet more to know of God.
Simplicity is the fundamental grammar of an attitude to God that
accepts he is other than us: mysterious, infinite, yet knowable by
creatures.

Lurking beneath these attitudes is often a third reason for
rejecting simplicity as unbiblical – an unduly low view of the
importance of church tradition. It is, of course, possible to give
theologians and creedal statements from the past too high a status
in our theology: to follow them unquestionably, or to let them elide
scriptural authority. Far more common, though, is the opposite
danger of imagining that faithful Bible reading should be
done without the confusing, polluting toxins of past endeavours.
Almost every patristic and medieval theologian and most of the
Reformation and Puritan era assumed or enthusiastically defended
the doctrine of simplicity. Most of the great confessions of the
Christian church uphold simplicity. So obviously biblical was it
to Reformed theologians such as Turretin that he could use it to
defend other doctrines under attack. As Stephen Holmes notes,
'Turretin had an acute mind, but seemed quite happy to argue
a controversial point on the basis of simplicity. He saw no
problem at all with one person of a simple God becoming incarnate: this was so trivial that it was something to be argued from,
not for.'[17]

With such a weight of tradition witnessing to the fact that great
theologians and church leaders have viewed simplicity as biblical,

---

17. Holmes, 'Something Much Too Plain', p. 59.

we ought to be cautious about assuming otherwise. We should not defend simplicity (or any doctrine) solely due to tradition; but surely even the most chastened view of tradition should allow it the role of challenging our assumptions that we know better than our forebears? By many accounts they often lived more passionately and sacrificially than we do, for the glory of God.

The above three reasons for thinking simplicity unbiblical are all instinctual assumptions rarely articulated as crudely as they are above. The fourth cause for dismissing simplicity as unscriptural has in recent years been documented and argued for at considerable length. This has resulted in both a scholarly and a popularized form of resistance to simplicity. The latter often is found where there is no awareness of the academic literature that has birthed it. This fourth reason for viewing simplicity as unbiblical is the championing of theology as drama or narrative – over and against what is unfairly caricatured as impersonal, timeless, doctrinal facts.

In its popular form, this objection flows from a totalizing vision of the Bible's redemptive-historical plotline. The biblical-theological or redemptive-historical methodology is made to bear more freight than it can carry. Many who were educated in theological institutions from the 1950s to the 1980s felt that they were indoctrinated into a way of reading the Bible that divided up Old and New Testaments, isolated sayings from their context, and consequently opened doors to unrooted interpretations and dry scholarliness. Encountering works from great theologians such as Vos, Kline, Goldsworthy and various covenant theologians was invigorating. Suddenly the whole Bible seemed to fit together. The Old Testament could be preached as Christian Scripture. The marriage of biblical theology[18] with

---

18. 'Biblical Theology examines the development of the Biblical story
     from the Old Testament to the new, and seeks to uncover the
     interrelationships between the two parts . . . Biblical theology
     is a methodical approach to showing these relationships so that
     the Old Testament can be understood as Christian scripture'
     (G. Goldsworthy, *According to Plan* [Nottingham: Inter-Varsity
     Press, 1991], p. 23).

expository preaching[19] seemed a match made in heaven. Only with time did it become evident that some of the parents and children in the family were being neglected.

It was thought that biblical theology could operate without systematic theology. Issues were deemed important in the Bible if they took central positions in the Bible narrative, regardless of whether they had been deemed important to previous generations of Bible readers. So matters such as the sacraments, the nature of God's being, ecclesiology, prolegomena and Christology were little studied. Not only content was forgotten by Christian leaders, but also ways of thinking and reading were lost. It has been wonderful to see the positive fruits of biblical theology joined with expository preaching: renewed confidence in the Bible, sensitivity to genre and (some) principles of interpretation elucidated. Still, systematic theology has been all too often seen in this venture as at best an awkward cousin, at worst the enemy. Dealing with theological matters by utilizing the narrative of Scripture feels very biblical. However, it is extremely reductionistic. A good sense of redemptive history is crucial for sensitive exegesis, which should shape and contribute to our systematic conclusions. To expect the narrative to do all the work for us is asking too much of it.

In addition to this popular privileging of biblical theology over systematic theology there has been a scholarly recasting of systematic theology as a form of narrative or drama. There is much that is exciting and stimulating to the presentation of the Bible as a form of drama. N. T. Wright describes it attractively:

> The Bible itself offers a model for its own reading, which involves knowing where we are within the overall drama and what is appropriate

---

19. 'All true Christian preaching is expository preaching . . . To expound Scripture is to bring out of the text what is there and expose it to view. The expositor prises open what appears to be closed, makes plain what is obscure, unravels what is knotted and unfolds what is tightly packed. The opposite of exposition is imposition, which is to impose on the text what is not there' (John R. W. Stott, *Between Two Worlds: The Art of Preaching in the Twentieth Century* [Grand Rapids: Eerdmans, 1982], p. 125).

within each act. The acts are creation, fall, Israel, Jesus and the church; they constitute the differentiated stages in the divine drama.[20]

Wright explicitly holds forth his view of the Bible as a drama as a way of dealing with the

> sterile debate between people who say, 'The Bible says . . .' and those who answer, 'Yes, and the Bible also says you should stone adulterers, and you shouldn't wear clothes made of two types of cloth.' We urgently need to get past this unnecessary roadblock and on to more serious engagement.[21]

Unfortunately Wright's descriptions of the sort of 'engagement' he envisions flowing from accepting Scripture as drama are not as fruitful or compelling as one might hope. A debate between people who believe the Bible teaches opposing things will not be settled by recasting doctrinal content as a dramatic performance. Wright too often sets the purpose of Scripture against its nature, by means of exaggeration. One example of this may be found in his work *Simply Christian*. There he concludes his chapter on the Bible with the comment 'The Bible is there to enable God's people to be equipped to do God's work in God's world, not to give them an excuse to sit back smugly, knowing they possess all God's truth.'[22] The assumption of Wright's observation is that there are only two options: either Christians use the Bible to do God's work (embracing the drama), or they embody lazy, smug pride (knowing the truth of doctrinal understanding). This is surely a crass caricature which gives the impression that seeking to define theological terms carefully and systematically automatically leads to pride and is opposed to using the Bible to do God's work. Such a mindset leaves little room for systematic, doctrinal reflection upon the nature of God's being. That

---

20. N. T. Wright, *The Last Word: Scripture and the Authority of God: Getting Beyond the Bible Wars* (New York: HarperCollins, 2005), p. 121.

21. Ibid.

22. N. T. Wright, *Simply Christian: Why Christianity Makes Sense* (London: HarperCollins, 2009), p. 157.

task has proven itself to require technical terms and has been born out of precisely the kind of 'The Bible says . . .' debates that Wright's promotion of the Bible as drama claims to transcend.

So there are popular and academic forms of setting narrative against systematic theology. The former lets redemptive-historical theology elide systematics; the latter reconfigures systematic doctrine as a drama. Despite real positive contributions from both, they should not be handled in such a way as to downplay the importance of systematic theologizing. It is indubitably the case that being precedes acting. There is a narrative to Scripture, and there is much insight to be gleaned from this. However, for that drama to be of any significance whatsoever there must be real actors in the play. If the metaphor of a drama has to be developed further, then it must be insisted that the scriptwriter is also real. The God who creates, speaks, directs, interacts and participates must be a real person before he can do any of these things. In the technical terminology, ontology is prior to revelation and salvation. Systematic theology recognizes this, and asks the entirely appropriate questions 'What kind of a being is he?' and 'What may we know of him from his words and actions?'

The Bible is indeed framed as a narrative, from creation to new creation, but throughout it are numerous statements which demonstrate that the Bible itself recognizes the priority of God's being, and reveals many things about him to us.

For example, we are told that 'God is one' (Rom. 3:30), 'your heavenly Father is perfect' (Matt. 5:48), 'God is Spirit' (John 4:24), 'the Father has life in himself' (John 5:26), 'with the Lord one day is as a thousand years, and a thousand years as one day' (2 Peter 3:8), 'God, who never lies' (Titus 1:2), Jesus Christ displays his 'perfect patience' (1 Tim. 1:16). These and countless other comments in the Bible make claims about the nature of God: his perfection, time-lessness, oneness, spirituality, truthfulness, and so forth.

Simplicity is not an unbiblical idea; it is the term used by generations of Christians and the church to describe the kind of existence God must have if he is indeed all the Bible says he is. Only if he is this simple God can he do all the gracious, loving things the Bible says he does. Systematic theology is not opposed to biblical theology, and simplicity is not an unbiblical doctrine. Quite the opposite – the doctrine of divine simplicity is a challenge to uphold the biblical vision of God in its disturbing, unsettling yet eternally satisfying totality.

Simplicity accords with threeness

Simplicity, abstracted from other distinctive Christian doctrines, can be affirmed by Muslims and Jews. Christians believe there is one God, who is a trinity of persons, each fully God. The threeness of God would seem a substantial obstacle to the idea that the one true God is simple. Augustine realized this would be an area of misunderstanding and argued that the threeness of God and simplicity accord. The relevant passage merits full quotation since it has proven itself one of the single most important texts in the development of the doctrine of God:

> This Trinity is one God; and none the less simple because a Trinity. For we do not say that the nature of the good is simple, because the Father alone possesses it, or the Son alone, or the Holy Spirit alone; nor do we say, with the Sabellian heretics, that it is only nominally a Trinity, and has no real distinction of persons; but we say it is simple, because it is what it has, *with the exception of the relation of the persons to one another.* For, in regard to this relation, it is true that the Father has a Son, and yet is not Himself the Son; and the Son has a Father, and is not Himself the Father. But, as regards Himself, irrespective of relation to the other, each is what He has; thus, He is in Himself living, for He has life, and is Himself the Life which He has. It is for this reason, then, that the nature of the Trinity is called simple, because it has not anything which it can lose, and because it is not one thing and its contents another, as a cup and its drink, or a body and its colour, or the air and the light or heat of it, or a mind and its wisdom. For none of these is what it has: the cup is not drink, nor the body colour, nor the air light and heat, nor the mind wisdom. And hence they can be deprived of what they have, and can be turned or changed into other qualities and states, so that the cup may be emptied of the liquid of which it is full, the body be discoloured, the air darken, the mind grow silly . . . According to this, then, those things which are essentially and truly divine are called

simple, because in them quality and substance are identical, and
because they are divine, or wise, or blessed in themselves, and without
extraneous supplement.[23]

Augustine here affirms the central claim of simplicity: God is his
attributes. God does not have life as a cup has the drink it contains;
God is life. Glorious implications are mentioned by Augustine: God
cannot lose his attributes, decline or change. He is supremely reliable
and self-sufficient. Crucially Augustine realizes that the relations
of the Trinity are an exception to the key teaching of simplicity.
It is not the mere fact of threeness that creates the exception to
simplicity; it is the inherent, inescapable other-person-centred relationality of the Father, Son and Spirit.

The Son, considered as the Son, cannot be contained within the
core definition of simplicity, because a Son requires a Father. A
being is simple if it is its attributes. Simplicity denies dependency
and speaks of self-sufficiency. The threeness of the Trinity involves
three persons in mutual relational dependence. The Father
would not be the Father without the Son. The Son would not be
the Son without the Father. The Spirit would not be the Spirit
of the Father and Son without the Father and Son. The exceptions
to simplicity are the relationships that form the mutual intimacy
between Father, Son and Spirit. Those relationships form a
beautiful dependence and other-person-centred love that is infinite
and self-sufficient.

The Augustinian relational exception must be read back into our
vision of simplicity. If this is done, it is abundantly clear that the
Christian doctrine of divine simplicity is not a modification or
addition to the Islamic and Jewish understandings of simplicity.
The Christian God is radically different from them. The Christian
God is the simple God who is three persons, each of whom is fully
that simple God and fully a person in relation with the others.
The Augustinian relational exception, then, rules out the caricatures
that so often lead to premature rejection of the doctrine of divine

---

23. Augustine, *City of God*, ed. H. Bettenson and G. R. Evans (London:
    Penguin, 1984), 11.10 (my italics).

simplicity. When we say God is simple, we are not believing he is static, inert, immobile, unrelational or inward looking. These would be as erroneous as the more crass mistake of thinking that God's oneness is, or is similar to, a created object's solidity. God's perfection is a relational self-sufficiency that joyously finds expression in the three persons of the Trinity looking beyond themselves in other-person-centred self-giving love. Saying that this God of threeness is simple is to affirm that his love, intimacy, outward-looking generosity and joyful passion are as perfect and infinite as can be imagined.

The Bible says that God is love (1 John 4:8) – simplicity is the philosophical and theological language that enables us to say that this is true, to a greater extent than we naturally assume. Simplicity is not opposed to the threeness of God. As Augustine discerned, simplicity is the insistence that the three persons of the Trinity are as loving, perfect and infinite as they possibly could be.

Simplicity is perfectly personal

The doctrine which insists that God is as perfectly personal as can be conceived is that of simplicity. Simplicity guards and counter-intuitively preserves glorious depths of trinitarian relationality. Such was the view of Calvin: 'For Calvin, divine simplicity functions . . . as a Biblically revealed divine attribute and as a basic rule of God language identifying God as non-composite, particularly for the sake of a right understanding of the doctrine of the trinity.'[24]

Muller correctly notes that Calvin realized simplicity, which emphasized oneness, far from opposing the relationality of threeness, was actually essential for a true view of that personal three-ness. Though Calvin affirmed this, he was content (as were Farel, Musculus and Zwingli) to agree with Catholic teaching on the matter and refrain from developing the doctrine of simplicity in any depth. Theologians wishing to reflect on the nature of God's personalness,

---

24. Muller, *Post-Reformation Reformed Dogmatics*, vol. 3, p. 274.

in so far as it is framed by the doctrine of simplicity, find more resources in the writings of Aquinas.[25]

Aquinas built on Augustine's theology to offer the church one of the richest defences of simplicity. He wrote:

> Augustine says in The Trinity 4.6.7 that *God is truly and absolutely simple* . . . It is clear that God is in no way composite, but is altogether simple. Since every composite being is posterior to its component parts, and is dependent upon them, but God is the first being. Further, every composite being has a cause, for things cannot be united unless something causes them to join. But God is uncaused.[26]

The description Aquinas gives of God in his *Summa Theologica* can appear unpalatable to modern readers. It seems that such a God is little more than a collection of impersonal philosophical denials and terms – hardly a personal God who would elicit worship and love. After recognizing this problem, Burrell argues that Aquinas is 'engaged in the metalinguistic project of mapping out the grammar appropriate *in divinis*. He is proposing the logic proper to discourse about God.'[27] In other words, simplicity is a technical way of explicating the assumptions and language necessary for believing all that Scripture reveals about God.

When Aquinas is read, we discover that the vision of God he finds consistent with his strong doctrine of simplicity is one of an intensely personal and loving God. Commenting on John 3:16, Aquinas extols God's love:

---

25. Those wishing to pursue another tradition's attempt to uphold personalness and simplicity may consult Oliver Crisp, 'Jonathan Edwards on Divine Simplicity', *Religious Studies* 39 (2003), pp. 23–41.

26. Thomas Aquinas, *Summa Theologica*, 5 vols. (Notre Dame: Ave Maria, 1948), 1a.1.q3.a7 (italics original). Previous arguments for simplicity given by Aquinas include a range of conclusions flowing from exploring claims about God that must be denied, e.g. that he has a physical body, a beginning, and so forth.

27. D. B. Burrell, *Aquinas: God and Action* (Chicago: University of Scranton Press, 2008), p. 19.

Here we should note that the cause of all our good is the Lord and
divine love. For to love is, properly speaking, to will good to someone.
Therefore, since the will of God is the cause of things, good comes
to us because God loves us. And God's love is the cause of the good
of nature: 'You love everything which exists' (Wis 11:25). It is also the
cause of the good which is grace: 'I have loved you with an everlasting
love, and so I have drawn you' i.e., through grace (Jer. 31:3). But it is
because of his great love that he gives us the good of glory. So he
shows us here, from four standpoints, that this love of God is the
greatest.[28]

He proceeds in the commentary to meditate on God's love from
the perspectives of God, sinners, the greatness of the gift, and the
fruit of the gift. In *Summa Theologica* Aquinas cites 1 John 4:16 and
observes, 'We must assert that in God there is love, because love is
the first movement of the will and every appetitive faculty.'[29] Aquinas
recognizes that simplicity may be thought to militate against the
personal nature of love. He notes that the objection could be put
thus: 'Dionysius says in *Divine Names 4* love is a uniting and binding
force. But this cannot take place in God, since he is simple. Therefore
love does not exist in God.'[30] Aquinas rejects this opposition of
simplicity to love:

An act of love always tends towards two things; to the good that one
wills and to the person for whom one wills it: since to love a person is to
wish that person good. Hence, inasmuch as we love ourselves, we wish
ourselves good; and, so far as possible, union with that good. So love is
called the uniting force, even in God, yet without implying composition;
for the good that he wills for himself, is no other than himself, who
is good by his essence. And by the fact that anyone loves another, he
wills good to that other. Thus he puts the other, as it were, in the place

---

28. Thomas Aquinas, 'Commentary on the Gospel of John, Lecture 3',
    Magi Books, http://dhspriory.org/thomas/english/John3.htm
    (accessed 10 Nov. 2013).

29. Aquinas, *Summa Theologica* 1a.1.q20.a1.

30. Ibid.

of himself; and regards the good done to him as done to himself. So
far love is a binding force, since it aggregates another to ourselves, and
refers his good to our own. And then again the divine love is a binding
force, inasmuch as God wills good to others, yet it implies no
composition in God.[31]

Aquinas then explicitly argues that God is love, and notes that
this in no way implies composition, which would deny the doctrine
of divine simplicity. Though his theology is often thought to
emphasize the oneness of God at the expense of his threeness,
Aquinas argues that the love of God is trinitarian: 'The Father loves
not only the Son but also himself and us by the Holy Spirit.'[32]

Commenting on this passage from Aquinas, Dodds explains
lyrically the implications of trinitarian love flowing from a simple
God:

> Unlike our love, which is awakened by the goodness perceived in
> the beloved, God's love is not caused by the goodness of its object.
> His love for himself is not caused by his own goodness since it is
> one with his goodness, and 'a thing cannot be its own cause' (*Summa
> Theologica* 1a.1.Q19.5). Nor is his love for creatures caused by his love
> for his own goodness since it is by one and the same act that God
> wills both his own goodness as his proper object and the existence
> of creatures as ordered to his goodness, and, again, a thing cannot
> be its own cause. And certainly his love for creatures is not caused
> by the goodness of creatures since it is the very source of whatever
> goodness is found in them. God's love is in no way caused. No change
> in his will is brought about by the goodness of the beloved. While our
> love has the character of both change and immovability in its
> inception, God's eternal and abiding love has only the character of
> immutability. As our love is the unchanging source of our deeds,
> God's love is the immutable source of his creative and providential
> action. But while our love gives rise to various desires and passions
> as it seeks to attain union with the beloved, God's love involves only

---

31. Ibid.
32. Ibid. 1a.1.q37.a2.

the boundless joy of eternal possession and complete union with his own goodness.[33]

Since simplicity coheres with the threeness of God, it is entirely possible to uphold a strong doctrine of simplicity and a stirring vision of God as love. Aquinas did just that. The vast majority of modern writers who reject simplicity do so on the basis of a secular philosophical account, which ignores the biblical portrayal of God as trinitarian. Such accounts refuse to treat the full sweep of arguments from writers such as Aquinas or Augustine, and so fail to appreciate that far from making the trinitarian God impersonal (a preposterous and idolatrous idea), simplicity is the insistence that the trinitarian God is eternally, perfectly, infinitely nothing less than personal love.

Simplicity guards God's 'Godness'

Divine simplicity is a rich, positive, creative insight into the nature of God. It is the doctrinal claim that guards God's 'Godness', ensuring that the claims we make for him do indeed conform reliably to the fullness of what he has revealed of himself in Scripture.

We find simplicity a difficult concept to understand because everything we encounter in creation is composed of parts, temporal, changing and has potential. God, since he is simple, has no parts, is atemporal, unchanging and fully realized. The meaning of some of these claims will be made clear in the following chapters; for now it is sufficient to observe that our experiences are bound up with things that are not simple. We become so used to this that we naturally transfer our assumptions to God. We think of God as if he were fundamentally like his creation.

Simplicity, then, is the doctrine that challenges us out of these idolatrous assumptions. God is not part of his creation. He is not

---

33. Michael Dodds, *The Unchanging God of Love: Thomas Aquinas and Contemporary Theology on Divine Immutability* (New York: Catholic University of America Press, 2008), pp. 207–208.

even the most powerful part of his creation. We do not arrive at a satisfactory concept of God by extrapolating from, or extending the power and might of, a created thing. God's power is of an absolutely different kind. God's existence is radically other.

There are similarities and meaningful connections between God's nature and humans. After all, we are made in his image. Analogical language is used throughout the Bible to reveal to us that God is loving, all-knowing and immortal. These descriptions have meaning for us; yet we have to accept that the way in which God exists, his perfection and his sheer Godness mean that we must avoid attributing to him an essentially creaturely gait.

So engrained are our habits of conceptualizing things that are part of creation, that it takes considerable mental and spiritual effort to describe a God who is different. The doctrine of divine simplicity is that act of humble, spiritual attention to Scripture that has led the church to guard the fundamental shape of its proclamation about God: that God is.

Simplicity is not one among many claims made of the Christian God; it is the grammar of all speech about God. As such the value and power of simplicity will become more apparent as we turn to consider other aspects of the doctrine of God. The usual reason that each of the other controversial claims about God is challenged is that the value of simplicity is not appreciated. So, for example, a way of conceptualizing God's perfect knowledge, which ignores simplicity, will (despite areas of biblical fidelity and limited truthfulness) hold inconsistencies and problems. Apart from utilizing simplicity, it will be the theological equivalent of trying to square a circle: giving a creaturely account of the Creator.

Simplicity guards God's Godness by maintaining that he is his attributes. Each of God's attributes is identical with the others. God's existence is perfect, infinite and undivided. Well may we say that we do not immediately or fully understand these things. We are creatures attempting to speak of our creator. Our struggles are a spur towards awe and wonder.

Meditation: wonder

> No one considers, nor is there knowledge or discernment to say,
> 'Half of it I burned in the fire; I also baked bread on its coals;
> I roasted meat and have eaten. And shall I make the rest of it
> an abomination? Shall I fall down before a block of wood?'
>
> (Isa. 44:19)

> You, O king, have made a decree, that every man who hears the
> sound of the horn, pipe, lyre, trigon, harp, bagpipe, and every kind
> of music, shall fall down and worship the golden image.
>
> (Dan. 3:10)

> The twenty-four elders fall down before him who is seated on the
> throne and worship him who lives for ever and ever. They cast
> their crowns before the throne . . .
>
> (Rev. 4:10)

Forgive me, O God, for the many times my heart has fallen down in wonder, worship and awe at things that are less than you.

Sometimes of my own volition, sometimes seemingly compelled from without, the end result is that I am painfully used to being impressed at things that are less than you.

Awaken my restless heart, Lord, to yourself: your infinite perfection, your beautiful love, your unique majesty. The angels before your throne avert their gaze from your glory. Moses took off his sandals. The apostle John fell at your feet as though dead. Give me a sense of the honour due to you. Enable me to think of you in your perfect Godness, in ways that are more true to who you really are. May that be one more step along the way, to that future day when you will let me see you as you really are, and permit me the honour of falling down before you, and laying all you have given me at your feet.

Amen.

3. BACK TO THE FUTURE

Struggling with time

Of old you laid the foundation of the earth,
    and the heavens are the work of your hands.
They will perish, but you will remain;
    they will all wear out like a garment.
You will change them like a robe, and they will pass away,
    but you are the same, and your years have no end.

                                      (Ps. 102:25–27)

Do not overlook this one fact, beloved, that with the Lord one day
is as a thousand years, and a thousand years as one day.

                                            (2 Peter 3:8)

Augustine struggled to explain the nature of time. He prayed:

There was never any time when you had not made anything, because
you made time itself ... What is time? Who could find any quick or easy
answer to that? Who could even grasp it in his thought clearly enough to

put the matter into words? Yet is there anything to which we refer in conversation with more familiarity?[1]

Augustine realized that if God had created all things, then time must be one of the things he created. Were we to speak of God's doing something before creation, that would technically be untrue. There was no time before creation in which he could be performing time-bound actions. Since all our language is time bound, we struggle to state truths about anything that may lie outside time. The word 'before' is a tensed word: technically it is incorrect to use it to refer to a state of timelessness.

It is all too easy to assume that God experiences time in a manner very similar to us, albeit with greater insight and vision. Even if we accept that God, as creator, must be radically different from his creation, we struggle with temporal words to express this. Many metaphors, claims and stories of the Bible use analogical language that has been taken by mainstream Christian theologians to teach that God, in his infinite perfection, is eternal. Clarifying what we mean by this is valuable for many reasons, not least for the pastoral benefit of giving confidence that God has infinite knowledge.

The eternal God

To be eternal is to have an existence that is timeless. Understanding and conceiving this is extraordinarily difficult for us. Easier to grasp are ideas such as 'everlasting'. The challenge eternality poses to our understanding is indeed one of the main reasons people reject it. However, as Paul Helm notes in his seminal defence of God's eternality:

> The rationale for introducing the possibility that God exists in a timeless eternity lies in the fact that this supposition will enable more sense to be

1. Augustine, *The Confessions*, tr. Maria Boulding, ed. John Rotelle, The Works of Saint Augustine, a Translation for the 21st Century, 11 vols. (New York: New City, 1997), 11.14.17.

made of what would otherwise be difficult, and so vindicate an
unattenuated Christian theism. It is agreed that the idea of a timeless
eternity is obscure and not fully graspable, but there is nothing novel
in the introduction of a concept such as electron or virus to make
sense of data otherwise unaccountable.[2]

As temporal creatures, all our knowing and relating is done in
time. I remember what I did yesterday. I imagine where I will be
tomorrow. It is difficult to imagine how two beings could relate
personally if one of them did not exist in time. The apparent impossibility of an eternal God relating personally to temporal creatures
is another reason many shy from the classical view of eternality. It
would seem to many that an eternal God is necessarily impersonal
and unrelational. As Swinburne observes, a timeless God would be,
'a very lifeless thing'.[3]

It also may seem that the great turning points of the Bible's
narrative militate against God's being timeless. In particular, do not
the creation and incarnation presuppose he experiences time?

It would seem that creation of a temporal world and involvement
with it as intimately as the Bible suggests require that God himself
be in time. Furthermore it has often been thought that God's
creation of the universe demands a change within himself. Does
not the decision to create signify a change within God's will?

Change is a temporal reality. Hence if it is thought that creation
involved God in change, then he cannot be eternal. Augustine
thought that the reality of God's creation of all things meant that
one of the things he created must have been time itself. Time is
something that did not exist before God created, and therefore the
God who created time could not be anything other than timeless
or eternal:

> What epochs of time could have existed, that had not been created by
> you? . . . There could not have been any passing times before you created

---

2. Paul Helm, *Eternal God: A Study of God Without Time*, 2nd ed. (Oxford:
   Oxford University Press, 2010), p. 23.

3. R. Swinburne, *The Coherence of Theism* (Oxford: Clarendon, 1993), p. 214.

times. If, therefore, there was no time before heaven and earth came to
be, how can anyone ask what you were doing then? There was no such
thing as 'then' when there was no time.[4]

As it is difficult to explain how a timeless God could changelessly
create a temporal world, it is challenging to understand how a
timeless God could become human at a particular point in time –
without undergoing any change that would require God to be not
eternal, but temporal. Augustine recognized that were God to have
changed (in creation or the incarnation), he would not be eternal:
'A will that is subject to change, and anything changeable is not
eternal. But our God is eternal.'[5]

It must be accepted, then, that there are weighty arguments
against the idea that God is eternal. The difficulty of conceptualizing
an eternal God, the challenge to personal relationality and the
assumptions that God must have changed in creation or incarnation
are among the most potent objections to eternality.

Nevertheless it is a key tenet of the classical doctrine of God that
the creator of the universe exists outside, and apart from, time. The
eternity of God was described by the sixth-century theologian
Boethius as

> [t]hat which embraces and possesses simultaneously only the whole
> fullness of everlasting life, which lacks nothing of the future and has lost
> nothing of the past, that is what may properly be said to be eternal. Of
> necessity it will always be present to itself, controlling itself, and have
> present the infinity of fleeting time.[6]

Boethius was a philosophical thinker, but that does not mean that
his insights are not necessary to make sense of the Bible's vision
of God. As Rob Lister recently argued, there were many pagan
philosophical concepts, some of which were utilized by Christian

---

4. Augustine, *Confessions* 11.13.6.
5. Ibid. 12.15.
6. Boethius, *The Consolation of Philosophy*, ed. V. E. Watts (London: Penguin, 1969), p. 164.

theologians, others of which were rejected as unscriptural.[7] For the mainstream of Christian teachers, for most of the history of the church, Boethius' definition of eternity was thought an inevitable implication of the Bible's statements about God's nature, knowledge and actions. So the Puritan Stephen Charnock preached that

> [e]ternity is a perpetual duration, which hath neither beginning nor end; time hath both. Those things we say are in time, that have beginning, grow up by degrees, have succession of parts. Eternity is contrary to time, and is therefore a permanent and immutable state; a perfect possession of life without any variation. It comprehends within itself all years, all ages; all periods of ages; it never begins![8]

Similarly, as Anselm worshipped God he was compelled to pray:

> Through your eternity you were, you are, and you will be. And since being past is different from being future, and being present is different from being past and from being future, how does your eternity exist always as a whole? Does none of your eternity pass by so that it no longer is, and is none of it going to become what, so to speak, it not yet is? Then, in no case were you yesterday or will you be tomorrow; instead, yesterday, today and tomorrow, you are. Or better, you simply are – existing beyond all time. You do not exist yesterday or today or tomorrow; for yesterday, today, and tomorrow are nothing other than temporal distinctions. Now, although without you nothing can exist, you are not in space or time but all things are in you. For you are not contained by anything but rather you contain all things.[9]

God's eternity, as understood by Boethius and Anselm, is very different from an idea such as 'everlasting'. God's 'eternity is not a

---

7. R. Lister, *God Is Impassible and Impassioned: Toward a Theology of Divine Emotion* (Wheaton: Crossway; Nottingham: Apollos, 2012), p. 60.

8. Stephen Charnock, *Discourses upon the Existence and Attributes of God* (London: T. Tegg, 1840), p. 175.

9. Anselm, *Monologion and Proslogion, with the Replies of Gaunilo and Anselm*, ed. T. Williams (Indianapolis: Hackett, 1996), p. 106.

different temporal mode, but strictly speaking, no-time'.[10] God's being eternal does not merely mean that he continues to exist for ever, or that he has always existed. This would be to try to conceptualize eternity as if language may be used of God in a univocal fashion. We do not arrive at an accurate conception of God's eternity simply by applying words and concepts to him that we use casually of ourselves, and multiplying them upwards. God's eternity is not simply a longer version of our time-bound lives. As Shults observes:

> Our experience of time has been shaped by our culture's framing of temporal experience in terms of the linear and mechanistic measurements of clock and calendar . . . most of our efforts to frame concepts operate unconsciously within this conceptual frame. Breaking out of this frame will require the kind of effort that is qualitatively different from replacing one concept with another. It may require a new way of ordering consciousness itself.[11]

Thus God's eternity means that temporal terms, strictly speaking, may not be applied to him. As Charnock observed, 'Eternity . . . is denying of God any measurement of time, as immensity is denying of him any bounds of place; as immensity is the diffusion of his essence, so eternity is the duration of his essence.'[12] God's eternity is a qualitatively different kind of existence to the one his creatures experience. God is outside and beyond time. God's omnipresence means that he is present everywhere. This is not a consequence of his having a much bigger body than us; it is a result of his having a qualitatively different form of existence: a spiritual, non-physical one. Similarly, God's eternity means that he is present to all times. This is not a consequence of his living longer than us; it is a result of his having a qualitatively different form of existence: an

---

10. Hannah Arendt, *Love and Saint Augustine* (London: University of Chicago Press, 1996), p. 56.
11. F. LeRon Shults, *Reforming the Doctrine of God* (Grand Rapids: Eerdmans, 2005), p. 199.
12. Charnock, *Discourses*, p. 175.

eternal, non-temporal one. This is difficult for time-bound creatures to imagine, but it should fill us with a sense of wonder and praise for God.

Being outside time does not mean that God cannot know what happens inside time, nor that he cannot interact with a temporal order. Quite the opposite! It does, of course, shape the way he does these things. God can interact with his physical creation, though he is spiritual. This is not entirely surprising, since he created physical reality. It would perhaps be odd for him to create something he could not interact with. Similarly God created time. It is part of the created order. And though God is not himself temporal, he can interact with, and know all that occurs in, the times he has made. Indeed, precisely because God is not temporal, he has perfect knowledge of all events in time. For us creatures who dwell in time, our experience and knowledge of temporal matters is gained by living through them, looking back at the past, or projecting expectations forward to the future. Our knowledge of past, present and future is always growing or becoming blurred – it changes. God, on the other hand never changes. He is always perfect and infinite. Were God to encounter time as we do, he would have to experience change and therefore not be perfect. So God's knowledge of time is of a different order to ours. For God, all times are present to him. He knows all things not by learning or experiencing them directly, but by comprehending, upholding and enfolding all reality and all times within himself. God shared his personal name with Moses – 'I AM' (Exod. 3:14). Jesus proclaimed that 'before Abraham was, I am' (John 8:58). Jesus is the one who is 'before all things, and in him all things hold together' (Col. 1:17). He is 'the Alpha and the Omega, the first and the last, the beginning and the end' (Rev. 22:13). Were God to experience time in the way we do, or in an analogous fashion, there would be an element of change, frailty and openness to doubt or failure within his nature. Only because the Bible everywhere assumes God's unique being is a timeless, that is an eternal, nature, can we praise him as the 'King of ages, immortal, invisible, the only God' (1 Tim. 1:17), and with all God's people say 'The eternal God is your dwelling place' (Deut. 33:27).

Alternatives to eternity

Three alternatives to the classical view of God's eternity have been promoted in recent years. In the light of the difficulty temporal beings have conceptualizing eternity it is understandable that alternatives have been proposed. It may be noted that diverging from the traditional understanding of eternality has not always been thought of as within the bounds of orthodoxy. Muller writes of the late Reformation era:

> There was hardly a doubt in the minds of the various major commentators of the age – as there was no doubt in the minds of the Reformers, when they encountered this text [Ps. 102:26] – that it taught the doctrine of eternity as held in traditional theological systems.[13]

The alternatives to eternality raise a number of problems for our view of God. They create more problems than they solve, and in at least one case the modern proposal is at least as difficult to understand as the classical vision of eternity.

The first alternative to the idea that God is eternal is a flat denial of that teaching. In place of eternity the conviction that God is temporal would be substituted. God is thought, then, to exist in time as we do. This appears to make the issue of how he relates to people in time quite straightforward. God can speak with us and intervene in history in much the same manner as I am typing these words. God's actions may be done with a greater power, insight and knowledge, but in all essentials his interactions with temporal creation would be merely more impressive versions of the same type of behaviour performed by me as I remember books I have read in the past, enter this knowledge into my computer in the present and look forward to your reading it in the future. To the extent that one can understand the process involved in my actions described, one can grasp the idea of God's acting in a similar fashion.

---

13. Richard Muller, *Post-Reformation Reformed Dogmatics*, 4 vols. (Grand Rapids: Baker, 2006), vol. 3, p. 351.

The idea of a temporal God seems to make his relationship to temporal reality more comprehensible; it does so only superficially. If God is temporal, then time could not have been created at creation – it would be a feature of his experience prior to creation. This would either make it an attribute of God, which can never be lost or improved upon, or it would be something external to God that in some sense he would be dependent upon. Neither option fits well with the Bible's vision of a God whose being is infinitely exalted and perfect.

It seems at first glance that a temporal God would find it easier to become incarnate. The birth of Jesus becomes easier to understand (it might appear) if the one being born is not eternal, but temporal. The difficulty is that the Bible emphasizes the mystery, wonder and surprise of Christ's birth. The whole point is that the God who dwells outside time took on flesh and was born in time. The mystery is not a problem that needs to be explained away – it is the whole point of the incarnation and as such motivated one of Charles Wesley's magnificent (but sadly underutilized) carols:

> GLORY be to God on high,
> And peace on earth descend!
> God comes down, he bows the sky,
> And shows himself our friend:
> God the invisible appears!
> God, the blest, the great I AM,
> Sojourns in this vale of tears,
> And Jesus is his name.
>
> Him the angels all adored,
> Their Maker and their King.
> Tidings of their humbled Lord
> They now to mortals bring.
> Emptied of his majesty,
> Of his dazzling glories shorn,
> Being's source begins to be,
> And God himself is born!
>
> See the eternal Son of God
> A mortal Son of man;

Dwelling in an earthly clod,
Whom heaven cannot contain!
Stand amazed, ye heavens, at this!
See the Lord of earth and skies;
Humbled to the dust he is,
And in a manger lies.

We, the sons of men, rejoice,
The Prince of peace proclaim;
With heaven's host lift up our voice,
And shout Immanuel's name:
Knees and hearts to him we bow;
Of our flesh and of our bone,
Jesus is our brother now,
And God is all our own.

Repeatedly in this carol the reason for praising and worshipping God is that the eternal God, the great I AM, has been born into the ravages of time. The good news of Christmas is not that a God used to time and temporal experiences visited our planet to do a bit more of what he had previously been doing. Rather it is that the eternal God, who dwells apart from time, entered temporality to show in time the love he timelessly enjoys within himself.

How would a temporal God know all things? The key to defending God's perfect knowledge (as we shall see) is his eternity. If God were temporal, then his knowledge would be temporal. This suggests he has not always known all things – either God has changed (growing in knowledge) or he does not possess total knowledge of all things. Temporality offers a superficially comprehensible God at the price of the glory of the incarnation and perfect omniscience.

A second alternative to eternity has been argued for by the Reformed theologian John Frame. He calls his view 'temporalism':

I shall argue that God is indeed temporal in his immanence, but that he
is (most likely) atemporal in his transcendence. He exists in time as
he exists throughout creation. But he also (I say with some reservations)
exists beyond time, as he exists beyond creation. So in this section we
will consider arguments to the effect that God is merely temporal, with

no supratemporal existence. That is the position I will refer to as
'temporalism.'[14]

Frame is not arguing that God is merely temporal. He suggests that
the main reason people argue for that is the influence of a libertarian
view of human free will, which he rejects. Rather, Frame is saying
that a vision of God as being both temporal and transcendent is the
best resolution to the issue:

> God is temporal after all, but not merely temporal. He really exists in
> time, but he also transcends time in such a way as to exist outside it.
> He is both inside and outside of the temporal box – a box that can
> neither confine him nor keep him out. This is the model that does
> the most justice to the Biblical data.[15]

Frame emphasizes that God is both in time and that he transcends
time. In my view his evidences for God's being in time (e.g. the
succession of events in the biblical narrative) are best understood
as not evidence that God is in time, but rather that God acts in time.
The question of whether a God who acts in time is himself best
described as in any sense temporal is a question unresolved by the
fact that he acts in time. In the end Frame's commendable attempt
to do justice to the full range of biblical affirmations leads him to
affirm too much. In doing so the content of terms such as 'eternity'
is changed. That is to say, if you say that God is both eternal and
temporal, you cannot be using the word 'eternal' in the manner it
was intended by theologians such as Augustine or Turretin, who
wrote, 'We maintain that God is free from every difference of time,
and no less from succession than from beginning and end.'[16] An
eternity that can be combined with temporality is not the eternity
that is a claim for the absence of temporality. Sure enough, Frame

---

14. John Frame, *The Doctrine of God: A Theology of Lordship* (Phillipsburg:
    P. & R., 2002), p. 549.

15. Ibid., p. 559.

16. Francis Turretin, *Institutes of Elenctic Theology*, 3 vols. (Phillipsburg:
    P. & R., 1992), vol. 1, 10.1.

finds it difficult to affirm simultaneously both aspects of what he claims for God, and instead emphasizes God's temporality:

> I see God's transcendence, not as his absence from the space-time world, but as his presence as the Lord. Eternity, for example, as I shall explain it, does not primarily mean that God is 'outside' time (though it is better to say that he is 'outside' than that he is 'inside'), but rather that he is present in time as the Lord, with full control over the temporal sequence.[17]

With this move, God's temporality swallows up his eternity. Frame appears to affirm God as eternal and temporal – indeed he states as much. In reality he redefines eternity to mean a form of temporal existence. While Frame's motivations and intentions are clearly good, and he does not personally follow the implications of his constructs, his temporalist model would most likely prove a shaky foundation for a robust doctrine of God that affirms all the Bible claims for him. So, in contrast to the classical view of the incarnation being the eternal God's entering a new form of existence, Frame writes:

> All Christians acknowledge that in the incarnation of Jesus Christ, the eternal God entered time and experienced to the full the passing of moments and the changes of human life. But in Christ, God entered, not a world that was otherwise strange to him, but a world in which he had been dwelling all along.[18]

A third alternative to the traditional concept of an eternal God has been argued for by the evangelist, philosopher and apologist William Lane Craig. This is that God is timeless apart from creation, and in time with creation. Craig suggests:

> At the moment of creation, God comes into the relation of sustaining the universe or at the very least that of coexisting with the universe, a relation he did not before have. As God successively sustains each

---

17. Frame, *Doctrine of God*, p. 543.

18. John Frame, *No Other God: A Response to Open Theism* (Phillipsburg: P. & R., 2001), p. 159.

subsequent moment or event in being a multiplicity of new relations result. So that even if God is timeless *sans* creation, his free decision to create a temporal world constitutes also a free decision on his part to enter into time and to experience the reality of tense and temporal being.[19]

Helm points out that Craig holds there to be 'two phases of God's life, one timeless and one temporal'.[20] There is a case for arguing that Craig's view is incoherent. Brian Leftow has done so[21] and Craig himself admits his position is 'extremely bizarre', 'startling and not a little odd'.[22]

Craig insists that his view is not fairly represented by a summary that presents these two phases of God's existence as temporally related. In other words Craig does not hold that God was at one time (before creation) timeless, and then he underwent a temporal change and became temporal. It is understandable that many have thought this is what he means, but Craig denies it. Rather he wishes to say that timelessness and temporality are modes of God's existence. They are modes in God's life, but are not best understood as phases that occur before and after each other. Craig does not explain how they are related to each other, but he denies the obviously incoherent idea that the timeless God changed at a point of time into a temporal God.

Were it not for the fact that Craig so strenuously opposes the classical teaching of God's eternality, one could argue that his view is a misstated view, actually compatible with traditional teaching.

---

19. William Lane Craig, 'The Tensed Versus the Tenseless Theory of Time: A Watershed for the Conceptions of Divine Eternity', in Robin Le Poidevin (ed.), *Questions of Time and Tense* (Oxford: Oxford University Press, 1998), pp. 221–250. Cited in Helm, *Eternal God*, p. 219.

20. William Lane Craig, *God, Time, and Eternity: The Coherence of Theism*, 2 vols. (Houten, Netherlands: Springer, 2001), vol. 2, p. 235. Cited in Helm, *Eternal God*, p. 219.

21. Brian Leftow, 'Eternity', in C. Taliaferro, P. Draper and P. Quinn, *A Companion to Philosophy of Religion* (Oxford: Wiley, 2010), pp. 278–284.

22. Craig, *God, Time, and Eternity*, vol. 2, p. 233.

That is, God is actually eternal. What Craig describes as God's temporal phase is actually a poorly worded attempt to describe the eternal God's relating to his creation. Some weight is given to this reading by the way in which Craig accepts that had God not created, he would remain eternal in the manner taught by Augustine and Aquinas. Underneath it all, in his most fundamental nature, Craig's God is then eternal. Nevertheless Craig vehemently rejects the classical teaching about God's eternity.

That Craig's doctrine of God teaches that God would, theoretically, be eternal if he did not create, is revealing. It suggests it is the relating of God to creation that pushes Craig to oppose the eternality of God. Perhaps the philosophical conceptions of the universe Craig uses in his apologetics drive this. Nobody would deny that the nature of God's relationship with creation is difficult to envision and articulate. Nevertheless Craig's approach is by his own admission bizarre. It is difficult to see how it affirms more of the biblical data than the traditional claim that God is eternal, and as the eternal God relates to his creation timelessly, tenselessly and perfectly.

Both Frame and Craig's approaches attempt to affirm and communicate multiple truths about God, in a manner that denies the full classical vision of God's simplicity. This is a pity, because the reality of God's eternity that flows from his simplicity offers stronger grounds to hold that he is omniscient, omnipresent, sovereign, free and perfect.

Eternal omniscience

Since God is simple, he is his attributes. This requires that we accept there is a beautiful, transcendent unity to God's being. As Scripture reveals various aspects of God's nature, we have solid grounds for speaking of genuinely distinct attributes. Yet, considered from the ultimate perspective of God's being, the doctrine of simplicity teaches that God is his attributes. It is often thought that this makes a nonsense of claims about God, for, if God is his attributes, then it follows that each attribute is identical with the others. How can God's eternity be his omniscience? Surely these attributes are distinct. The former has to do with time, the latter with knowledge.

It is possible to make the doctrine of simplicity appear non-sensical. However, a sympathetic hearing opens the possibility that the identity of attributes is a function not of incoherence, but sublime divine perfection and unity. From our creaturely perspectives we are legitimized by Scripture's language to speak of distinct attributes such as eternity and omniscience. However, there is a fundamental and radical disjunction between a creature's knowledge of God, and God's knowledge of himself. Perhaps from God's perspective his eternity is indeed his omniscience. As a concession to our time-bound, composite creatureliness God reveals himself as holding these two attributes. If simplicity is the grammar of God's being, then it is perfectly logical and rational to believe that perfect, infinite eternity is perfect infinite knowledge. Eternity means that God's knowledge is not a vaster, more learned, better informed version of our human learning. Rather God's perfect, infinite knowledge is timeless eternal knowing. Only eternal knowledge can truly be omniscience.

Augustine understood the connections I am making. He realized that a consequence of God's being eternal is that he knows all things perfectly, and in a manner different from how creatures know things. He reflected, 'Eternity belongs to you, O Lord, so surely you can neither be ignorant of what I am telling you, nor view what happens in time as though you were conditioned by time yourself.'[23]

In this comment Augustine links God's perfect knowledge with his eternity. The fact that God cannot experience tensed time is precisely what gives him perfect knowledge. Omniscience is eternity.

I experience things temporally. This means that my knowledge is tensed. I know that I ate a banana for breakfast this morning: I remember peeling and eating it in my kitchen. This is a piece of knowledge I have. It is temporal – it is a remembered experience from the past. As I type these words, I can recall the place I stood, and remember dropping the banana skin into the bin. I considered emptying the bin as it was nearly full – but decided against it as I wanted to get to my study to clear some emails. All this is knowledge

---

23. Augustine, *Confessions* 11.1.1.

I have. God knows everything I have just written. However, the way he knows it is radically different from the way I know it. I remember it, but God knows it eternally. It is not possible for him to look back in time and recall something he has forgotten. God knows my banana-eating perfectly, but his knowledge is infinite and timeless. As such it is on a different plane to my self-knowledge, rather than being merely on a grander scale. God's omniscience is a perfect knowledge of everything gained not from looking back (or forward) through time, but by way of timeless self-knowledge. God simply is. As a necessary function of his existence, God knows all things. That God's omniscience is his eternity ought not to be a cause for people to claim incoherence resides within the classical doctrine of God. Rather it is the basis upon which we can with relief say that God knows things in a different manner to us, and necessarily holds perfect knowledge of everything.

Aquinas preached a sermon on Luke 2:52, in which he wondered what it could mean for Jesus to grow in wisdom. Aquinas held to the classical doctrine of God I have been expounding, so he remarked, 'We must be amazed that eternity advances in age, for the Son of God is eternity.'[24] Aquinas knew that if God were perfect, eternal and simple, he could not change. This rules out the possibility of God's growing in wisdom. What then to make of the claim in Luke 2:52? Aquinas realized that the passage is speaking of the incarnate Christ. This was God's becoming human, for our benefit. Aquinas knew that other passages such as John 1:14 teach that Jesus was 'full of truth'. On that basis he reconciled the two verses:

> He was full of every grace and truth because he was the only-begotten Son . . . But what is meant by advancing in wisdom and grace? We must say that someone is said to advance in wisdom, not only when he acquires a greater wisdom, but also when the wisdom in him is more evident. It is true that Christ from the beginning of his conception was full of wisdom and grace, but he has not shown it from the beginning,

---

24. Aquinas, *The Academic Sermons*, ed. C. P. Mark-Robin Hoogland, The Fathers of the Church, Mediaeval Continuation (Washington: Catholic University of America Press, 2010), p. 88.

but at that age when others usually show it. In that case we speak of
advancing in wisdom, not in the absolute sense of the word, but in
view of the effect through which he advanced amidst other people.[25]

Shrewdly Aquinas notes that, were it otherwise, the incarnation itself
would have been challenged: 'If he had willed to show his wisdom
when he was seven years of age, people would have doubted the
truth of the assumed human nature.'[26]

The grammar of simplicity means that God's omniscience is
eternal. God's knowing is a perfect, infinite, timeless expression of
his being. It cannot be otherwise, if God is the Creator. For creatures
such as ourselves, our knowing is different. It is temporal, limited,
partial, tensed, forgotten, muddled and exaggerated. What a relief
that we can pray to one who is radically other than us, perfect in
knowledge. Out of love to us he became a human and veiled his
glory, knowing fully the painful implications he would endure to
restore us to a loving knowledge of himself.

Benefits for time-bound creatures

What benefit does God's eternal omniscience offer us?

One of our deepest longings is to be understood and known.
God's omniscience means that he knows us in the fullest manner
conceivable:

> O Lord, you have searched me and known me!
> You know when I sit down and when I rise up;
>   you discern my thoughts from afar.
> You search out my path and my lying down
>   and are acquainted with all my ways.
> Even before a word is on my tongue,
>   behold, O Lord, you know it altogether.
> (Ps. 139:1–4)

---

25. Ibid., p. 89.
26. Ibid., p. 90.

Understanding that God's omniscience is timeless – that each attribute is identical with his being – leads us to a deeper appreciation of what it means to be truly known by God. We realize that God knows us perfectly, but not in the same manner we know ourselves:

> In the same way a sighted person cannot know what it is like to be blind from birth, but the sighted person has a better grasp of what blindness means in the sense that she grasps what is missing, God does not understand us as we understand ourselves. That would be impossible. But perhaps he understands us better than we understand ourselves.[27]

Our knowledge is always temporal. The interconnections between past and present interject a temporal fragility to our understanding. 'Our experience of the present very largely depends upon our knowledge of the past.'[28] Eagerness to affirm that God knows everything can lead us naively to portray him as merely a better-informed version of ourselves. Accepting that God knows all things in a manner radically different from the way our knowledge is acquired preserves the Creator–creature distinction. This gives a more solid basis upon which to uphold the perfect vision of all things God eternally enjoys. We may doubt, forget, overlook, but God truly knows. It is deeply reassuring that the God we trust knows us better than we know ourselves, and loves us.

Many people intellectually resist the claim that God genuinely knows everything. It can seem that such a God squeezes out our human responsibility. How can my actions be genuinely mine if God knows all before it is done? How can I be culpable for that which God foreknows? Our intellectual frameworks, culture, church traditions and instincts may lead us to imagine that it is incoherent to hold both that God knows all things, and we as creatures are fully responsible for our decisions and lives. With regard to God's

---

27. Katherin Rogers, *Perfect Being Theology* (Edinburgh: Edinburgh University Press, 2000), p. 90.

28. P. Connerton, *How Societies Remember* (Cambridge: Cambridge University Press, 1989), p. 2.

sovereignty J. I. Packer famously argued that though we may disagree intellectually about the issue, all Christians who pray affirm a sovereign God in their requests:

> How then do you pray? Do you ask God for your daily bread? Do you thank God for your conversion? Do you pray for the conversion of others? If the answer is 'no', I can only say that I do not think you are yet born again. But if the answer is 'yes' – well, that proves that, whatever side you may have taken in debates on this question in the past, in your heart you believe in the sovereignty of God no less firmly than anybody else. On our feet we may have arguments about it, but on our knees we are all agreed.[29]

In the same way we may have intellectual debates and struggles about how God's knowledge interfaces with ours, and his perfect knowledge may appear to weaken the reality of our responsibility. Such matters do not trouble us when we talk to God in prayer. For when we cry out to him, our posture and senses lead us to feel that we are as we are – creatures. The sense of need and dependence are essential aspects of conversation with God. Where they are absent, we forget the Creator–creature distinction and continue to munch on the forbidden fruit of self-determination. It is reassuring that Augustine, who did so much to promote the classical vision of God as all-powerful, perfect, eternal and omniscient, penned his most famous book, *Confessions*, as a long heartfelt prayer. A fresh glimpse of God's eternal omniscience drives us to prayer, and undergirds all true conversation with the Creator.

A friend recently shared with me how painful it was that as part of his job he had to tell numbers of people in his company that they were losing their jobs. He remarked how it always came as a shock, and was particularly upsetting for those who had homes and families to provide for. There are moments in life where the future is painfully uncertain. Others include the seasons after a close bereavement, or an experience of life-changing illness. At such

---

29. J. I. Packer, *Evangelism and the Sovereignty of God* (London: Inter-Varsity Fellowship, 1966), p. 17.

times it is deeply encouraging to know that God knows all things. He not only knows the future, which is unseen to us; he also knows the fear, disappointment and pain we may hide from others. Some may question how it is possible for an infinitely perfect God to have a relationship with his creatures. The problem may be framed in precisely contrary terms: How would it be possible to be in relationship with a God who did *not* know everything about all the recesses of our hearts? Others may not, indeed as Proverbs teaches, *cannot* understand:

> The heart knows its own bitterness,
> and no stranger shares its joy.
> (Prov. 14:10)

God does know. Perfectly. And he shares in the bitterness.

The basic fact that God knows everything is something that many would wish to affirm. As we have seen, however, it is possible to do so in a way that suggests God's means of knowing are nothing more than more powerful and effective versions of knowing than ours. If God's knowing is temporal, like ours, then it is imperfect. The desire to make God's knowledge intelligible to us erodes its perfection. The classical approach I have explored here is, it must be admitted, not my instinctive approach. It is difficult to understand and is open to the charge of being an unnecessary confusion. Is it not adequate simply to affirm the truth that God knows everything, and read the Bible verses that teach this? On one level, if people do this, then it is enough. God can use that to grow people's relationship with him, and to keep them in his love. However, from another perspective, such an approach of merely affirming truth claims is fragile. Under the pressure of secular philosophy, sceptical theology and suffering lives, such unconnected claims are brittle. The vision of God's knowledge as eternity flows from the doctrine of simplicity. It has been affirmed by the great catholic theologians of the church. The connections it makes enable us to speak of God in a way that affirms in a deep, grounded way all the claims made of him in the Bible. God is God. He is not like us. He knows all things. Perfectly and exhaustively. Eternally. This is a comfort not easily swept aside by life's vicissitudes.

Meditation: living in time

> You have been born again, not of perishable seed but of
> imperishable, through the living and abiding word of God; for
>
> 'All flesh is like grass
>   and all its glory like the flower of grass.
> The grass withers,
>   and the flower falls,
> but the word of the Lord remains for ever.'
>
> And this word is the good news that was preached to you.
>
> (1 Peter 1:23–25)

O God, I dwell in time and can barely express what time is. My rushing around and constant search for the next thing is little more than a futile attempt to numb myself to the unbearable reality – time is slipping away from me. I feel the claim on being that your image grants me; I feel that my life should not fade away to nothing. Yet every graveside I visit, every quiet moment of stillness, hauntingly mocks me. Time marches on and, as you have said, I wither and fall like the grass in a field.

You are so different. Always living, always there, all-knowing. I have studied books and languages. Sometimes paying attention, but often not. You have never grown in wisdom, for you are wisdom. I have forgotten and confused so many things; you are knowledge.

Outside time you know perfectly. You never age or weaken. And yet your perfection is not a splendid isolation – surely the thing that surpasses all others in beauty is that you graciously deign to speak with me, one of your mortal creatures. Your perfect knowledge is shared with me, wills good for me, and is all-loving despite knowing my sin more deeply than I do.

Forgive me for not talking enough with you, for imagining that you are as little as me, and for my futile attempts to overcome my creaturely limits. Awaken in me a more passionate dependence upon you, a more humble reverence for your perfect knowledge.

Amen.

4. ALL POWERFUL AND ALL GOOD

The problem of suffering

The painful reality of evil and suffering in our world is thought of by many as one of the most compelling reasons to doubt the existence of a good, all-powerful God. Any time I speak to a group of people about the claims of Christianity, I am aware, in all likelihood, there are several listeners who are struggling with the pain of a bereavement, injustice or illness that afflicts somebody close. I have travelled to some areas of the world where the realities of poverty, illness and brutality are so extreme that it is difficult to express them in words. Some of my first years of church ministry were in an urban parish with high levels of poverty and suffering. We need not only to have credible responses to the very understandable challenge to faith posed by suffering, but we also must feel within ourselves the intimate, childlike trust in God that guides us through our own times of darkness. Our knowledge of God and ourselves is, as Calvin wrote, 'intimately connected'.[1] Engaging with the doctrine of God is

---

1. John Calvin, *Institutes of the Christian Religion*, tr. Ford Lewis Battles, ed. John T. McNeill, 2 vols. (Philadelphia: Westminster, 2001), 1.1.1.

therefore a crucial part of exploring how we are to live life – nowhere is this more apparent than the juncture where we feel the shadow of grief, and wonder if God cares. As David Ford writes, 'The issue at stake is the whole shape of living. To attend to that when we are being overwhelmed is no easy matter. But it is hard to imagine any adequate way of coping that does not try to answer the big questions about life, death, purpose, good and evil.'[2]

I am conscious that the classical doctrine of God, expounded in this book, is often dismissed as cold, impersonal and overly philosophical. I for one would not wish to teach or live out the implications of such a theology. As I write this chapter my wife is pregnant with a daughter whom we know will not be able to live more than a few minutes or days after birth. Philosophical niceties are not what sustains us as we talk to God about our grief and love for a child whose life on earth is to be so brief. As Helm observes in his highly philosophical text, 'The problem of evil is not an invention of philosophers or theologians, but starts life as an acute personal difficulty. Its primary context is not calm reflection but anguish of spirit.'[3] For myself, then, as much as those to whom I seek to commend the Christian God, I desire to know how, in the face of suffering, God can be trusted as both all-powerful and perfectly good.

Biblical affirmations of omnipotence and goodness

Before considering how the classical doctrine of God helps us affirm his goodness and omnipotence in the face of suffering, we would do well to open our hearts to the intensely personal ways the Bible testifies to God's goodness and power. These attributes of God are not affirmed there in a merely technical or cursory fashion; they are emblazoned across God's self-revelation.

---

2. David Ford, *The Shape of Living: Spiritual Directions for Everyday Life* (Grand Rapids: Zondervan, 2002), p. xix.

3. Paul Helm, *The Providence of God* (Leicester: Inter-Varsity Press, 1993), p. 194.

God's goodness is first seen in his creation of a world teeming with beauty, relationships, order and love. The trees were 'pleasant to the sight and good for food' (Gen. 2:9). God saw and declared that his creation is 'good', indeed 'very good' (Gen. 1:21, 31). Since the world was made by God, it bears the shape and stamp of his character: the creation's goodness flows from the Creator's goodness. This is assumed within the language of Creator and creation, and is most explicitly noted with regard to humanity, who are made in God's 'image' (Gen. 1:27).

God's creation of a good world is a profound declaration not only of his goodness, but also his power. Since the world was created out of nothing by God, it was and remains absolutely dependent upon him for its existence. The God who called all things into existence is necessarily the most powerful being who can be conceived by a creature. So creation is a beautiful display of both goodness and power.

Adam plunged the world into sin and rebellion by not believing and loving God's word. The goodness of God stands out all the more clearly as it is set in relief against a backdrop of anger, murder, deception, pride, selfishness and theft. God begins in the immediate aftermath of the fall to reveal the form his goodness will take for much of the Bible narrative: patience, acts of undeserved kindness and 'mini' rescues that anticipate the future salvation. So we read of God's giving Adam and Eve animal skins as they are evicted from Eden (Gen. 3:21), Cain's punishment for murder is commuted (Gen. 4:15) and Noah with his family are rescued from the flood (Gen. 8:18).

God's power is seen throughout this in his ability both to punish and save, together with the sense that he could do more than he chooses to do at a given moment. God could destroy the whole world in the flood; even his restraint is a hidden display of power. The thoughtful reader of Genesis also cannot fail to begin theologizing about the extent to which God is in control of sin, suffering and evil. It may be appealing in some ways to think that God is not fully in control of sin, but such a view is difficult to reconcile with the absolute power over creation seen in the biblical portrait of his freely creating all things out of nothing.

Total control and power over suffering, sin and evil is declared:

> As for you, you meant evil against me, but God meant it for good, to
> bring it about that many people should be kept alive, as they are today.
> (Gen. 50:20)

> Is a trumpet blown in a city,
>   and the people are not afraid?
> Does disaster come to a city,
>   unless the LORD has done it?
> (Amos 3:6)

The human heart is desperately sinful, mysterious and subtle. God's
control over it is complete:

> The king's heart is a stream of water in the hand of the LORD;
> he turns it wherever he will.
> (Prov. 21:1)

Calvin reflected on this verse:

> Does God work in the hearts of men, directing their plans and
> moving their wills this way and that, so that they do nothing but what
> He has ordained? . . . The question is whether He has in His power also
> the depraved affections of the ungodly, moving them here and there
> so that they will what He has decreed they should do. Certainly when
> Solomon declares (Prov. 21:1) that the heart of kings are [sic] in the
> hand of God so that He inclines it as He pleases, he shows that in
> general the will not less than external works are governed by the
> determination of God.[4]

It is often thought that suffering and evil resist or challenge
God's power. The Bible's logic is that the sinful world provides a
forum in which God displays all the more clearly the reality of his

---

4. John Calvin, *Concerning the Eternal Predestination of God*, ed. J. K. S. Reid
(Cambridge: James Clarke, 2000), p. 174.

omnipotence. In the midst of all the sin, suffering and evil that blight his good creation, God is still praised as unreservedly good:

> For I know the plans I have for you, declares the LORD, plans for welfare and not for evil, to give you a future and a hope.
> (Jer. 29:11)

> I say to the LORD, 'You are my Lord;
>   I have no good apart from you.'
> (Ps. 16:2)

> Oh, taste and see that the LORD is good!
>   Blessed is the man who takes refuge in him!
> (Ps. 34:8)

> Truly God is good to Israel,
>   to those who are pure in heart.
> (Ps. 73:1)

> For the LORD is good;
>   his steadfast love endures for ever,
>   and his faithfulness to all generations.
> (Ps. 100:5)

So throughout the Old Testament account of Israel's sin and the suffering of a fallen world God is revealed as both good and all-powerful.

The Prophets open out a fuller vision of God's goodness, preaching that God's good rescues of people through Abraham, Moses, Joshua and David were harbingers of a greater rescue. This future day of salvation would free people from death, sin, suffering, Satan and sadness. Such a universal, supernatural rescue would be a magnificent display of God's goodness and power:

> The wolf shall dwell with the lamb,
>   and the leopard shall lie down with the young goat,
> and the calf and the lion and the fattened calf together;
>   and a little child shall lead them.
> (Isa. 11:6)

> And he will swallow up on this mountain
>> the covering that is cast over all peoples,
>> the veil that is spread over all nations.
> He will swallow up death for ever;
> and the Lord GOD will wipe away tears from all faces,
>> and the reproach of his people he will take away from all the earth,
>> for the LORD has spoken.
> (Isa. 25:7–8)

Having previously commanded his people to 'remember' the rescue from Egypt, God declares that the future rescue will cause the earlier salvation to be forgotten:

> 'Remember not the former things,
>> nor consider the things of old.
> Behold, I am doing a new thing;
>> now it springs forth, do you not perceive it?
> I will make a way in the wilderness
>> and rivers in the desert.
> (Isa. 43:18–19)

The power of God is verified by the fact that his good rescue was prophesied, and in due course came to pass. The immense power required to predict the future accurately was given by God as one of his calling cards (Isa. 48:5), and is the mark of a true prophet (Deut. 18:22).

Jesus frequently did things that demonstrated he had God's power: calming a storm (Mark 4:41), forgiving sins (Mark 2:7) and raising the dead (Mark 5:42).

In the many encounters between Jesus and people, we see a humanity restored to kind, loving other-person-focused love. Whether with an educated religious seeker, the marginalized or immoral, Jesus repeatedly demonstrated a goodness not only attractive but believable. So good was Jesus in his dealings with people that when his enemies sought to find a pretext to charge him with, they had to rely on false charges. Even then it was impossible to find false witnesses who could fabricate a convincing accusation (Mark 14:55–56). The Old Testament had revealed God as perfectly good and infinitely powerful. When the gospel accounts are read, we discover, in the words of N. T. Wright, that the Old Testament vision of God 'fits Jesus like a glove'.[5]

In Jesus' life we see a beautiful joining of power and goodness. A great deal of Jesus' attractiveness is the perfectly apportioned arrangement of both power and goodness – within a humanity that is both so far from our experience, and yet so genuinely human. The idea that Jesus is beautiful because he embodies multiple virtues, simultaneously and in perfect harmony, was a theme Jonathan Edwards returned to frequently. In one sermon Edwards points out that Revelation 5:5–6 portrays Jesus as both a lion and a lamb. In this way Jesus is seen as possessing both infinite power and infinite humility. The harmonious conjoining of these virtues renders him all the more beautiful to us:

> There is an admirable conjunction of diverse excellencies in Jesus Christ. The lion and the lamb, though very diverse kinds of creatures, yet have each their peculiar excellencies. The lion excels in strength, and in the majesty of his appearance and voice: the lamb excels in meekness and patience, besides the excellent nature of the creature as good for food, and yielding that which is fit for our clothing and being suitable to be offered in sacrifice to God. But we see that Christ is in the text compared to both, because the diverse excellencies of both wonderfully meet in him.[6]

All too often our 'goodness' is ineffectual as we lack the power to implement it. Our power is all too often exerted without due moral presence, as an impersonal or even bullying coercion. The presence of both perfect power and perfect goodness in Jesus makes him all the more attractive to us. An excellent conjoining of virtues is what our humanity feels it was designed for.

In his death Jesus hid his power in shame and suffering. Only those whose eyes are opened in faith, by the Holy Spirit, can see that it is on the cross God's power is truly revealed (1 Cor. 1:18–25;

5. N. T. Wright, *The Challenge of Jesus* (London: SPCK, 2000), p. 121.

6. Jonathan Edwards, *Sermons and Discourses 1734–1738*, Works of Jonathan Edwards, 26 vols. (New Haven: Yale University, 2001), vol. 19, p. 565.

2:6–12). When the Spirit enables us to see past our sinful assumptions, we are liberated to find, on the cross, God's goodness and power revealed. In 1517 Martin Luther wrote in his Heidelberg Disputation:

> That person does not deserve to be called a theologian who looks upon the invisible things of God as though they were clearly perceptible in those things which have actually happened [Rom. 1:20]. He deserves to be called a theologian, however, who comprehends the visible and manifest things of God seen through suffering and the cross.
>
> A theologian of glory calls evil good and good evil. A theologian of the cross calls the thing what it actually is. That wisdom which sees the invisible things of God in works as perceived by man is completely puffed up, blinded, and hardened.[7]

So in the death of Jesus we see true goodness and true power. A goodness that would use power to serve the undeserving; a power that would plunge the eternal God into the depths of death. Such goodness is beyond our fallen abilities – we need God's power if we are to embody anything like it. So when Jesus returned to the heavens, he sent his Spirit, who empowers Christians to love with God's cross-shaped power. We are to 'walk by the Spirit' (Gal. 5:25) and so love as Christ loved us (John 13:34; Eph. 5:2).

The future beyond the grave, for all who have the Spirit, is an eternal world of love. This world is brought about by the power of God. We can trust he will bring it, because we have seen him exert amazing power to keep all his other promises. When all other powers are conquered, God will be seen to be the absolute ruler. Such is his goodness that at that point of total victory God will desire to wipe away the tears of his people (Isa. 25:8; Rev. 21:4).

Throughout the Bible story we find that God is always perfectly good and infinitely powerful. The Bible is very aware of the reality of sin, suffering and evil in the creation. Nevertheless these are not challenges to God's power or goodness; they are the arena within

---

7. Martin Luther, 'Heidelberg Disputation', in *Luther's Works*, 55 vols. (Philadelphia: Fortress, 1957), vol. 31, pp. 52–53.

which his goodness and power are most wonderfully displayed. Non-Christian forms of thought set concepts against each other in a win-or-lose fashion. So, for example, the rights of one group in society are protected, at the cost of another's. Such a non-Christian way of arguing struggles to believe in both God's goodness and his power. Suffering and evil seem to suggest that God cannot be both perfectly good and omnipotent. Surprisingly even many popular Christian ways of describing God fall into a similar trap of setting one attribute against another. This can be the case even with systems of thought aiming to harmonize biblical data about God: the systems of doctrine about God colloquially known as Arminianism and Calvinism both struggle with this weakness. To the extent that Calvinists or Arminians reject the classical doctrine of God's simplicity, they are forced into a system that sets attributes against each other. This means that, despite the best of intentions, both systems (at least as popularized in contemporary Christian circles) fail to do justice to God's goodness and omnipotence. While the Calvinist will affirm more fully God's sovereignty, where this is unsupported by simplicity it will be a brittle doctrinal claim, unable to maintain its consistency under close examination. The classical theist does not merely weigh up the goodness or otherwise of God's actions. Since God is simple, his goodness is what and who he is. As Augustine prayed, 'You are Goodness itself and need no good beside yourself.'[8]

Imperfect systems

Arminianism and Calvinism are two schools of thought that attempt to relate God's sovereignty to his relationship with creatures. Both the writings of Calvin and Arminius were richer and more nuanced than the summaries of them that have become popularized in various strands of contemporary Christianity. Each school of thought has its own attractions and weaknesses when used to analyse

---

8. Augustine, *The Confessions*, tr. R. S. Pine-Coffin (London: Penguin, 1961), 13.38.

the problem of how God can be perfectly powerful and perfectly good. Whichever tradition we feel most comfortable with, it is instructive to be wary of the dangers.

Arminianism owes its leading ideas to the Dutch theologian Jacobus Arminius (1560–1609). Roger Olson, a leading contemporary Arminian scholar observes the role played by the problem of evil in Arminianism: 'Arminians reject the narrow definition of sovereignty – absolute and meticulous control – because it cannot avoid making God the author of sin and evil, in which case, Arminians believe, God would be morally ambiguous.'[9]

Arminius did defend a grand doctrine of God, including perfection, simplicity and infinity. In this sense he may be described as a 'perfect being theologian'.[10] However, since it is assumed a high view of God's sovereignty will lead to a situation where God is responsible for evil, Arminian theology contends that there is an initial aspect of the human will that is in some way receptive, willing or open to the Spirit's enlightening:

> Underscoring that humanity is a willing recipient of divine grace and
> faith, Arminius left space for responsiveness in the divine–human
> relationship. The relationship is one of mutuality; God takes the
> initiative, but salvation is a cooperative process. God desires the salvation
> of all; nothing can prevent the demonstration of God's mercy except a
> refusal to repent.[11]

The weakness in Arminianism is that it is difficult to see how such a cooperative view of salvation is consistent with the infinite perfection of God. What makes one a 'willing recipient'? If it is a desire or will that arises from within the creature, rather than God, then this desire (however slight or imperfect) is something created from the creature rather than the Creator. It is possible to conceive of a

---

9. R. Olson, *Arminian Theology: Myths and Realities* (Downers Grove: InterVarsity Press, 2009), p. 118.

10. K. Stanglin and T. McCall, *Jacob Arminius: Theologian of Grace* (New York: Oxford University Press, 2012), p. 79.

11. Ibid., p. 188.

God outside whose will and power lie nothing at all. Such a God would be more perfect than the God of Arminius. Indeed the very attempt to divide up the universe into aspects God is sovereign over and areas the human will is responsible for is a failure to appreciate the Creator–creature distinction. This posits that God and creatures are of a fundamentally different order of being. It is not a situation where God is sovereign over most things, but some things are under the control of the human will. Rather if God is radically other than us, then his sovereignty and power are of a different order to ours. God is completely, perfectly and fully in control of all things, including whether a person desires to will a positive response to salvation. Human power, control and responsibility are genuine and meaningful, but they operate in a fundamentally different and complimentary manner to that of God. God's sovereignty is that which is appropriate to the infinite, perfect Creator; our powers are those that are meet for creatures made from nothing but God's word.

Despite protestations to the contrary, Arminianism's reservation of some powers of will to the human will is evidence that the vision of God posited is not the classical perfect-being deity. Certainly the God of Arminianism is (much) more powerful than humans, but his power is of a greater degree, rather than a different order. Simplicity has not been worked through the theological system as the fundamental grammar of God's being, which permits all his attributes to be believed fully, simultaneously, consistently and perfectly.

The theology of John Calvin is, again, a richer fount of constructive theological insight than the summaries assumed by many today to align with his convictions. Many contemporary Christians believe that if they hold a strong doctrine of God's sovereignty, they are 'Calvinists' – even if they marginalize the sacraments, are Baptists or are ambivalent about creedal confessions. Calvin would have found such attitudes bizarre, to say the least. Kenneth Stewart has warned us about the ease with which Calvin can be misrepresented.[12]

---

12. Kenneth Stewart, *Ten Myths About Calvinism: Recovering the Breadth of the Reformed Tradition* (Downers Grove: InterVarsity Press; Nottingham: Apollos, 2011).

Nevertheless it was perhaps inevitable that the theology of such a voluminous writer as Calvin would be summarized and codified in slogans.

One of the most significant statements derived from Calvin's theological legacy was the insight agreed at the Synod of Dort in 1618–19. Responding to the teachings of Arminius, the Reformed leaders (including the Bishops of Winchester and Salisbury) offered four points, with fifty-nine subpoints. These were famously summarized in the late nineteenth century under five headings, with the acronym 'TULIP'.[13] The TULIP acronym affirms the following:

T: Total depravity of humanity
U: Unconditional election
L: Limited atonement
I: Irresistible grace
P: Perseverance of the saints

The developments in language since these slogans were coined has made them misleading. 'Total' depravity does not mean to imply that people are as sinful as possible, but rather that all parts of people are tainted and damaged by sin. 'Limited' atonement intends to teach not that the atonement is in some sense limited in power, but rather that it saves all those it was intended to save. In a certain sense Christ died for his elect, the sheep. D. A. Carson therefore suggests the term should be revised to 'definite' or 'intentional' atonement.[14] 'Perseverance' as it is used today suggests a focus on the works done by the saints (Christians). It is intended to guard rather the idea that God will ensure the 'preservation' of his people, from conversion into eternity.

---

13. The original Synod of Dort had treated the third and fourth point of TULIP together.
14. D. A. Carson, *The Difficult Doctrine of the Love of God* (Leicester: Inter-Varsity Press, 2000), pp. 84–85. See further Lee Gatiss, *For Us and for Our Salvation: 'Limited Atonement' in the Bible, Doctrine, History, and Ministry*, Latimer Studies 78 (London: Latimer, 2012).

Despite R. T. Kendall's misleading thesis,[15] it has been demonstrated that all points of TULIP, including limited atonement, follow naturally from various doctrinal statements Calvin made on closely related matters.[16] The latter-day Calvinists who explicated limited atonement were therefore in substantial agreement with the theology of John Calvin. Although some today still maintain that Calvin did not teach limited atonement, in his commentary on 1 John 2:2 he at least showed awareness of it.[17] He noted that it is 'said that Christ suffered sufficiently for the whole world, but efficiently only for the elect. This solution has commonly prevailed in the schools. Though then I allow that what has been said is true, yet I deny that it is suitable to this passage.' This is a revealing aside, not discussed further by Calvin as it would not have been helpful in commenting on the verse under consideration.

While Calvin affirmed each of the points of TULIP, he clearly taught much more than those five statements. The summary of TULIP, when it is separated from Calvin's broader theological concerns, has misled many today to think they are 'Calvinist' because they affirm them. Not only is this reductionistic, but it fails to realize that the affirmation of each doctrinal point in isolation from a rich vision of simplicity has unintended consequences around the problem of suffering. Without an appreciation of the way God's simplicity enjoins upon us a radical Creator–creature distinction, modern-day proponents of TULIP are left merely asserting the five truths. Integration of the truths with each other, and with a genuine role for human responsibility, is not possible apart from this Creator–creature distinction. It is only on the basis of God's simplicity, and

---

15. R. T. Kendall, *Calvin and English Calvinism to 1649* (Eugene: Wipf & Stock, 2011).

16. Paul Helm, *Calvin and the Calvinists* (Edinburgh: Banner of Truth, 1982); 'Calvin, Indefinite Language, and Definite Atonement', in David Gibson and Jonathan Gibson (eds.), *From Heaven He Came and Sought Her: Definite Atonement in Historical, Biblical, Theological and Pastoral Perspective* (Wheaton: Crossway, 2013), pp. 97–120.

17. John Calvin, *Commentary on Hebrews–Jude* (Grand Rapids: Baker, 2005), p. 173.

the consequent Creator–creature distinction, that we can say that God's sovereignty is infinite and perfect, and there is at the same time a genuine, human responsibly and culpability for decisions. The human freedom is genuine, but is of a different order to that of God.

Both popular Arminian and Calvinist theology fail to provide adequate resources for addressing the problem of suffering, if they are held apart from God's simplicity and the consequent Creator–creature distinction. The truths each affirms may appear to console (in differing ways), but they are not coherent systems unless God is simple. Affirming the Creator–creature distinction is a doxological and pastoral process that opens our hearts both to meaningful intellectual responses to suffering, and the heartfelt affections commended in Scripture.

The classical God and Felix Culpa

One of the main reasons the classical doctrine of God is resisted by theologians is that it is thought to envision a God who is inert, static and therefore impersonal. Such a God would be of no more consolation in times of suffering than the concept of chance. Thankfully, the perfect, simple God is not like that. He is infinitely personal, and perfectly so. His capacity for love and desire to shower love upon the undeserving is greater than we dare imagine. Due to his radical otherness, which arises from the distinction between Creator and creatures, we are invited to contemplate what it is like to trust a God who is not like us. This is of great comfort to us, for it enables us to trust him with suffering in a way we cannot trust any other human. The Bible calls this 'faith'.

When we consider the reality of suffering, sin and evil, we stand at the edge of human intellectual and emotional endeavour. We strain at the frontiers of what is possible for us to know – even on the basis of scriptural revelation. Our considerations of the shortcomings in popular Arminian and Calvinist schemes forewarns us of thinking that there is an answer or intellectual solution to the problem of why there is suffering in the world. At a fundamental level we accept that there is no inherent reason, justification, sense or joy in suffering. A fallen world is a damaged world, and the damage is not good. Every tear that falls, every child that dies, every lonely pensioner, every famine, every angry word – all are within themselves without meaning and rationale. From our creaturely perspective they are all without justification and explanation. Their meaninglessness is another part of their fallen nature. Often pastoral care in a time of suffering would be foolish to venture beyond a tear-soaked sharing in that absurdity: 'Weep with those who weep' (Rom. 12:15).

Nevertheless there is within the vision of the classical doctrine of God an invitation to trust that from God's perspective there is meaning, beauty and a joy that wipes away every tear. We see within the pages of the Bible only hints of this bigger picture. It is a context for suffering, but since it is viewed from God's perspective, we are called to trust not the explanation but the God who we believe will in his time and manner renew and restore all things. This theological frame was known to theologians and pastors such as Aquinas as the 'Felix Culpa',[18] the 'Happy Fault'. The teaching is that Adam's sin was a happy fault, for, since he permitted that sin, God can be trusted to bring a blessedness to his people that is better than anything that could have been enjoyed had there never been sin and suffering. As Augustine put it, 'God judged it better to bring good out of evil, than to allow no evil to exist.'[19]

The doctrine of Felix Culpa could be misrepresented as a harsh teaching that attempts to solve suffering intellectually: God let evil into the world so that he could bring more good later. Therefore you should get over your suffering because it will all turn out for the best. This is nothing like what Aquinas and Augustine intended by the teaching. That would be to read these perfect-being theologians as if they were contemporary preachers who get their theology from nothing more profound than yesterday's news. Felix Culpa is an invitation to trust that the perfect, infinite God has within himself perfect

18. Thomas Aquinas, *Summa Theologica*, 5 vols. (Notre Dame: Ave Maria, 1948), 3.1.q3.a3.

19. Augustine, 'Enchiridion on Faith, Hope and Charity', in Boniface Ramsey (ed.), *On Christian Belief* (New York: New City, 1996), p. 27.

goodness and power over his creation. The good that comes out of the fall is not a solution to suffering, but a greater revelation of God:

> Any Christian theodicy must not only have a man-ward emphasis but also, and perhaps predominately, a God-ward aspect as well. In the permission of moral evil lies the prospect of God's own character being revealed in ways which, but for the evil, it could not be.[20]

He has a timeless knowledge of all things, and wills all reality into existence. If Adam's fall were not from God's perspective the 'Happy Fault', then God would not be perfect, timeless, omniscient, omnipotent and good. He would not be worth trusting in times of suffering or happiness. God is the one who timelessly knows the nature of the good he will bring out of evil. He has not laid out the details of that plan for us, and he certainly does not invite us to explain or rationalize our sufferings in some kind of mechanistic manner by comparing them with a larger number of good things. 'The sufferings of this present time are not worth comparing with the glory that is to be revealed to us' (Rom. 8:18). This is an invitation not to intellectualize a solution to suffering; it is cruel theology that says it is all worth it because the future will be better. Rather Romans 8:18 is an affirmation that the original sin was indeed a Happy Fault, and so we trust God. We look to the God who is perfect, not the intellectual answer we think we have formulated (even if the formulation is derived from truths in Scripture). God is God, and he knows what he is doing.

Pastoral value

The Felix Culpa does not give us a straightforward intellectual answer to suffering, since it is a doctrine that speaks of creation from God's perspective. There is intellectual content to it, but it is primarily a call to accept that God is other than us, and we can (indeed should) trust him as we suffer.

---

20. Helm, *Providence of God*, p. 214.

So Job found he was confronted by the overwhelming reality of a God who is no mere creature:

Then the LORD answered Job out of the whirlwind and said:

'Who is this that darkens counsel by words without knowledge?
Dress for action like a man;
   I will question you, and you make it known to me.
"Where were you when I laid the foundation of the earth?
   Tell me, if you have understanding.
Who determined its measurements – surely you know!
   Or who stretched the line upon it?
On what were its bases sunk,
   or who laid its cornerstone,
when the morning stars sang together
   and all the sons of God shouted for joy?"'
(Job 38:1–7)

God in his majestic exaltation as the Creator confronts Job, a fearsome experience that forms the attitude that is able to face suffering, with God as the ultimate comforter. The classical doctrine of God seeks to affirm his omnipotence and goodness in their perfection. As such it is a way of speaking about God that promotes the kind of attitude Job developed after he was confronted by God.

A similar emotional overwhelming by God's power is expected when we read the doxology at the end of Romans 11:

Oh, the depth of the riches and wisdom and knowledge of God! How unsearchable are his judgments and how inscrutable his ways!

'For who has known the mind of the Lord,
   or who has been his counsellor?'
'Or who has given a gift to him
   that he might be repaid?'

For from him and through him and to him are all things. To him be glory for ever. Amen.
(Rom. 11:33–36)

We may feel the desire for explanations or solutions to suffering, sin and evil. In the absence of such it is tempting to impugn God's character by believing the lie that he cannot be both perfectly good and omnipotent. God takes the first step towards helping us in our suffering by confronting us with his glorious presence. He is not like us. His ways are not our ways. Our limitations do not restrict him. So when God offers to comfort, love and sustain us through the valley of the shadow of death (Ps. 23:4), we can be assured that he will in no way let us down. The person who knows God will have a humble reticence about slogans or systems of theological thought. They contain truths, and to some degree we all have to depend upon them to shape and hold our knowledge. Nevertheless all systems distort and obscure as well as communicate truth. In the final analysis it is God himself with whom we have to do business, not an explanatory framework.

If we are convinced that God is of a superior order to us, fundamentally a different kind of being to his creatures, we find this fosters within us a trust that his love is (unlike ours) perfect, infinite and timeless. When we read in the Bible that God loves us, we sense that his love to us cannot be resisted, lost or transcended. God's love is perfect; the classical doctrine of God assures us of this. In times of suffering we long to feel that God's love is real and available to us. A perfect-being theology gives us the confidence that the love we read of in Scripture is infinite and perfect. So we are given encouragement to follow the advice Martin Luther gave the Queen of Hungary in 1526: 'Anyone who has come to the point he can see and feel in the scriptures the Father's love towards us will easily be able to bear all the misfortune that there may be on earth.'[21] It is ironic and sad that many have thought the classical doctrine of God is a portrait of a cold, lifeless deity. Nothing could be further from the truth. The perfect God is perfect in power and goodness. We trust in a God fundamentally different from us. In a world full of grief, death and suffering it is of inestimable comfort to know that God is fully able to implement his loving plans to shepherd his people.

---

21. Martin Luther, *Luther's Works*, 55 vols. (St. Louis: Concordia, 1958), vol. 14, p. 210.

Meditation: God is good

> Cancer has been a turning point in my life that I never could have
> dreamed of, and I know that my life will never be the same. But
> despite the hard times and the multitudes of tears, the Lord has
> been protecting me every step of this journey. Whether I live, and
> one day become cancer free, or I die, I know without a doubt that
> God is good, and that does not change based on my circumstances.
> (Perrin Thompson, aged 22)[22]

O God, in times of suffering, life closes in. My struggles and pain
seem to surround me. Please open my heart to you. Lift my eyes to
see your goodness. Help me to believe that you are not only all good,
but good to me. You have given me so many good gifts, which I do
not deserve. Even the pain and sadness are a gift from your kind
hand, though I cannot yet understand your purposes.

When life seems out of control, help me to accept that you are in
control. I cannot see beyond today; I trust that you know the end
before the beginning. You have foretold your saving plans in Scripture.
Your faithfulness and power have been proven many times.

Forgive me the times I have become so enveloped by my suffering
that I have forgotten you, blamed you and doubted you. Thank
you that you have never changed: you have been, and always will be,
the same perfectly good God. Give my heart a sense and taste of
your sweet goodness: your beautiful kindness and generosity. I long
to be refreshed by a sight of your perfection. When I look at this
fallen world, twisted by sin and suffering, it is difficult to believe that
it could ever be better. Yet I know that you are all-powerful; you are
able to bring about your perfect purposes for your people. Please
do so not as I, but as you, would have it. As a sinful creature, limited
in so many ways, I am content to trust you.

Amen.

---

22. *Washington Post*, 26 Mar. 2012, http://www.washingtonpost.com/
blogs/guest-voices/post/despite-cancer-god-is-good/2012/03/26/
gIQAgfjXcS_blog.html (accessed 10 Nov. 2013).

5. THE IMMORTAL DIES

> 'Tis mystery all! The Immortal dies:
> Who can explore His strange design?
> In vain the first-born seraph tries
> To sound the depths of love divine.
> 'Tis mercy all! let earth adore,
> Let angel minds inquire no more.
>
> (Charles Wesley)

Jesus is at the centre of God's plans for the universe, 'For all the promises of God find their Yes in him' (2 Cor. 1:20). A Christian is somebody who has been awakened to enjoy the beauty of a life lived serving Jesus rather than self. Since it is the case that in Jesus 'all the fullness of God was pleased to dwell' (Col. 1:19), it is – from one perspective – impossible to make too much of Jesus. We can never be deeply enough moved, or thankful enough, for the sacrifice Jesus made for us on the cross.

Nevertheless it is problematic to view Jesus in isolation from the teachings about God we have been considering. It is unscriptural to magnify Jesus in such a way that he is thought of as all there is to know about God. One helpful doctoral thesis shows that both John Calvin and Karl Barth sought to put Jesus at the centre of their theological systems. They did so in different ways. There was a fundamental 'difference between Calvin's soteriological christocentrism and Barth's principial christocentrism'.[1] It follows from the different

---

1. David Gibson, *Reading the Decree: Exegesis, Election and Christology in Calvin and Barth* (Edinburgh: T. & T. Clark, 2009), p. 201.

ways of focusing upon and magnifying Jesus that not all ways of doing so are equally valid or helpful.

All too often the default method of talking and preaching about Jesus ignores the classical doctrine of God, which is revealed in Scripture and ought to form the theological frame within which Jesus is seen to be who he is. The classical doctrine of God insists upon God's perfection. From this follows the belief that God cannot change, fail, doubt or suffer. At first reflection such a vision of God appears to be far removed from the Bible's record of Jesus' life and death. How can a God who by definition cannot suffer be said to have died on a cross? How can a God who is love not change? This chapter will suggest that rather than letting a theologically isolated Christ totalize the classical doctrine of God, faithful Scripture reading leads us to view Jesus as the perfect God who is love, becoming human. When we do so, God's love is seen as all the more wonderful. Indeed the love that God unchangeably is is as infinite as God himself:

> How great, then, is the Supreme Spirit's love – a love so mutual to the Father and Son? If the Supreme Spirit loves himself to the extent that he remembers and understands himself, and if he remembers and understands himself in proportion to his essence – as cannot fail to be the case – then surely the Supreme Spirit's love is as great as this Spirit himself.[2]

God is love

We are told in 1 John 4:8 that 'God is love.' If people in the Western world know anything about Christianity, it is that the God talked about in Scripture is one of love. It is a normal part of witnessing to God in today's culture to explain that the world's assumptions about love are not necessarily shared by God. The culture assumes it is loving to let people do whatever they want to. However, the God

---

2. Anselm, *Monologion and Proslogion, with the Replies of Gaunilo and Anselm*, ed. T. Williams (Indianapolis: Hackett, 1996), p. 63.

of love read about in the Bible intervenes in people's lives. God's love is a holy love, morally pure and implacably opposed to all that is selfish, unkind or independent from him. We are familiar with the idea that a word such as 'love' ought not to be defined in any way the culture deems fit. We need to ensure our assumptions about the nature of God's love come from the Bible, not secular culture.

Reflecting on how God's love relates to the classical doctrine of God and the death of Jesus is a crucial part of making sure our understanding of God's love is biblical. The theologian who upholds the classical tradition of Augustine, Aquinas and Calvin maintains the Creator–creature distinction. This means that we do not view God's love as merely a more powerful version of human love. God's love is of a different order to our love. At a fundamental, qualitative, ontological level, God's love is other than our love. This flows from the fact that he is the Creator, while we are his creatures. The love of the uncreated Creator must be infinite, perfect and independent. God's love cannot be dependent upon his creatures. If God needed his creation, he would not be the sovereign, free God he declares himself to be. As God put it:

> If I were hungry, I would not tell you,
>   for the world and its fullness are mine.
> (Ps. 50:12)

Ironic poetry is used to communicate to us the awesome reality of God's being God – he does not need us. So with God's love. If his love is truly perfect, infinite and distinct from our love, it must be free from rather than dependent upon creatures. We are used to thinking that love is elicited by the beauty within the beloved. This is true in the instance of human love. The patriot loves his country's heritage; the wife loves her husband's kindness; the student loves her teacher's wisdom. However, when God revealed to his people that he loved them, he explicitly said that his love was not due to anything within them:

> For you are a people holy to the LORD your God. The LORD your God
> has chosen you to be a people for his treasured possession, out of all the
> peoples who are on the face of the earth. It was not because you were

more in number than any other people that the LORD set his love on you
and chose you, for you were the fewest of all peoples, but it is because
the LORD loves you and is keeping the oath that he swore to your fathers,
that the LORD has brought you out with a mighty hand and redeemed
you from the house of slavery, from the hand of Pharaoh king of Egypt.
(Deut. 7:6–8)

Disorientating and unnerving it may be, but in this passage God
says that he loves Israel simply because he loves them. He is the
source and cause of his own love. God's love is unlike our love, in
that it is free, independent and unconstrained. This must be so, for
otherwise God's love would not be perfect and infinite.

Though God's love is radically other to our love, Scripture can
reveal to us something of what his love is. Words can be used to
communicate truth about God's nature and character. Language is
used, as we have seen, analogically. This is obvious in the case of
ironic poetry, as for example in the above quotation from Psalm 50.
However, it is also the case that language used of God is analogical
when we are talking about a word such as 'love' in 1 John 4:8. The
word 'love' when used of God has a genuine correlation with what
we mean by love in human relationships, but God's love is nevertheless ontologically different.

Simplicity is the basic grammar of language about God. When
Aquinas wrote about simplicity, he was 'engaged in the metalinguistic
project of mapping out the grammar appropriate *in divinis*. He is
proposing the logic proper to discourse about God.'[3] I have
discussed how the grammar of simplicity means that God does not
have attributes such as patience, truthfulness or omniscience. Rather
God is perfect patience, truth and knowledge. So 1 John 4:8 does
not say that God is loving, or that he feels love; it states that 'God
is love.' Simplicity has several implications for God's love.

First, the fact that God is his attributes – that he does not just
love, but is love – means that when he loves us, he gives himself to
us. God's love for creatures is not merely a grand gesture from a

---

3. D. B. Burrell, *Aquinas: God and Action* (Chicago: University of Scranton
   Press, 2008), p. 19.

Roman cross. God's love is not distant. God's love is God. God's love would not be his love if it were something that could only be talked about, described or understood. Since God is love, when people receive God's love they experience God himself. This is precisely what we are taught in one of the verses Augustine most frequently quoted in his writings: 'Hope does not put us to shame, because God's love has been poured into our hearts through the Holy Spirit who has been given to us' (Rom. 5:5). Similarly, God said.

Do not be afraid, Abram.
  I am your shield,
    your very great reward.
(Gen. 15:1 NIV)

When God loves, he gives himself to those he loves. Spiritual intimacy, a deep sense of being loved, a realization that God's love is infinite – these are realities for those whom God loves because God is simple. God does not just love: he is love.

Secondly, the doctrine of simplicity means that God's love is as reliable and powerful as God himself. God is his love. God can no more cease to love than he can cease to exist. We cannot even imagine his not being love – for such a God would be a different (non-existent) 'god'. In the moment we think God is not perfect love towards us, we are worshipping not God, but an idol. Since God cannot be other than perfect love, his love is exercised with the omnipotence proper to him. This is wonderful news for us. It means that God's love can overcome any and all opposition ranged against it. No nation, ideology, book or heart can ever defeat his love. If that were possible, God would not be love. At various times we all doubt his love, or struggle to believe he loves us. When shadows of doubt cloud our vision, God has within himself the power to reawaken our hearts to his love, for God is love.

Thirdly, since simplicity means God is his attributes, it is also the case that each attribute is identical with the other attributes. From our human, creaturely perspective it makes sense to distinguish between God's omniscience and omnipresence. However, when God is seen as the simple, infinite Creator, we begin to realize that, in a mysterious way, omniscience and omnipresence both refer to the same thing, God's presence, from the different perspectives of time and space. Love and wrath appear to humans as vastly opposed attributes. However, from the perspective of the simple God there is no division, part or conflict. Rather love and wrath are how the saved and unrepentant experience the same reality of God from their differing situations. This interchangeability of attributes means that no act or aspect of God's nature is opposed to or independent of his love. Simplicity means that God's omnipresence, omniscience, wrath, patience, eternity and holiness are all also his love. We need the distinctions to help us understand something of what he is like. We also need to remember the unifying role of simplicity, which ensures no attribute is set against another. God is not loving one day, but wrathful another. He is not omniscient in a way that is independent of love. Rather his knowledge is his love. His wrath is his love. This does not mean that God is incoherent or contradictory. It means his knowledge is a form of love; his wrath is an expression of love. All that God does is love, for he is love. Every action and attribute is love-shaped and is a form of love. We often, due to our creaturely limitations, have to think of an attribute of God in isolation from his love. However, as we do so we conceive a being less than God. For God is love, and does not cease to be so in any part of his being at any time. He has no parts and is timeless: God is love.

Reflection on all that Scripture reveals about the simple God of love led theologians such as Aquinas to conclude that when God revealed his name as 'I AM' (Exod. 3:14), he revealed himself as a verb rather than a noun. Weinandy comments on Aquinas's insight:

> God's very nature . . . is not then designated or signified by a noun, but by a verb. Being pure act (pure verb) as *ipsum esse* does not mean that God is something fully in act, such as a creature might actualise its full potential, but rather that God is act pure and simple.[4]

---

4. Thomas G. Weinandy, *Does God Suffer?* (Edinburgh: T. & T. Clark, 2000), p. 122.

This means that God is not an inactive substance, or even, strictly speaking, a being who does things. Properly speaking, God is pure act and perfect potentiality. This means that rather than thinking of God as a being who loves, we ought to see him as a being of pure, infinite love – God is one eternal act of perfect love, eternally in motion, reaching towards the other in love. God is a pure, timeless act of infinite love. This is not how we are accustomed to conceive of ourselves or God. The reason is surely that all too often we imagine God's love is, in the final analysis, quite like our love: fickle, dependent, conflicted and impure. It may be unsettling to realize that God is not a creature, but, given our desperate need for a love that is genuinely and fully from God, it is good news.

Without suffering or change

The majority of Christian theologians and church confessions have taught that God neither suffers passions nor changes. So the Anglican Church declares, 'There is but one living and true God, everlasting, without body, parts, or passions.'[5]

John Calvin wrote that 'God does not have blood, [and] does not suffer.'[6] Similarly, the Westminster Confession teaches:

> There is but one only, living, and true God, who is infinite in being and perfection, a most pure spirit, invisible, without body, parts, or passions; immutable, immense, eternal, incomprehensible, almighty, most wise, most holy, most free, most absolute.[7]

If we turn to some of the earliest theologians, we find clear teaching that God does not suffer or change. Justin Martyr believed

---

5. *The Book of Common Prayer* (Cambridge: Cambridge University Press, 2005), art. 1, p. 611.

6. John Calvin, *Institutes of the Christian Religion*, tr. Ford Lewis Battles, ed. John T. McNeill, 2 vols. (Philadelphia: Westminster, 2001), 2.14.2.

7. A. A. Hodge, *The Confession of Faith* (Edinburgh: Banner of Truth, 1992), p. 46.

God is 'unchangeable and eternal'.[8] He is the 'unbegotten and impassible God'.[9] Irenaeus contended:

> The [Gnostics] endow God with human affections and emotions. However, if they had known the Scriptures, and had been taught by the truth, they would have known beyond doubt that God is not like men. His thoughts are not like the thoughts of men. For the Father of all is at a vast distance from those dispositions and passions that operate among men.[10]

Reformed theologians have explained immutability as follows: 'Immutability is an incommunicable attribute of God by which is denied of him not only all change, but also all possibility of change, as much with respect to existence as to will.'[11]

Baptist preachers such as Charles Spurgeon have found immutability unexceptional: 'The very existence, and being of a God, seem to me to imply immutability.'[12]

The doctrines of immutability (that God does not change) and impassibility (that God does not have passions) are essential parts of the classical vision of God. Understandably people today find it difficult to see how an immutable, impassible God could possibly be loving. It does indeed appear counter-intuitive. Our modern view of love assumes that love opens itself to hurt, suffering and rejection. This is portrayed in the contemporary novel *One Day* by David Nicholls. The book follows twenty years of an on-and-off relationship between Dexter and Emma. From university to eventual marriage and tragedy a consistent theme of the book is that Emma's love for Dexter hurts her. He mistreats, misunderstands and ignores

---

8. Justin Martyr, *The First and Second Apologies of Justin Martyr*, tr. L. W. Barnard (Mahwah, N.J.: Paulist Press, 1997), 1.13.

9. Ibid. 1.25.

10. Irenaeus, *Against Heresies* 2.13.3, http://www.newadvent.org/fathers/0103213.htm (accessed 10 Nov. 2013).

11. Francis Turretin, *Institutes of Elenctic Theology*, 3 vols. (Phillipsburg: P. & R., 1992), vol. 1, 3.11.

12. Charles Spurgeon, Sermon 1, http://www.spurgeon.org/sermons/0001.htm (accessed 18 Nov. 2013).

her. The pain and confusion Emma feels as a result of his ineptitude serves to make Emma's love seem all the more real. At one point in the book Dexter displays his social incompetence by getting drunk at a party, and during a game nearly breaking his then girlfriend's nose. As she attempts to staunch the flow of blood, Dexter reflects on the situation. He feels he ought to say something. Inspired, he kisses her shoulder and whispers, 'Well you know what they say – '. He pauses for effect. 'You always hurt the one you love!' This is pretty clever, pretty adorable, he thinks, and there's a silence while he waits, eyebrows raised expectantly, for the implication to sink in. 'Let's get some sleep, shall we?', she says.[13]

The comment 'You always hurt the one you love' is poignant. For Dexter is indeed hurting the one who loves him – Emma – by having a relationship with somebody else. That this other girl has just had her nose bloodied, and is not impressed at his wise crack, raises the possibility that while modern love seems irretrievably bound up with hurt and pain, we are not entirely satisfied with this.

Still it is difficult to understand how a God can be loving if he cannot change or feel passions. Surely it is of the essence that love be open to hurt and rejection? When we love, are we not binding our happiness up with another, who may hurt us? Surely vulnerability and tenderness require, at the very least, an open-ness to pain and change? If we love somebody deeply, surely this changes us?

The conviction that love must involve ability to feel passions, and be hurt, is deeply felt in our culture. Christians are quick to realize that our culture's views on love, relationships and feelings are the insights of a rebellious, sinful world that is burdened by the effects of Adam's sin. This is all true, but for our purposes it may be even more important to realize that these insights come from reflections upon the experience of love between people, who are creatures. Due to the Creator–creature distinction we must be very wary of assuming that observations about human relationships can be applied to God. Love between people who are creatures may well involve inevitable exposure to suffering, rejection, change and hurt.

---

13. D. Nicholls, *One Day* (London: Hodder & Stoughton, 2009), p. 261.

That God experiences love in the same way as us is no more likely than his having two arms and legs. The Bible teaches that God is love. We want God to love us. Why should it be the case, and why would we desire it to be the case, that God's love be as weak, damaged and flawed as ours so often is? As Rogers observes:

I have a hard time seeing why one would prefer a God incapable of unconditional love. Hartshorne's view of love seems to be that the lover needs the beloved in order to become more joyful. I find in myself (and I can only ask the reader to introspect to see if this is a shared phenomenon) a longing to be loved, wholly and completely, by someone who does not want anything from me. I do not think such a thing has a place in the created universe, since we are all by nature contingent and hence needy beings. As far as I can tell, the most likely candidate for a being who can perfectly will good for us without demanding anything in return is the God of Augustine and Anselm and Aquinas . . . I find the idea of a God who is made to suffer by us, and who needs us to be fulfilled, a depressing conception of divinity. In any case, it does not square with the other attributes of a perfect being, like simplicity and immutability.[14]

The real reason we struggle to grasp how God can be loving if he does not change or suffer passions is that we so rarely reflect deeply on the fact that God is not like us. We all too easily think that he is a slightly bigger version of us, existing, loving and feeling as we do. In reality that is an absurd view to hold – how could the Creator be more or less similar to his creatures? We are made in his image, which means there is some kind of likeness that enables relationship and communication. But before an image is like the original, it is different. The image is like the source, but it is only an image! So with God and people. A fundamental starting point for faithful theology is that God is not a creature. We learn about God not primarily by assuming he is like his creatures, but by learning what he has revealed about himself as God. When we do so, we are

---

14. Katherin Rogers, *Perfect Being Theology* (Edinburgh: Edinburgh University Press, 2000), pp. 52–53.

confronted by a God who is perfect, infinite and simple. God is immutable because if he changed he would not be perfect. Any improvement or decline would mean God is not the most perfect being that Scripture reveals him as. This does not prevent his being loving – quite the opposite.

The immutability of God does not mean he is inert or static. God is not immobile like a stone. Rather the unchangeableness of God means he is unchangeably, irrevocably and necessarily the most passionately loving being that can be imagined. God's love is infinite and perfect. Such a love must be immutable. It cannot weaken, increase or vary. As Augustine taught:

> You will not find any change in God, anything that is now like this, a moment ago like that. Where you find 'now like this, now like that' a kind of death has taken place . . . whatever dies – both from better to worse and from worse to better – is not what God is, because it is not possible either for the highest good to become better or for the truly eternal to become worse. The truly eternal has nothing to do with time . . . What does 1 Tim. 6:16 mean if not that God alone is beyond all change, because he alone has true eternity? So then, there is no change where God is.[15]

God's love must be immutable since it is perfect:

> The divine attribute of love is fully in act. The trinity of persons subsist in relation to one another, as the one God, with their love for one another fully and completely actualized. They are immutable and impassible in their love for one another, not because their love for one another is static or inert, but because it is utterly dynamic and totally passionate in its self-giving. It is impossible for the Trinity to be more loving, for the persons of the Trinity possess no self-actualizing potential to become more loving.[16]

---

15. Augustine, *Homilies on the Gospel of John 1–40*, tr. Edmund Hill, ed. Allan Fitzgerald, The Works of Saint Augustine, a Translation for the 21st Century (New York: New City, 2009), 23.9.

16. Weinandy, *Does God Suffer?*, p. 161.

Immutability and impassibility do not negate God's love; they maximize and guard his love, ensuring that this love is (unlike ours) perfect. The Creator–creature distinction must be observed in all our language about God, not least when we theologize about his passionate love:

> God is both impassible and impassioned . . . God's passion transcends ours both in an ontological sense and an ethical sense . . . The critical point here is that God transcends humanity not only in his impassibility, but also in his impassionedness . . . Both senses of God's transcendent passion grow out of the Creator–creature distinction.[17]

No theologian in church history who has defended the teaching that God cannot change has thought that God is incapable of love – quite the opposite. That God cannot change is an insistence upon the unique, perfect, unsurpassable reality of his divine love.

It may seem that declaring God is 'without . . . passions'[18] rather rules out the idea that God can be infinitely passionate in his love. This is a misunderstanding arising from our modern casual use of language. 'Passion' is an English word derived from Latin (via French). In its original sense it meant a deep, overwhelming feeling or emotion that can overcome a person. In that sense a passion, by definition, is something suffered by a person; hence the Latin origin, *passio*, giving us the term 'Christ's Passion'. With this in mind we see the intention of saying that God is without passion: we are claiming that nothing outside God can make him suffer. Nothing can act upon him in such a way that he feels lack, want, loss, pain or hurt. God is sovereign, perfect and self-sufficient. If he had passions, he would be none of these things: he would be enslaved, imperfect and dependent. Modern casual use of language means that we assume denying passions of God involves rejecting the possibility of any relationality. To deny passions of God in this manner in no way assumes that God is not personal and relational; it merely insists

---

17. R. Lister, *God Is Impassible and Impassioned: Toward a Theology of Divine Emotion* (Wheaton: Crossway; Nottingham: Apollos, 2012), pp. 251–252.

18. *Book of Common Prayer*, art. 1, p. 611.

that he experiences his inner life in a way that is not subservient, or enslaved, to anything. God is God and as such is infinitely free. His love is not a passion, but it is beautifully and freely passionate, and infinitely so. These matters are well put by Shedd:

> In defining God to be 'a most pure spirit without passions,' it must be remembered that the term passion is used etymologically. It is derived from *patior* (to suffer). Passion implies passivity. It is the effect of an impression from without. . . . God has no passions. He stands in no passive and organic relations to that which is not himself. He cannot be wrought upon and impressed by the universe of matter and mind which he has created from nothing. . . . He is not operated upon and moved from the outside, but all his activity is self-determined. All the movement in divine essence is internal and from himself. Even when God is complacent toward a creature's holiness and hostile toward a creature's sin, this is not the same as a passive impression upon a sensuous organism, from an outward sensible object, eliciting temporarily a sensation that previously was unfelt. Sin and holiness are not substances; and God's love and wrath are self-moved and unceasing energies of divine nature. He is voluntarily and eternally complacent toward good and hostile toward evil . . . It is important to remember this signification of the term passion and the intention in employing it. Sometimes it has been understood to be synonymous with feeling or emotion, and the erroneous and demoralizing inference has been drawn that divine nature is destitute of feeling altogether. . . . It denudes God of those emotional qualities that necessarily enter into personality and are requisite in order to love, worship and obedience on the part of the creature . . . While therefore God as a most pure spirit has no passions, he has feelings and emotions. He is not passively wrought upon by the objective universe, so that he experiences impressions and organic appetites physically, as the creature does, but he is self-moved in all his feelings.[19]

Often people try to use the different range of modern relational words to stand for differing degrees of feeling. So an emotion,

---

19. W. G. T. Shedd, *Dogmatic Theology*, 3 vols. (New York: Scribner, 1888), vol. 1, pp. 170–178.

feeling, passion and affection are thought to bear various amounts of strength, and have various ranges of legitimate connection to rationality. A feeling may then be thought of as inappropriate to God, as it might be weak or transient, and an affection more fitting for God because it is said to have a certain depth or connection to reason. Such an approach has an appearance of wisdom, but in the end is doomed to failure. For it forgets that all these terms are modern words, used analogically of God. They are all used (in various ways) to point towards something of God's reality, and they can do so, but since they are analogical they bear with them much that is meaningless when applied to God. Much better to use all the words – feeling, emotion, affection and passion – in combination with careful systematic theology, to encourage the scriptural belief that God is infinitely relational, loving and emotional in a way only the perfect God can be.

What then would it mean for God not to change? It is to say that, due to the Creator–creature distinction, all our language about God, including the revelation of him in Scripture, is analogical. Our words, which are earthed in creation and human-focused contexts, are misleading when applied in an unthinkingly univocal way to God:

> God cannot change, because even if he does something which might look to us like 'change' he would still be the same as he was before . . . a word like 'change' simply makes no sense when it is applied to God. Classical theism is not perfect, and it does not have the answer to every question. But fifty generations of Christians have not been wrong to insist on the basic principles which that traditional theology has sought to uphold.[20]

The Bible is replete with stories of how God stopped having mercy and poured out his wrath (and vice versa) and how he repented of his decision to punish. The classical tradition holds that such assertions are describing how God appears to us, but the language used to describe God's 'changing' is used analogically. That is,

---

20. Gerald Bray, *The Personal God: Is the Classical Understanding of God Tenable?* (Carlisle: Paternoster, 1998), p. 74.

something about God's real desires and passion is being communicated to us; but in the strict sense of the word, God is not actually changing – we are experiencing his reality in differing circumstances. Consider the nation God promises he will punish, but then they stop sinning and he repents from his promised wrath. He appears to have changed from being wrathful to being in solidarity with the people. But in reality God has not changed. Both before and after the people stopped sinning, he was perfectly holy, sovereign and loving. The people are the ones who have changed – and as they have changed they have experienced the same perfectly holy, sovereign and loving God in a different way. How could it be any other way? After all, change is a temporal experience and only creatures live in time. God is eternal.

Open to change?

It is understandable that people struggle to see how an impassible and immutable God can be loving. The best way to affirm God's free, sovereign love is to realize that the classical vision of God is nothing less than an attempt to promote his perfect love as a form of love appropriate to the Creator. We all want to proclaim and experience God's love. As one theologian who rejected the classical view said, 'The Bible's God has a heart.'[21] Sadly many do not realize that the classical tradition is the best way to affirm the emotional, passionate love of God. Instead they turn to elements of another theological school: Open Theism.

The Openness of God: A Biblical Challenge to the Traditional Understanding of God was published in 1994. As the title states, it sought to rebut the view of God known as Classical Theism. The authors were fully aware they were rejecting the views held for centuries as a faithful reading of Scripture. As Clark Pinnock wrote in one of his other books, 'It is astonishing, when you think about it, that impassibility could have become orthodox belief in the early centuries. Here

---

21. Colin Gunton, *Act and Being: Towards a Theology of the Divine Attributes* (London: SCM, 2002), p. 129.

perhaps more than anywhere else we find the bankruptcy of conventional theology.'[22]

In the original *Openness of God* manifesto a number of key beliefs were identified. One of these was that 'God always desires our highest good, both individually and corporately, and thus is affected by what happens in our lives.'[23] As God is 'affected' by his creatures, the Openness theologians envision God's joy and pain increasing or decreasing. They believe such a state of affairs increases the value and legitimacy of God's emotional life and capacity to love. The classical theologian sees such a view as misguided: impassibility is actually the claim that God is as fully, eternally and perfectly emotional as is possible. The Openness view diminishes God's capacity for love.

Clark Pinnock reads Scripture as if its statements about God are univocal: that is, assuming the words used of God function in the same way as when they refer to creatures. This hermeneutic leads him to note the many affirmations in the Bible of God's loving his people, and conclude that he must in a straightforward sense, suffer:

> God, as a loving person, is involved in the world and is affected by creatures. This challenges the traditional view of the impassibility of God. Far from being aloof or abstract, God maintains a personal and intimate relation to the world. He is moved by what happens and reacts accordingly. God is a subject and events arouse in him joy and sorrow, pleasure and anger. He experiences pathos, for example he loves, laughs, repents, can be delighted and become angry. It is said that when God was sorry that he made humankind, it grieved him to his heart (Gen. 6:6). Love leads to suffering. God feels the pain of rejection. He suffers because of his people and also with and for them. The world affects God emotionally and he is moved by the sufferings of his creatures. The fact that God is love rules out the doctrine of impassibility, which entails that God has no desires that can be thwarted; he cannot suffer or be in any way vulnerable. A. M. Fairbairn declared a century ago, 'Theology has no

---

22. Clark Pinnock, *Most Moved Mover* (Grand Rapids: Baker Academic, 2001), p. 89.

23. Clark Pinnock (ed.), *The Openness of God: A Biblical Challenge to the Traditional Understanding of God* (Downers Grove: InterVarsity Press, 1994), p. 156.

falser idea than that of the impassibility of God.' Most theologians today
agree with him and reject it. Scripture speaks of the suffering of God.
God's heart can be close to breaking (Hos. 11). God knows his people's
condition and feels their pain (Exod. 3:7f). God laments and mourns
over them. Even for Moab God says, 'My heart cries out' (Is. 15:5). The
issue for Christians is not whether God could suffer but how God could
not suffer. God made a world with suffering in it and he would be less
than God if he ignored it. He would be less than God if he lacked
sympathy or refused to share in the suffering of creatures.[24]

The views Pinnock and his co-authors argued for had roots in
many earlier movements, not least Origenism, Socinianism, Arminianism and Hegelianism. The publication of *The Openness of God* in
1994 was the bringing into the public arena of a debate about God
which had till that point been more or less limited to university
theology and philosophy departments.[25] Until 2003 a large number
of books and articles were published about Open Theism – a veritable
war of words between evangelicals who rejected Open Theism and
others who embraced it. For a few years after 2003 the focus of
debate became the Evangelical Theological Society, which wrestled
and voted over whether members should be expelled for affirming
Open Theism. The debate was protracted, since the actual terms of
discussion became whether Open Theism contradicted inerrancy,
something required of the Society's members but which had not (in
2003) been defined by them. Clark Pinnock died in 2010. His death
was notable in that there was not any significant furore within
evangelical groups surrounding his teachings on Open Theism. The
reason was not merely the appropriate respect accorded at the point
of somebody's funeral. The sociological reality is that Open Theism
had several years previously ceased to be an intra-evangelical debate.
Open Theism became a recognized body of views, but was no longer
a movement (as it was in the wake of the 1994 book). This does not

---

24. Pinnock, *Most Moved Mover*, p. 88.
25. An important exception is R. Rice, *The Openness of God: The Relationship
    of Divine Foreknowledge and Human Free Will* (Hagerstown: Review &
    Herald, 1980).

by any means imply that the teachings associated with Open Theism have become historical artefacts. Quite the opposite: they are now unquestioned assumptions of many strands of the Christian world, some of which are associated with massively successful churches, publishing and media movements.

In 2003 supporters of Classical Theism observed that Open Theist 'conclusions find a receptive audience today because they fit comfortably within recent currents in American thought'.[26] Since that was observed, the culture has become even more receptive to the vision of God propounded by Open Theists, which is why the original literature is still important to understand, and why its conclusions will continue to be popular. One of the main appeals of an Open Theist view of God is that it renders God more intelligible to humans (at the cost of eliding the Creator–creature distinction). This vastly reduces mystery: we appear to understand more of God. However, as D. A. Carson wisely counsels, 'In my experience, if you locate what is mysterious at the wrong place, sooner or later the mistake will come back to haunt you.'[27] The classical doctrine of God, with its leading role for perfection and simplicity, is often wrongly accused of attempting to systematize away the mystery in God. Far from it. The concept of simplicity is far from being straightforwardly comprehensible: it is counter-intuitive and profoundly mysterious. Sustained meditation on the relationships between attributes and the essential otherness of God does not reduce the mystery of God's being; it locates it in the correct place and ensures his glorious splendour is maintained.

One of us

We have seen that Aquinas was one of the church's firmest defenders of the classical conviction that God, being perfect, cannot change.

---

26. John Piper (ed.), *Beyond the Bounds: Open Theism and the Undermining of Biblical Christianity* (Wheaton: Crossway, 2003), p. 120.

27. D. A. Carson, *How Long, O Lord? Reflections on Suffering and Evil* (Grand Rapids: Baker; Leicester: Inter-Varsity Press, 2006), p. 20.

Typical of his observations was this: 'Since every creature has something of potency, in that God alone is pure act, it is necessary that all creatures be mutable, and God alone immutable.'[28]

If views such as Open Theism that embrace change within God's being are rejected, what is to be made of what appears to be the record of the greatest change in God, the incarnation, where God became a human? Surely we read in the gospel accounts of so many changes in the life of Jesus, who is fully God, that immutability is an untenable belief? Jesus hungered, wept, sailed across a lake and died. Do these incarnate actions not prove God changes, and signal the lunacy of believing the classical doctrines of simplicity and immutability?

Theologians such as Aquinas were far from unaware of the incarnation. He knew that Jesus, the man, was God. A bit of reflection on the key doctrines convinced him that God became a human without undergoing any change. The alternative would do immeasurable damage to God's glory and nature. In a sermon entitled 'The Boy Jesus' Aquinas taught about an aspect of the incarnation that appears to offer some of the strongest biblical evidence that the incarnation meant God changed. Aquinas dealt with the text 'And Jesus increased in wisdom and in stature and in favour with God and man' (Luke 2:52).

Aquinas believed this text of Scripture, but he knew the crucial issue was one of interpretation. What did it mean for God to tell us that the boy Jesus grew in wisdom? As Aquinas put it:

> Someone is said to advance in wisdom, not only when he acquires a greater wisdom, but also when the wisdom in him is more evident. It is true that Christ from the beginning of his conception was full of wisdom and grace, but he did not show it from the beginning, but at an age when others usually show it. In that case we speak of advancing in wisdom, not in an absolute sense of the word, but in view of the effect through which he advanced amidst other people.[29]

---

28. Thomas Aquinas, *Scriptum Super Libros Sententiarum*, ed. S. E. Fretté and P. Maré, Opera Omnia (Paris: Vivè, 1882–9), I.8.3.2.

29. Thomas Aquinas, *The Academic Sermons*, ed. C. P. Mark-Robin Hoogland, The Fathers of the Church, Mediaeval Continuation (Washington: Catholic University of America Press, 2010) p. 89.

Not only, as Aquinas argued, is this an accepted usage of language, but it would be rather counter-productive for Christ to display his wisdom earlier: 'If he had willed to show his wisdom when he was seven years of age, people could have doubted the truth of the assumed human nature.'[30]

Such a shrewd observation from Aquinas fits well with Calvin's use of the concept 'accommodation', that God in revelation accommodated himself to our creaturely limitations. The idea of accommodation and linguistic effect are together weighty responses to those who think records of 'change' in Jesus disprove God's immutability. The changes are accommodations to our creaturely capacities, which speak of impacts upon us rather than actual ontological changes within God's being. If this is unsatisfying and seems to demean God, then consider the alternative. It is that God does not have to accommodate his revelation to us, which means the creator God is not much more powerful, knowledgeable or glorious than us. This was presented by Satan in Genesis 3:5 as an insidious temptation.

What of Jesus' death? Did God die on the cross? If so, that would seem to be a massive change within his being. The classical view of God would then be utterly untenable. 'Explaining how the impassible and immortal God could suffer and die was the greatest single challenge the early Christians faced.'[31]

Augustine preached that 'God died', but explained his claim as follows: 'God died, that he might make compensation in a certain kind of divine exchange, that humanity might not see death. So Christ is God, but he did not die in the aspect by which he was God ... For he put on what he was not, he did not lose what he was.'[32]

---

30. Ibid., p. 90.
31. Gerald Bray, 'Does God Have Feelings?', in Michael Jensen (ed.), *True Feelings: Perspectives on Emotions in Christian Life and Ministry* (Nottingham: Apollos, 2012), p. 101.
32. Augustine, *Sermons*, ed. John Rotelle, trans. Edmund Hill, The Works of Saint Augustine, A Translation for the 21st Century, 11 vols. (New York: New City, 1991), vol. 3, 80.5.

Augustine agonized over the problem of how one who cannot die could suffer and be killed.[33] Augustine wanted to preach that God had died – he felt the emotional and theological power of being able to say that 'the immortal one put on mortality, that he might die for us, and by his death kill our death'.[34] Augustine made strong statements like this, despite insisting that Christ 'did not die in the aspect by which he was God'.[35] This is instructive for us. It shows that classical theologians distinguish between technical, philosophical statements about God's being and things that may be said about him, in sermons for example. Many things may be said about God in preaching that are true of him in an allegorical sense. Said in any other sense they would portray God as less than he is. In the case of Augustine's saying that God died, Augustine feels free to say something about God that is true in so far as it applies to Jesus, God incarnate. The person Jesus did die on a cross, but it would be incorrect in a technical theological sense if one said that the divine nature died. The tradition of 'Communicatio Idiomatum' (Latin: Communication of Properties) has developed, by which it is held to be legitimate to speak of something that, properly speaking, only one nature of Christ can experience as applying to the other. So, for example, only the human nature could hunger, but one can say, 'God hungered.' This approach gave support to Augustine's statement that 'God died.' Such a radical thing can be said, on the understanding that it is a statement within the bounds of traditional Christological orthodoxy. God died in the sense that Jesus experienced death through his human nature. At this point we stand on the edge of the greatest mystery of the universe. There is much we do not understand, and there is mystery. We are free to use language about God's dying that might appear to support Open Theism. In reality it is language used with the understanding that, amazingly and wondrously, God became human in a way that preserved his perfect, immutable nature. Such a claim is essential, for denying it destroys the incarnation:

---

33. Ibid., vol. 10, 375B.4.
34. Ibid., vol. 2, 23A.3.
35. Ibid., vol. 3, 80.5.

The words of John's Gospel 'the Word became flesh' must not be interpreted in a way that makes the Incarnation a mere fantasy. God truly becomes human. But in doing so, he does not cease to be the unchangeable God. When properly understood, the Incarnation, far from denying the immutability of God, rather requires it. For if God changed in becoming human, he would no longer be truly God, and Jesus Christ would not be truly God and human.[36]

Meditation: love for me

'I live by faith in the Son of God, who loved me and gave himself for me.'

(Gal. 2:20)

O God, at the centre of your unchanging being is love. Love that is so pure, so perfect, so infinite, so raw and alive that it pursued me to the cross. Forgive me for ever wanting to hurt you, and for my doubting your love. Thank you that you sent your Son into the world, and your Spirit into my heart, to make me feel the supernatural reality of your love for me.

Not love in general, not mere words, gestures or ideals. But the intimate joy of heaven, poured out on a person such as me, who not only fails to understand it but who does not deserve it.

I praise you that your love cannot weaken, fade or change. I thank you that you are the source of your unchanging love, for you are your love. It is with such relief that I realize your love depends not on me, but on you. I cast myself upon you, with love that is awakened by your love, sustained by your grace and bound for your glory.

Amen.

---

36. Michael Dodds, *The Unchanging God of Love: Thomas Aquinas and Contemporary Theology on Divine Immutability* (New York: Catholic University of America Press, 2008), p. 200.

PART 2

THE RELATIONAL GOD

6. GOD'S LOVE AND THREENESS IN SCRIPTURE

Scripture contains much diversity of genre, ethos and historical setting. This diversity deepens our appreciation of the unchanging, fundamental message of the salvation it reveals. Church of England ministers are forbidden in their confession from 'expound[ing] one place of Scripture, that it be repugnant to another'.[1] This instruction assumes both diversity and unity in Scripture. Diversity, since one text may appear to conflict with another; unity, since all texts can be expounded coherently. As anybody who has sat under a faithful preaching ministry that has expounded vast tracts of Scripture, over a period of twenty or so years, will testify, the diversity of Scripture serves to bring home the central message of salvation all the more evocatively and powerfully.

In a similar way we find that the threeness of God ensures that the reality of his love is experienced in its fullness. Far from undermining his unity, God's trinitarianism undergirds it. The simple God

---

1. *The Book of Common Prayer*, art. 20, p. 620.

who is love can be perfect love only because the simple God is three fully divine persons.

When we explore Scripture, we find that God reveals himself as a God who is Father, Son and Spirit. Each of the three persons is fully divine, yet there is one God who is simple. This is a sublime enrichment of what it means for God to be love. As Warfield observed, 'To Calvin the conception of the trinity gave vitality to the idea of God.'[2] The distinctive contributions of the three persons of the Trinity are revealed increasingly through salvation history.

The Father's loving plan

God the Father is revealed most clearly once the Son steps onto the world stage. There is a new revelation through Jesus: 'Jesus seems to have addressed Israel's god as "father" in a way which, even if not completely unique, is at least very remarkable.'[3]

So at Jesus' baptism we are told that a 'voice from heaven' addressed him as 'my beloved Son' (Matt. 3:17). The appearance of the Son means there is a Father. While the familial terms in no way imply the physical procreative acts associated with our normal linguistic usage, the terms 'Son' and 'Father' communicate genuine analogical truth about the being of God. If there was a Son with no Father, then the word 'Son' would not be a meaningful revelation of anything about God. When the Father speaks to Jesus at the start of his earthly ministry, the communication is one of love. The Father wants us to know that he loves his Son. Their relationship is one of perfect, infinite, satisfying love. The rejection, homelessness, thorns, scourging and nails suffered by the Son in no way suggest the Father's love is lacking. When the Son is revealed to the world in his baptism, the nature of God is unfolded and seen to be love.

---

2. B. B. Warfield, *Calvin and Augustine* (Philadelphia: P. & R., 1956), p. 192.
3. N. T. Wright, *Jesus and the Victory of God* (London: SPCK, 2001), pp. 649–650. The author did not capitalize the term 'god' in this classic work, a decision he explains at the start of his book.

Jesus' teaching on living as disciples in God's kingdom is summarized in Matthew 5 – 7. At least seventeen times in those chapters Jesus mentions his 'Father'. The Father is perfect (Matt. 5:48), sees what is done in secret (6:4), knows what you need before you ask (6:8, 32), forgives (6:14), rewards (6:18), gives good things (7:11) and has a will that must be obeyed (7:21). Each reference to the Father teaches something important about his distinctive role. However, it is also vital to see that the weaving of references to the Father through this discourse reveals that the Father is in some sense the prime person of the Trinity. The Father is seen in these references as the person who plans and initiates the kingdom. Jesus repeatedly shows a deference and submission to his Father, which the Father is not revealed in Scripture as mirroring. God is love, and his kingdom is one that brings love to those who do not deserve it. That the Father's distinctive role in the work of loving salvation is to plan and initiate is taught in a number of other verses:

> The God and Father of our Lord Jesus Christ . . . [made] known to us the mystery of his will, according to his purpose, which he set forth in Christ as a plan for the fullness of time, to unite all things in him, things in heaven and things on earth.
> (Eph. 1:3, 9–10)

> The works that the Father has given me to accomplish, the very works that I am doing, bear witness about me that the Father has sent me.
> (John 5:36)

> The living Father sent me, and I live because of the Father.
> (John 6:57)

> I do as the Father has commanded me.
> (John 14:31)

> [Jesus] said to them, 'It is not for you to know times or seasons that the Father has fixed by his own authority.'
> (Acts 1:7)

The Father is the person of the Trinity who plans the work of salvation. He sends the Son, sets the times and instructs the Son.

The Father is by no means a proud ruler or selfish leader – he wills that all would honour the Son (John 5:23). Nevertheless even when affirming that all things must be laid at the feet of Jesus, we are taught that the Son will subject himself to his Father (1 Cor. 15:28). Similarly the Father's priority is seen in the Son's having life in himself – but this being 'granted' by his Father (John 5:26). Scripture repeatedly reveals that the Father is the person of the Trinity who plans and leads. The Son's role is different, though this in no way suggests the Son is less fully God than the Father.

In our status-driven culture it is easy to assume that the Father's role of planning must in some way relegate the Son to a second-rate position. This is not at all how Jesus viewed it. Jesus said, 'I have come down from heaven, not to do my own will but the will of him who sent me' (John 6:38). Jesus humbled himself to do his Father's will even when it led to the cross (Phil. 2:8). In all these experiences the Son remained the beloved Son (Matt. 3:17).

The intention of God in revealing the distinct role of the Father and Son in this way is surely to open to us the incredible depth of love that exists in the Trinity. We see in the Father and Son that this love is flavoured by humility and submission to the Father's plan. That plan pours out of a heart that is infinitely loving. Contemplating these nuances of God's love, in the distinct roles of the Father and Son, should move us to feel within our hearts a sense of dependence on and trust in the Father's plans. When we realize that the Father plans only that which is for our good, that he is perfect, all-powerful and kind, we begin to talk with him as our Father (Matt. 6:9) and sense that we have no need to worry over the details already planned out by him (Matt. 6:31–32). As Calvin wrote:

> Until men recognise that they owe everything to God, that they are nourished by his Fatherly care, that he is author of their every good, that they should seek nothing beyond him – they will never yield him willing service. Nay, unless they establish their complete happiness in him, they will never give themselves truly and sincerely to him.[4]

---

4. John Calvin, *Institutes of the Christian Religion*, tr. Ford Lewis Battles, ed. John T. McNeill, 2 vols. (Philadelphia: Westminster, 2001), 1.2.1.

Seeing more clearly the distinctive role of the Father in planning salvation helps us feel his 'Fatherly care', an essential prerequisite for placing our happiness in him. As people who experience the lavish love of God, Christians are to share the message of God's salvation with others. We do so in a way that preserves the distinct roles and persons of Father, Son and Spirit.

Having begun his ministry with a word from his Father, Jesus inaugurates the church's mission with a command to baptize people from all nations in the 'name of the Father and of the Son and of the Holy Spirit' (Matt. 28:19). The mission of the church is to be carried out with due awareness that God is Father, Son and Spirit. Only an experience of God in all three persons will provide sufficient endurance and virtue for the task of making disciples of all nations.

It is usually obvious to people from their first encounter with Christianity that the Father is divine. The distinctive features of the Father's ministry more closely align with our natural expectations of what 'God' might be like. The challenge is to realize that the Father is indeed the Father – meaning that he has a Son. This Son, being perfectly worthy of the Father's love, is himself perfect, infinite and necessarily divine. This has important implications for the Father. He is deeply relational, other-person-focused and, in his plans for the Son, loving. When secular persons think they entertain similar ideas to the Christian conception of God, they may appear to have grounds for such a belief in that Christianity does teach there is a divine person who plans, initiates and controls all things. The shocking, new revelation of Christianity is that that God is the Father. He has a Son and so can never be correctly thought of as a solitary, monistic being.

The Son's loving service

The New Testament states in a small number of places that Jesus is God.[5] That Jesus is in fact what these verses claim – the fully divine God – is evidenced by his birth, words, deeds and the Old Testament.

---

5. Verses where the word *theos* – a strong term for 'God' – are applied to Jesus include John 1:1; 20:28; Rom. 9:5; Titus 2:13; Heb. 1:8; 2 Peter 1:1.

The virgin birth of Jesus is a claim made in the Gospels (Matt. 1:23; Luke 1:34–35) and solemnly affirmed in the Apostles' Creed, Nicene Creed, Athanasian Creed and Chalcedonian Definition. In 1930 Gresham Machen published a landmark book in which he painstakingly considered the pagan and Jewish writings that could be suggested as precedents that could perhaps have enabled the gospel writers to concoct a mythical virgin birth. Machen concluded that the New Testament teaching on the virgin birth is unique – it simply has no precedent. He concludes:

> The problem of the virgin birth idea has not been solved by . . .
> the most elaborate of all attempts, any more than it was solved
> by the many previous theories that have succeeded one another
> in the long history of modern naturalistic criticism. The conclusion
> to which we are obliged to come after examination of the whole
> subject of alternative theories is that if the doctrine of the virgin
> birth of Christ did not originate in fact, modern critical
> investigation has at any rate not yet succeeded in showing how
> it did originate.[6]

Since those words were written, those who reject the virgin birth have still not managed to explain how the early Christians could have come up with the idea, had the claims not actually been true. N. T. Wright presented the argument with the rhetorical force it merits. The theory that the gospel authors invented the virgin birth 'asks us to believe in intellectual parthenogenesis: the birth of an idea without visible parentage. Difficult. Unless, of course, you believe in miracles, which most people who disbelieve the virginal conception don't.'[7]

On its own the virgin birth does not prove the divinity of Jesus, but none of the evidences of his divinity were intended to be considered in isolation from the others. At the very least the virgin birth

---

6. G. Machen, *The Virgin Birth of Christ* (London: James Clarke, 1958), p. 379.

7. M. Borg and N. T. Wright, *The Meaning of Jesus: Two Visions* (London: SPCK, 1999), p. 177.

of Jesus is part of a historically credible portrait of a human being who was divine.

The words of Jesus show that he believed himself to be God. So Jesus identified himself as 'I am' in John 8:58. This was the divine personal name God revealed to Moses at the burning bush. A higher claim to be God from within a Jewish cultural context is difficult to imagine. The response of those religious leaders present for the declaration was to pick up stones to kill him; they understood his comment was a claim to be God. Since they were unwilling to believe this, they viewed it as blasphemy, punishable by stoning under Jewish tradition. At his illegal trial before the Jewish council, Jesus claimed to be the 'Son of Man' (Mark 14:62). This was a term he used of himself at numerous points in his ministry. The Son of Man refers to a person predicted in Daniel 7:14 as receiving a kingdom that is everlasting and will not be destroyed. The high priest who heard Jesus' words 'tore his garments and said, "What further witnesses do we need? You have heard his blasphemy"' (Mark 14:63–64). The high priest understood Jesus' words to be a claim to make himself equal with God, as he had argued previously with regard to the Sabbath (John 5:17–18). This was held to constitute blasphemy.

The critic may challenge the accuracy of the words recorded of Jesus. So much seems to hang on a few words. The reliability of the gospel documents is best explored via the arguments of John Wenham, who guided readers through an inductive argument that permits a degree of scepticism as part of the process.[8] No uneducated leaps of faith are required! Nevertheless the words of Jesus testify to his divinity and, powerful as they are, God has not insisted that they be believed in a vacuum. They are entwined with other evidences, including his deeds.

Jesus did many things only God could do. Some of these the Gentile pagans would recognize as the prerogative of God alone, such as walking on water (Mark 6:45–52). Other actions make sense as evidences of Jesus' divinity only when the first-century Jewish cultural context is understood. Even his actions that cross cultures

---

8. John Wenham, *Christ and the Bible* (London: Tyndale, 1972).

to the Gentiles make more sense when the Jewish background is discovered. So when Jesus walked on water he acted as the psalmist said God did (Pss 89:9; 107:29), and he said to his disciples, 'Take heart, I AM. Do not be fearful' (Mark 6:50, my tr.). The resonances are obscured in most translations, but Jesus was echoing the divine personal name, and God's repeated refrain to his people through the prophets 'Do not fear' (e.g. Isa. 41:14). N. T. Wright is perhaps the modern theologian who has done most to highlight the importance of paying attention to the actions of Jesus in our efforts to understand his identity. Wright observes:

> Jesus acted as, and saw himself as, a prophet, standing within Israel's long prophetic tradition. One of the things that prophets like Isaiah, Jeremiah and Ezekiel did was to act symbolically, often in relation to Jerusalem and the temple, sometimes in prediction of its destruction. Isaiah's nakedness, Jeremiah's smashed pot, and Ezekiel's brick come to mind as obvious examples. We have seen that Jesus was capable of acting symbolically, and with deliberate scriptural overtones.[9]

Jesus performed many memorable and striking actions during his three-year ministry: he cleansed the temple, healed people, cast out demons, raised the dead, cursed a fig tree, turned water to wine and multiplied loaves of bread. These and many other actions were symbolic deeds, not implying that they were fictional or unhistorical but that they were done consciously to reveal that God was in Jesus doing all he had promised in the Old Testament. The return from exile, the cleansing from sin, the propitiation of wrath, defeat of evil powers, the renewing of creation and undoing of death. To be sure we ought not draw a straight, logical line from Jesus' actions to his divinity. As Wright warns, 'Some will want to jump without more ado into a full Nicene Christology, and will have to be severely restrained.'[10] Although it cannot be made too quickly, unreflectively or thoughtlessly, the move from Jesus' actions to his divinity can and

---

9. Wright, *Jesus and the Victory*, p. 415.
10. Ibid., p. 197.

must be made. Taken as a whole, the cumulative weight of Jesus' actions led the inspired authors of the New Testament, and the church that reflected on their witness, to conclude that Jesus' actions indicated that he was doing things that could be done only by God himself. As some of Jesus' contemporaries said, 'Who can forgive sins but God alone?' (Mark 2:7).

The Old Testament is the skeleton that gives shape and structure to the New Testament revelation of Jesus' birth, words and deeds. And the Old Testament's promises and expectations that God would deal with sin, draw near to his people and overcome death enable us to see the fulfilment in Jesus as nothing less than the Father's plan enacted. The prophecies of Scripture, the pattern of God's dealings with his people, repeated refrains – all these give a context into which Jesus is born, speaks and acts. Viewed through the lens of Old Testament Scripture it is then possible to see that all God's promises have found their 'yes' in Jesus (2 Cor. 1:20), and God himself has come to his earth. This being the case, Jesus could accept the 'worship' of creatures, something only God can do without sin (Matt. 28:17).

Jesus serves his Father by doing his will: being born as a human and dying to ransom many people (Mark 10:45) and make all things new (Rev. 21:5). It is natural that as we have considered the way Jesus serves the Father's plan of salvation some time has been spent highlighting the way in which we should go about evaluating evidence that Jesus is actually who Christians believe he is. The distinctive role of service Jesus had led him to be the person of the Trinity who came to earth and walked on our planet as a human. Consequently Jesus is the divine person who left his mark on history. His actions and words made waves that still crash on the shores of cultures and nations. Few people today are competent at evaluating evidence that is by its nature historical: in popular language and culture 'evidence' is something associated with an idealistic misunderstanding of science, not history. However, historical matters must be examined with the tools of history. When this is done, it is discovered that much that we know has occurred in history, for example the spread of the Christian church, the invention of a new virtue, humility, and the writing of the New Testament are simply inexplicable unless Jesus was who he said he was: God.[11] Since Jesus' service was done in history, he invites us to evaluate it with historical tools. Not with a radical scepticism (that would be shoddy historical research) but with an appropriately enquiring evaluation of the evidence as a whole. Enabling us to do this was a crucial outcome of Jesus' earthly ministry.

The Bible's invitation to explore the evidences left behind by Jesus of his divine identity and mission mean that the Son is the person of the Trinity who brings God's love to us in a substantive manner. God is simple: his love is perfect. God's love is of a different order to our love. It is natural to wonder how we can ever experience his love, if he is so radically different from us. The Son is the person who crosses the Creator–creature distinction to bring God's love to sinful people. In his incarnation Jesus became one of us; in his death he died for us. God the Son is the person of the Trinity who unfolds God's love to us, deals with the sin which separates us from that love, and through his historical situatedness invites us with all our creatureliness to behold God's love, and then 'taste and see that the LORD is good' (Ps. 34:8). God the Father's plan is one of love; God the Son's service is to enact that plan.

The Spirit's loving intimacy

'The Lord is the Spirit' (2 Cor. 3:17). As such, the Holy Spirit is divine. When God spoke through the Old Testament prophets, it was the Spirit speaking (Acts 28:25). Many of God's attributes are predicated of the Spirit, including eternality (Heb. 9:14) and omniscience (1 Cor. 2:11). Citations could be multiplied to demonstrate that the Bible reveals the Spirit as no less divine than the Son or Father.

People often make the error of thinking the Spirit to be a mystical force or power that is less personal than the other trinitarian persons.

---

11. P. Barnett, *Jesus and the Logic of History* (Leicester: Apollos, 1997), presents these historical arguments well. John Dickson, *Humilitas: A Lost Key to Life, Love, and Leadership* (Grand Rapids: Zondervan, 2011), shows how the ancient world's view of humility was transformed by Jesus.

Scripture refutes this view as it describes the Spirit's doing things that are deeply personal: he speaks (Acts 13:2; 1 Tim. 4:1), leads (Rom. 8:14), wills (1 Cor. 12:11), forbids (Acts 16:6) and can be grieved (Eph. 4:30). All of these observations show that the Spirit is a relational person, not an impersonal force. It would be deeply offensive to his majesty to refer to him as an 'it' or a 'thing'.

As the divine third person of the Trinity, the Spirit has a distinct ministry. He unfolds and makes real God's love, in particular ways. When Jesus was preparing his disciples to live on earth without his physical presence, he reassured them by saying, 'I will ask the Father, and he will give you another Helper, to be with you for ever, even the Spirit of truth' (John 14:16–17). Jesus' use of the word 'another' means that the Spirit is like a replacement Jesus. The Spirit will do for the disciples what Jesus knows is best for them, in a manner fitting for the situation they will be in after the Son returns to heaven. The Spirit by his nature is perfectly suited to do the distinctive work that must be done in God's people, between the first and second coming of Jesus.

The Bible often associates the Spirit with the work of sharing the intimacy of God's love with his people. So one of the verses most frequently cited by Augustine was Romans 5:5: 'God's love has been poured into our hearts through the Holy Spirit who has been given to us.' This is clearly a deeply personal, intimate, relational and emotional experience. In Romans 1:24 we read that the heart is the inner throne room of human desires where sexual desires (among other passions) develop and reign. The experience of God's love in our heart can no more be a cool rational matter than sexual desires can be. Since God pours his love into our hearts, we have grounds for trusting that he can renew, restore and heal our passionate desires that have been distorted by sin. He does not promise to do so fully until he returns, but the Spirit is the one who can operate in the otherwise unsearchable waters of human hearts (Jer. 17:9; Prov. 25:3).

Jonathan Edwards observed this distinctive role of the Spirit in bringing God's love deep into our hearts. He wrote:

> The scripture seems in many places to speak of love in Christians as if it were the same with the Spirit of God in them, or at least as the prime

and most natural breathing and acting of the Spirit in the soul. Phil. 2:1, 2 Cor. 6:6, Rom. 15:30, Col. 1:8, Rom. 5:5, Gal. 5:13–16.[12]

There is a radical difference between the Creator and creatures. If we are to have a genuine relationship with God, we need more than correct information about him. We need more than an accurate understanding of the gospel or doctrine. We need God himself to come close to us, to dwell in our hearts and implant new desires for holiness and divine love. It is the distinctive glory of the Spirit that he is perfectly suited to this ministry. In Romans 8:15–16 we are told of a crucial instance of the Spirit's intimate ministry: 'You have received the Spirit of adoption as sons, by whom we cry, *"Abba! Father!"* The Spirit himself bears witness with our spirit that we are children of God.'

The Spirit brings God's love home to our weary hearts with such effective power that we not only understand that God has adopted us; we feel the Spirit bearing witness that this supernatural reality is our own most intimate experience. We may deduce and conclude that we are children of God, but far more gloriously we are not left to rely on our own strength and intelligence. The Spirit testifies with our spirits that we genuinely are God's children. Such a deep, relational, experiential certainty is a work of the most sublime power. Bringing God's loving intimacy deep into our hearts is the distinctive ministry of the Spirit. When we are brought to know, in our deepest longings and desires that we are God's children, we feel a desire to talk with the Father. We realize that he wants to give us good gifts, that Jesus has taught us what to say to him and our most basic spiritual instinct is to cry out, *'Abba!* Father!' Such an intimate cry of dependence and trust in our Father is the work of the Spirit, who pours God's love into our hearts. We call out to our Father by him. We have barely begun to understand the reality of prayer if we think it is just a case of our talking to God using our natural intellectual and linguistic abilities. Prayer is so much more than that – it is our

12. Jonathan Edwards, *Writings on the Trinity, Grace, and Faith*, Works of Jonathan Edwards, 26 vols. (New Haven: Yale University Press, 2003), vol. 21, p. 125.

hearts being brought before the Father, in the Spirit's power. As we pour out our deepest longings and hopes, we find that the Spirit is at work in those desires, enabling us to call out to our Father in joyful trust.

As the Spirit enables us to experience God's love we begin to realize that God's love is a holy love. As God the Spirit works in our hearts we find ourselves awakened to desires for deeper intimacy with God. This demands the pursuit of holiness. We seek to become like that which we love. The Mosaic Law is fulfilled in love (Gal. 5:14), but that love cannot be experienced by any amount of obedience to commandments, human decisions or will power. Rather this law-fulfilling love is the experience of those who are 'led by the Spirit' (Gal. 5:18) and 'walk by the Spirit' (Gal. 5:25). Such people feel within themselves desires they realize are from the Spirit – they cannot arise from natural human capacities. There are contradictory desires battling within our inner selves. However, the battle is not straightforwardly between the believer and sin; the conflicting desires are more fundamentally between the flesh and Spirit. Christians are called, then, not to join the battle in their own strength, but rather to depend upon the Spirit. The Spirit is committed to growing his holy fruit within us (Gal. 5:22) and we are to keep in step with that work. There is an active-passivity to being led by the Spirit. We are passive in the sense that we recognize the desires for holiness are from God, and in the most fundamental sense it is God the Spirit who will grow his fruit. We are active in the sense that we are to 'crucify the flesh' (Gal. 5:24), which means we remove and fight against all that would oppose what the Spirit is doing in us. Merely trying in our own strength to obey the Law would ironically be a way of cultivating holiness that resists the Spirit's distinctive ministry of growing his fruit within us. This is not the approach Paul commends as the Christian way – it would be a falling away from grace and a negation of Jesus' value (Gal. 5:2–4). Those who pursue love must do it in the only manner open to sinful creatures: walking by the Spirit and following his leading (Gal. 5:16, 18). The distinctive ministry of the Spirit is to impart a holy love for God deep within our sinful hearts. Only God the Spirit can do such a miraculous work.

Development in salvation history

God's perfect, infinite love is unchanging: it can neither increase nor decrease, for if it could do either, it would lack perfection. While God's love does not alter, our personal experience of it does change. This is commented on by Vos:

> The saints are addressed as the beloved of God. The love of God is shed abroad in their hearts through the Holy Spirit given unto them. It is put on a line with the peace which is not merely subjective, but objectively also, is an exclusively Christian possession. Nor does the Apostle represent this unique love which rests upon believers as something first originated at the moment of their introduction into the Christian state. On the contrary, with the greatest possible distinctness, and in entire harmony with our Lord's Johannine teaching, he prolongs it backwards to a point where it enters a region of the absolute eternal life of God.[13]

There is a point in our lives when we are brought into a conscious experience of God's love. The Spirit pours God's love into our hearts and awakens us to the Father's love that led him to give his Son up to death for us. The fact that we have come to a fresh experience of God's love does not mean that his love was imperfect before that, nor that it has increased or decreased when we encountered it. The vast majority of Bible references in this chapter have been taken from the New Testament. This should not be taken as suggesting that God became more loving after the Old Testament. He is unchanging, and was just as perfectly loving in the Old as in the New Testament times. However, as our personal experience of God's love changes in time, so the progression of salvation history through the Bible records that he has revealed things in varying degrees throughout times. Some matters were less fully revealed in Old Testament times, which have since been more fully declared. So, for example, we read that 'Jesus . . . brought life and immortality to light through the gospel' (2 Tim. 1:10). This explains why the doctrines

---

13. Gerhard Vos, 'The Scriptural Doctrine of the Love of God', *Presbyterian and Reformed Review* 49 (1902), p. 33.

of resurrection and eternal destiny are not as clearly taught in the Old as in New Testament. So it is consistent with Christian experience and other doctrines that God's love, and the distinct roles of the persons of the Trinity, are most clearly revealed in the New Testament:

> The Old Testament is the veiling of the New Testament, and the New Testament is the unveiling of the Old Testament . . . The veil is being made void, in order that what was obscure may be understood. This was, of course, shut away as a closed book, because the key of the cross was not yet available.[14]

This process of ever-increasing revelation will continue, and when Jesus returns to his earth, God's love and the Trinity will be yet more fully revealed to us.

All readers of the Bible need to be sensitive to the way in which salvation history develops. D. A. Carson has argued that one of the most pressing issues in theology

> is how simultaneously to expound the unity of New Testament theology (and of the larger canon of which it is a part) while doing justice to the manifest diversity; or, to put it the other way, how simultaneously to trace the diversity and peculiar emphases and historical developments inherent in the various New Testament (and Biblical) books while doing justice to their unifying thrusts.[15]

Since the earliest days of Christianity allegations that the Old Testament contradicts the New have been made, most famously by Gnostics and Manicheans. However, the solution is not to pretend

---

14. Augustine, *Sermons*, ed. John Rotelle, trans. Edmund Hill, The Works of Saint Augustine, A Translation for the 21st Century (New York: New City, 1991), vol. 9, 300.3.

15. D. A. Carson, 'New Testament Theology', in R. Martin and P. Davids (eds.), *Dictionary of the Later New Testament & Its Developments: A Compendium of Contemporary Biblical Scholarship* (Downers Grove: InterVarsity Press; Leicester: Inter-Varsity Press, 1997), p. 810.

that the Testaments are identical – there is too much development and change for that to resolve the problem. To be sure, the God of the Old Testament is the same loving God of the New Testament. Nevertheless we have seen that the persons of the Trinity are not clearly revealed in their distinctiveness until the latter stages of the biblical revelation. The development of salvation history has implications for our appreciation of the love of God, which is so central to each divine person's ministry.

In the early church the main forum for theological reflection was the sermon, arguably something that ought never to have been changed. In a sermon on the love of God Augustine argued that since the law and prophets depend on the love of God and neighbour (Matt. 22:37–40), and as Jesus' new commandment is to 'love one another' (John 13:34), it is the case that 'every page of the scriptures'[16] is about love. Augustine proceeded to reflect on the complex development and diversity within the Bible's narrative, and its implications for our appreciation of love:

> If you are wondering, perhaps, how the Law is both called the Old Testament or covenant, and also depends on love, though love . . . belongs to the new man, here is the reason. It is an old covenant that is drawn up, because it makes an earthly promise, and it was an earthly kingdom that the Lord there offered his worshippers. But even then there were to be found lovers of God who loved him freely for his own sake, and cleansed their hearts by longing for him. They peeled off the outer shells of the old promises, and came upon the prefiguration of the new covenant that was to come. They grasped that all the things that are commandments or promises in the old covenant . . . are figures or symbols of the new covenant, which the Lord was going to fulfil at the last times, as the apostle says so plainly: 'Now these things happened to them as symbols, but they were written for our sake, upon whom the end of the ages has come' (1 Cor. 10:11). So the new covenant was being foretold in a hidden way, and being foretold in those figures or symbols.
>
> But when the time for the new covenant came, the new covenant began to be proclaimed openly, and those figures and symbols came to

---

16. Augustine, *Sermons*, vol. 10, 350A.1.

be interpreted. Explanations were given of how the new was to be understood even there in the old. So the preacher of the old covenant was Moses; but while he proclaimed the old, he himself grasped the new. He was preaching the old to a fleshly, earth-focused people – he himself was fully aware of the new.

The apostles however, were both preachers and administrators of the new covenant; but this does not mean that what was later made publicly known through the apostles was not there at that earlier time. Love is there in the old and love is there in the new. But in the Old Testament love is more hidden away; fear more in the open. In the New Testament love is more publicly manifest, fear altogether less so. To the extent, you see, that love grows, fear diminishes. As John says, 'perfect love casts out fear' (1 John 4:18).[17]

This sermon shows that from early times preachers have wrestled with how best to communicate the development in salvation history that shapes the biblical revelation. As the trinitarian persons are more clearly revealed in the New Testament, so is the love that animates their distinctive ministries more fully proclaimed there. This does not mean that the Old Testament presents us with an unloving God, nor that there is no benefit to reading the earlier books of Scripture. Far from it.

The Old Testament hints at plurality within God, for example by recording him as saying, 'Let us make' (Gen. 1:26), or by the person of God sometimes being described as the 'angel of God' (Exod. 14:19). However, by far the greatest burden of the Old Testament revelation concerns those aspects of God that relate to his oneness: his perfection, holiness, sovereignty, timelessness and goodness. God is revealed in the Old Testament as the God of love, but crucially he is a God of love whose inner diversity is only hinted at. The full extent of God's love cannot be seen until the distinct ministries of each person are unveiled. Perfect, infinite love cannot actually be experienced by an infinite being who is only one person. Such a 'love' would actually be a form of selfishness. Only the trinitarian God can be perfect love. The Father's loving plan,

---

17. Ibid. 350A.2.

the Son's loving service and the Spirit's loving intimacy reveal a perfection of love that thrills our hearts and draws adoration from us.

The full divinity of Son and Spirit are crucial in maintaining the perfection of God's love. Only God himself can perfectly serve the Father's will, and only God himself can cross the Creator–creature distinction. Were there any less than fully divine persons in the Trinity, God's love would include some elements of unworthiness and be less than perfect. Until Athanasius many of the church fathers struggled to do justice to the love of God, because they began in their relating Old and New Testaments by assuming that the God of the Old Testament was the Father. The implication was that when the Son and Spirit were revealed more clearly in the New Testament, they had to be fitted into a doctrine of God in which the Father was more fully God than the Son and Spirit. This way of thinking is far from uncommon today. Many Christians believe that

> the Father is God in absolute terms, whereas the Son and Holy Spirit are God only in a relative sense, because they supposedly derive their divinity from him. The Father is therefore considered to be the default person of the Godhead, which means that unless a Biblical text specifies that 'God' refers to the Son or Holy Spirit, it should be taken as referring primarily to the Father.[18]

The 'Athanasian Insight', as Thomas Weinandy called it in his lectures, was that 'God' is not a title most properly held by the Father, but rather 'God' is Father, Son and Spirit. We do not develop a biblical vision of God by starting with any one of the divine persons' divinity and then trying to fit the other two in. Rather we start from the revelation that there is one God who is a trinity of divine persons.

This has important implications for the doctrines that have been considered in our study: simplicity, perfection, omniscience, eternality and love. It would be all too easy to associate all these with the Father, and then try to fit the Son and Spirit around them. The

---

18. Gerald Bray, *God Is Love: A Biblical and Systematic Theology* (Wheaton: Crossway, 2012), p. 172.

correct way to proceed, as Athanasius realized, is to realize that the one true God – who is simple, perfect and eternal – is actually three persons who are each fully divine. The simple God is not inert, impersonal or unrelational, because he is Father, Son and Spirit. This is nothing more than a restatement of the classic text on simplicity from Augustine:

> This Trinity is one God; and none the less simple because a Trinity. For we do not say that the nature of the good is simple, because the Father alone possesses it, or the Son alone, or the Holy Spirit alone; nor do we say, with the Sabellian heretics, that it is only nominally a Trinity, and has no real distinction of persons; but we say it is simple, because it is what it has, with the exception of the relation of the persons to one another.[19]

The classical attributes may seem more comprehensible when applied to a God who is unitary; but in Christian theology they must be understood as referring to the one God who is three persons, each of whom is divine. The Christian God is simple and perfect. The only way this can be so is if that God is trinitarian – a monistic being would not be able eternally, omnisciently and omnipotently to be perfect love.

Given the difficulty we fallen creatures have in articulating or understanding these matters, it is perhaps not surprising that God chose to reveal his nature to us in stages, through a Bible structured by salvation history. It is part of God's 'accommodation' to our frailty. So commenting on the differences between stages of biblical revelation, Calvin wrote, 'God ought not to be considered changeable merely because he accommodated diverse forms to different ages, as he knew would be expedient for each.'[20]

There are benefits to readers who take time to read through and ponder the Old Testament revelation in its entirety. The New Testament then breaks upon us with a fresh force and vigour. The God of infinite, timeless, perfect power – this God – was born a

---

19. Augustine, *City of God*, ed. H. Bettenson and G. R. Evans (London: Penguin, 1984), 11.10.

20. Calvin, *Institutes* 2.11.13.

human and died on a cross. The Christian God is both simple and relational, both one and three. Furthermore he can only be either because he is the other. Scholastic philosophical theologians can elucidate the classical attributes of simplicity and eternality. Modern-day preachers and Christians often revel in the relationality and threeness of Father, Son and Spirit. However, the only way to preserve either the oneness or threeness of God is to insist on both. Downplaying either Old or New Testaments leads to a lopsided doctrine of God that futilely tries to preserve either relationality apart from simplicity, or simplicity apart from relationality. God is both, and we need to read the whole Bible, in the company of the whole church, past and present, to hold on to that.

Meditation: love

O God, warm my cold heart with the fire of your love.

Eternally you are love: Father, Son and Spirit. I am so slow to learn that I can trust your plans; I struggle to believe that your intentions are truly good. So thank you that you have taken such pains to reveal again and again that you love creatures like me who have been caught up in sin and disordered loves.

Your plan of salvation foretold to Israel, your coming to earth to live, cry and bleed, your awakening of a heart that did not care – these are your divine works. Left to my own devices, without the perfect God of love, my heart would still be cold.

Amen.

7. GOD'S LOVE AND THREENESS IN CHURCH HISTORY

Simplicity is a doctrine that emphasizes the oneness of God. Cognizant of this, many theologians reject the doctrine. So D. A. Carson wrote of one of simplicity's key entailments, impassibility, that he is 'unwilling to endorse the doctrine of the so-called impassibility of God. That doctrine is too tied to just one side of the Biblical evidence.'[1] As Carson goes on to say, he wholeheartedly affirms the Bible's teaching on both God's relationality and transcendence. He rejects the caricatures – and lopsided presentations – of immutability. This is precisely what the classical doctrine of God does. Those who have used the language of simplicity are more than aware of the dangers of its emphasis on the oneness and transcendence of God: 'The danger must certainly be recognised that, in the interest of maintaining the absolute immutability of God, one might deny the Incarnation.'[2]

---

1. Carson, *How Long, O Lord? Reflections on Suffering and Evil* (Grand Rapids: Baker, 2006), p. 216.
2. Michael Dodds, *The Unchanging God of Love: Thomas Aquinas and Contemporary Theology on Divine Immutability* (New York: Catholic University of America Press, 2008), p. 200.

Our first four chapters have focused on the classical doctrines that flow out of simplicity. These are all associated with the 'oneness' of God, a phrase popularized by Colin Gunton,[3] but with a distinguished pedigree. For instance, Van Til noted that '[t]he philosophy of history is . . . an aspect of the perplexing One and Many problem.'[4] Simplicity, perfection, eternity, omniscience, omnipresence, omnipotence, immutability and impassibility are all doctrines associated with the 'oneness' of God. A God who is perfect and simple in these ways could be misconceived as being unrelational, unloving, impersonal and static. Such a caricature would in no way be faithful to the vision of Christians who have over the centuries championed these teachings. As was intimated in the previous chapter, when he became a human, God was perfect, impassible and simple. Simplicity is merely the doctrinal grammar which enables us to say that God is as fully loving, perfect and relational a being as can be imagined.

Our culture tends to favour the intimate and relational. That has not always been the case – arguably the Victorian era had a bias towards hierarchy and distance. It runs with the grain of our culture, then, that Christians have been publishing book after book about the love and relationality of God. When we want to emphasize the love and relationality of God, we focus not on the oneness of God, but his threeness. Undergirding the turn to relationality has been a rediscovery, or revival, in trinitarian theology. The revival of interest in trinitarianism owes much to Karl Barth, who famously opened his *Church Dogmatics* with a lengthy treatment of the Trinity. This stood in stark contrast to Schleiermacher, who relegated the Trinity to an appendix to his major work, *The Christian Faith*. To the extent that God is Three, not only One, renewed appreciation for the Trinity is praiseworthy. Some have, however, offered cautionary remarks about this renewed focus on the Trinity:

---

3. Colin Gunton, *The One, the Three and the Many: God, Creation and the Culture of Modernity* (Cambridge: Cambridge University Press, 1993).

4. E. H. Sigward (ed.), *The Articles of Cornelius Van Til* (New York: Labels Army, 1997), electronic ed. 'Defending the Faith', *Torch and Trumpet* 1.1 (1951), p. 18.

> My interest in trinitarian theology springs from my interest in the
> theology of the church and the theology of Christian spirituality . . .
> It is an interest in the so-called renaissance of trinitarian theology that
> has taken place in recent decades. This, however, is not merely a revival
> of interest in this part of Christian doctrine. It is, rather, a new
> conception of theology that makes the Trinity into the key to the
> whole of Christian theology and requires every topic of theology to
> be restructured in trinitarian terms. While I believe that all subjects of
> theology can be legitimately developed in the trinitarian way, I do not
> in every instance see the point of doing so.[5]

As modern writers get excited about love, relationship, intimacy
and personalness, they have tended to denigrate the doctrines associated with God's oneness. These then get misrepresented as being
antithetical to love and relationality. There are at least two serious
problems with this; the first concerns church history and the second,
systematic theology.

First, it is a woefully superficial reading of church history that
presents a modern rediscovery of trinitarianism as legitimating
rejection of oneness doctrines such as simplicity. As Fred Sanders
has protested, 'Everything that is routinely praised as belonging to
the excitement of the trinitarian revival of recent times is fairly easy
to find in those older sources.'[6] As we have seen in our study of
theologians such as Augustine, Aquinas and Charnock, those who
affirmed simplicity also in no uncertain terms proclaimed God's
intimate, relational love. There was, for them, no contradiction.

Secondly, from a systematic perspective, it should concern us
if the form of relationality and love promoted by Christians is
antithetical to the oneness of God. Stephen Holmes warns of this
danger:

---

5. Marcel Sarot, 'Trinity and Church: Trinitarian Perspectives on the
   Identity of the Christian Community', *International Journal of Systematic
   Theology* 12.1 (2010), p. 37.

6. Fred Sanders, 'The Trinity', in John Webster, Kathryn Tanner and Iain
   Torrance (eds.), *Oxford Handbook to Systematic Theology* (Oxford: Oxford
   University Press, 2007), p. 42.

> Much recent theology associated with what has become known as
> the trinitarian revival looks to categories of person and relationship
> as points of contact between the divine and created ... In popular
> presentation, it rather invites the ancient error that different divine
> persons instantiate different divine perfections ... some particular
> attributes fare rather more badly under this sort of scheme: is difficult
> to see how a doctrine of simplicity might be retained; aseity also
> becomes difficult.[7]

The classical tradition maintains that the God who is loving and
relational is precisely the God who is other than us: simple, perfect,
eternal and immutable. A God who is approachable and relational
because he has been stripped of the oneness attributes is a God
refashioned in the image of our times. We may think we have made
God more comprehensible and approachable, but in reality we have
collapsed the undergirding truths that make it worth hearing that he
loves us and became one of us. The love found in the threeness of
God does not require jettisoning his oneness: it is predicated upon
it. The threeness of God began to be reflected on in the previous
chapter, as we considered the incarnation. As we proceed to see
more of the love God reveals through his threeness, we are not
contradicting or forgetting earlier affirmations of God's simplicity
and perfection. Quite the opposite: we can be sure that God
will never cease to be the God who is love, because he is perfect
and immutable.

We shall in this chapter consider Augustine, Richard of St Victor
and Jonathan Edwards. Each of them made distinctive contributions
to our appreciation of the nature of the divine love that arises from
God's threeness. Such love is all the more dependable, beautiful and
mysterious because it is the love of the One God who is perfect,
simple, eternal, impassible and immutable.

---

7. Stephen Holmes, 'The Attributes of God', in John Webster, Kathryn
   Tanner and Iain Torrance (eds.), *Oxford Handbook to Systematic Theology*
   (Oxford: Oxford University Press, 2007), p. 63.

Augustine

Augustine has often been noted for his love of friendship. 'Having read the life of this extremely inward looking man, we suddenly realise, to our surprise, that he has hardly ever been alone. There have always been friends around him.'[8] Augustine often reflected on the nature of love, and the relationship between our love of self and God.[9] He concluded that God's love enveloped and enabled all other loves: 'Augustine believed the love of self could be right only in relation to the love of God; it was a means and not its own ultimate reason.'[10]

As Augustine wrote, 'It is God who causes us to love our brother ... The first object of our love must be the very love with which we love our brother.'[11]

So far as friendship was concerned, this meant that 'He loves his friend truly who loves God in him, either because God is in him or in order that He may be in him.'[12]

God, in Augustine's theology, was impassible and simple. Nevertheless Augustine lived not only a life full of loving friendships, but believed that this was enabled by God's love. Our love for each other is a gift given to us through God's love: 'We cannot say that agape has no presuppositions, for God presupposes that which he himself has already given in agape.'[13] As one study on Augustine's theology of love makes clear, our love and God's love are intimately related: 'In his sermons on the Trinity, Augustine reaches a new psychological level of love talk. First of all, God is love. Secondly, we are

---

8. Peter Brown, *Augustine of Hippo* (London: Faber & Faber, 2000), p. 174.

9. Oliver O' Donovan, *The Problem of Self-Love in St. Augustine* (New Haven: Yale University Press, 1980).

10. M. A. McNamara, *Friends and Friendship for Saint Augustine* (New York: Alba House, 1957), p. 223.

11. Augustine, *The Trinity*, tr. Edmund Hill, ed. John Rotelle, The Works of Saint Augustine, a Translation for the 21st Century (New York: New City, 1991), vol. 10, 8.11.

12. Augustine, *Sermons*, 361.1.

13. O'Donovan, *Problem of Self-Love*, p. 159.

made in the image of God's self-love, so that our self-love must somehow reflect God's love.'[14]

Reflection on Augustine's theology led Hannah Arendt to make profound connections between God's love and our love of neighbour:

> The lover reaches beyond the beloved to God in whom alone
> both his existence and his love have meaning. Death is meaningless
> to love of neighbour, because in removing my neighbour from the
> world death only does what Love has already accomplished; that
> is, I love in him that being that lives in him as his source. Death is
> irrelevant to this love, because every beloved is only an occasion
> to love God.[15]

It is difficult to see how Augustine could have been the source of such rich insights on love if his understanding of simplicity made God an inert, impersonal or unrelational being. We must recall that in Augustine's view simplicity in no way negated the relational threeness of God: 'This Trinity is one God; and none the less simple because a Trinity.'[16]

God's oneness does not obliterate, but rather establishes and confirms, his threeness. The simple God is one God who is Father, Son and Spirit. There are many places we could look at to see Augustine encourage love between people, as the fruit of God's love. One such place is his sermons on 1 John. These were preached against the backdrop of the Donatist controversy.

There were social factors in the division between Donatist and Catholic Christians of fourth-century North Africa. Nevertheless there was an irreducible doctrinal disagreement. The Donatists, who comprised the majority of North African Christians and included

14. James A. Mohler, *Late Have I Loved You: An Interpretation of Saint Augustine on Human and Divine Relationships* (New York: New City, 1991), p. 51.

15. Hannah Arendt, *Love and Saint Augustine* (London: University of Chicago Press, 1996), p. 96.

16. Augustine, *City of God*, ed. H. Bettenson and G. R. Evans (London: Penguin, 1984), 11.10.

many of the poorer people, wished to preserve the holiness of God's people. They believed that baptisms and ordinations performed by ministers who subsequently capitulated to the state under violent persecution were invalid. Baptized Christians would therefore have to be rebaptized. Augustine viewed the Donatist approach to these matters as a failure of love. He argued that his opponents were failing to enter into the reality of God's love for his church. God's love led him to overlook infirmity, forgive sin and welcome the repentant sinner home. Donatists sought to hold people to higher standards than God did; in Augustine's view this revealed they themselves did not know God's love:

> We have established a contract with our God in The Prayer that, if we want him to forgive our sins, we should also forgive the sins that have been committed against us. But there is no forgiveness apart from love. Remove love from the heart and it holds onto hatred and cannot forgive. Let love be there and it forgives with a sense of security and is not made narrow. See if this entire epistle, which we have undertaken to preach on, commends anything else than this love.[17]

Augustine held that it was beyond the power of church leaders to make a congregation become loving. This was the work of God:

> There is no need for your heart to be enlarged by us. Ask God that you may love one another. You should love all people, even your enemies, not because they are your brothers but so that they may become your brothers, so that you may always be aflame with brotherly love, whether towards one who has become your brother or towards your enemy, so that by loving him he may become your brother.[18]

On the basis of Romans 5:5 Augustine believed that the Spirit poured God's love into the hearts of all who put their faith in Jesus:

---

17. Augustine, *Homilies on the First Epistle of John*, tr. Boniface Ramsey, ed. John Rotelle, The Works of Saint Augustine, a Translation for the 21st Century (New York: New City, 2008), 7.1.

18. Ibid. 10.7.

The true faith of grace is the sort that works through love. Now to have love, and to be able to do good works as a result of it, is surely not something we can give ourselves. Since it is written 'The love of God has been poured out in our hearts through the Holy Spirit which has been given to us' (Rom. 5:5). So completely is love or charity the gift of God that it is even called God, as the apostle John says – 'God is love.'[19]

Augustine realized that God does far more than merely tell people to be loving. He does more even than awaken love within the believer. God enables people to love, by giving himself to them. God is love, and it is the God of love making his home within us that enables us to love. Augustine shared his reflections on how God created love within his naturally cold heart in his famous book *Confessions*. He also preached about it:

If we open ourselves wide, God can walk in us. But for us to make space within ourselves, God must set to work within us. If love, you see, which is innocent of narrowness, creates space, notice how God makes a space for himself within us – 'The love of God has been poured out in our hearts through the Holy Spirit which has been given to us' (Rom. 5:5). It is due to this space, I'm saying, that God can walk in us.[20]

So we can see that Augustine championed the love of God. The God of love is simple, immutable and perfect. Yet there is a threeness to God as well as a oneness. The Spirit is God's love, able to dwell in the hearts of all who put their faith in Christ. And so Augustine realized there is a distinct member of the Trinity who has the role of bringing the unchanging, eternal, perfect God of love to live in sinful creatures' hearts. A love that was anything less than the perfect, eternal love that is God himself would not transform us in the ways

---

19. Augustine, *Sermons*, tr. Edmund Hill, ed. John Rotelle, The Works of Saint Augustine, a Translation for the 21st Century, 11 vols. (New York: New City, 1991), vol. 5, 156.5.

20. Ibid. 163.1.

God desires. So God does not merely tell us to be loving, nor does he show us only what it is like to be loving. Rather God the Holy Spirit comes in person to give us the greatest gift the God of love can give: his loving self.

Richard of St Victor

Crucial to maintaining that God is indeed overwhelmingly loving is the difference, multiplicity or diversity that exists in the Trinity. A God who was only 'One', a monistic God, might be construed as inert and unrelational along the lines of caricatures of the classical Christian position. We have seen how Augustine highlighted the role of the Spirit in bringing God's love to us, one of Augustine's great contributions to subsequent Christian thought. Augustine's appreciation for the distinctive ministry of the Spirit is one of the reasons his book *The Trinity* is (until now) the high point of trinitarian theology. Astonishing though it may be, since Augustine wrote in the fourth century, Edmund Hill writes, 'We might ask ourselves where Augustine left the tradition of theological reflection on the Trinity for his successors. I have already stated my opinion that he did not, unfortunately, have any real successors.'[21]

Future generations of theologians managed only to ossify Augustine's teachings, or emphasize one or another part of Augustine's legacy, doomed, as they did so, to rediscover every few centuries something he had already taught, and then to overemphasize it to the detriment of some other crucial part of his trinitarian thought. Nevertheless the centuries of mining Augustine's writings on the Trinity did lead to some significant, isolated insights. One of these came in the twelfth century, from Richard of St Victor.

Richard, possibly from Scotland, spent most of his life as a theologian and monk in Paris. As subprior at the Augustinian Abbey of Saint Victor, Richard's ministry was 'bedevilled'[22] by his

---

21. Augustine, *Trinity* Intro.5.114.
22. J. Walsh, *The Pursuit of Wisdom and Other Works*, Classics of Western Spirituality (Mahwah, N.J.: Paulist Press, 1988), p. 13.

'incompetent'[23] superior, Ernisius. He squandered large amounts of money on vain building projects, and was too proud to accept the help of others he worked with. Bullying appears to have been rife at the Abbey: Ernisius ruthlessly suppressed those who became aware of his character defects. Despite Richard's prominence and popularity wider afield, Ernisius used his power to restrict Richard's ministry. 'Richard must have found it difficult to be the second ranking official under such a person.'[24] The situation was seen by the wider church as an embarrassment. Eventually appeals were lodged with the pope to intervene, and after several years Ernisius was ousted and Richard given his job. Sadly Richard died shortly afterwards. Richard wrote about forty theological treatises. It is remarkable that, in the midst of the stress of living and working at a place so damaged by seedy abuses of power and bullying, Richard was able to write one of the church's greatest books about God's love.

Written in the methodical, penetrating scholastic style of his day, Richard's work *The Trinity* was steeped in Augustine's book of the same title. 'For the Victorines, the primary authority is the sacred scriptures. After the scriptures, Augustine is certainly who has the most impact on their thought.'[25] Augustine helped Richard realize that the diversity within the Trinity is essential to God's love. He followed Augustine's traditional exegesis by seeing that each of the persons in the Trinity is described in Scripture as being sent, or proceeding from a different source: 'Just as in the divinity there is only one person who is from himself, likewise, there can be only one person originating from one, single person. And there can be only one person possessing his being from two persons.'[26]

23. H. Feiss, *On Love: A Selection of Works of Hugh, Adam, Achard, Richard, and Godfrey of St. Victor* (New York: New City, 2012), p. 304.

24. G. A. Zinn, *The Twelve Patriarchs; The Mystical Ark; Book Three of The Trinity*, Classics of Western Spirituality (Mahwah, N.J.: Paulist Press, 1979), p. 4.

25. Feiss, *On Love*, p. 42.

26. R. Angelici, *Richard of Saint Victor, On the Trinity: English Translation and Commentary* (Eugene: Cascade, 2011), 5.10.

In other words, the Father is different from the Son, and the Spirit is different from them both. The reason the Father is a genuinely distinct person from the Son and Spirit is the fact that he is the Father, not the Son or Spirit. On the basis of these real, relational differences between Father, Son and Spirit, Richard discerned implications for the necessity and nature of God's love.

Richard surmised that if there were a being who was perfect, he must be perfect in all attributes. This includes love: a perfect being must be perfectly loving. That requires the perfect being to have another perfect person worthy of receiving perfect love. That is, if the Father is perfect, there must be a Son who is also divine and perfect:

> Perfection of a single person necessarily postulates coexistence with another one . . . Fullness of charity-love, for its part, wants each person to love the other as each loves himself . . . it is necessary for this person to have someone worthy of him, in order to rightly love him as he loves himself. Then, if it is true that the first person is supremely good, he will be completely unable to not want that which the highest charity-love implies. And if it is really true that this person is omnipotent, everything that he wants will happen.[27]

The implications of these reflections are seismic. Richard is saying that a 'God' who was not more than one person could not be perfect. He would lack either perfect love or perfect power. If there really is a God who is perfect, he cannot be a simple being who just comprises a oneness with no diversity. Richard was a firm believer in the doctrine of simplicity. He affirmed 'the simplicity and unity of that supreme good . . . the divine substance is identical to power itself, identical to wisdom itself'.[28] There are many criticisms made of simplicity by modern detractors: it is a doctrine that makes God out to be unloving and impersonal. Richard, as a strong promoter of simplicity, proves that such criticisms are a non-Christian caricature of simplicity. They may hold true for a non-trinitarian conception

27. Ibid. 5.7.
28. Ibid. 2.17.

of simplicity, but that is never what Christian theologians have taught. Ironically, the criticisms of simplicity collapse under their own weight. For Richard argues that if it were possible to postulate a perfect simple being who was of a unitary nature (such as critics of classical theism accuse the traditional view of espousing), such a being would, due to the requirements of perfection, have to be a relational God comprising more than one perfect being. The perfect Father must have a perfect Son; both must be divine. A profound theological irony resides in the much-misunderstood relationship between simplicity and relationality, between the one and the many. Far from abrogating relationality, perfect simplicity establishes and demands it.

The genius of Richard lay not only in grasping the above insight; it had been hinted at in the shape of Augustine's trinitarian theology. Richard pressed the theological implications further and considered the number of persons in the Godhead. If a perfect God had to comprise more than one perfect divine person to fulfil the nature of perfect love, where did this leave the Spirit? Richard realized that perfect love required that there be three divine persons, neither more nor less: 'It must be rightly underlined that in the divine persons the perfection of one of them requires the addition of another. And consequently, between the two persons, perfection of both requires the association of a third one.'[29]

Due to the nature of love, which is centred on the good of another and the sharing of joy, two perfect loving persons will desire to share their love with each other:

> When two reciprocally loving persons hug each other with the greatest desire and enjoy their mutual love very much, the supreme happiness of the one consists of the intimate love of the other and, conversely, the prime joy of the latter, resides in the love of the former.[30]

These two perfectly loving persons will, if their love is truly infinite and perfect, require a third to share in their happiness:

---

29. Ibid. 3.15.
30. Ibid.

They necessarily have to have another one to be loved in the same
manner. Consequently if the two persons who love each other are so
generous to be willing to communicate every perfection of theirs, it is
necessary that both of them require with equal desire and for the same
reason a third person to be loved in the same fashion.[31]

God is love. The nature of love rules out the possibility of a supreme
being of love who is a monad: the required number of persons for
perfect love is neither one nor two, but three. A monadic person
cannot be perfect love; two perfectly loving beings who love each
other will have an infinite desire to share that love with another.

Does this mean that God could perhaps have been four or more
divine persons? If that would increase the love of God, then the
Trinity as traditionally understood would not then be the perfect
God. Richard argued that there was 'no room'[32] in the divinity for
a fourth divine person. His reasoning for this was that all the roles
of giving, receiving and being love are perfectly accounted for
with the Trinity revealed in Scripture. There can be only one person
who has his being from himself: the Father. There can be only one
divine person who receives his being as the perfect image from
another: the Son. There can be only one divine person who shares
and communicates the perfect love that exists between the others:
the Spirit. If there were another perfect divine being, that person
would either destroy the perfection of one of the others, or would
have to be a person who consists of 'only . . . possessing, without
giving and without receiving'.[33] Such a fourth being would not be
perfectly loving, and would damage rather than sustain the Trinity's
love. In this way Richard showed that the trinity of love is the most
perfect love that can be imagined or conceptualized. The simple
trinity of divine persons is love and cannot be improved upon.

Richard of St Victor showed that the simple God had to be a
God of threeness, not oneness. The classical doctrine of God is
a vision of the most loving being that can be thought of. Thankfully,

---

31. Ibid.
32. Ibid. 5.15.
33. Angelici, *Richard of Saint Victor* 5.15.

such a God is not merely an abstract imagined idea; he is revealed
in Scripture and is as real as the desk upon which I write these words.
Simplicity does not oppose love; it demands it. 'Without a doubt, in
sovereign simplicity, being and loving coincide with each other . . .
the fact that there are multiple persons in one, single divinity means
precisely this: that a plurality possesses one single and same affection;
the supreme affection.'[34]

Jonathan Edwards

Jonathan Edwards was one of the most significant theologian-
preachers of early modernity. One of his most attractive features is
his rootedness in a specific locale: dealing with missionary concerns,
pastoral matters and revivals. Alongside that he was immersed in
the Enlightenment's intellectual developments. In an age that ruthlessly promoted rationality to an idolatrous position Edwards
wrestled with the nature of the powers that reason and the heart
could exert.

The God Edwards extolled was a being of supreme beauty, joy
and love. 'God made man to be happy in the beholding of God's
own excellency.'[35] In Jesus we discover God's beauty: 'Before Christ
is found, there is nothing that is truly lovely that is ever found or
seen.'[36] Edwards's God was an immense deity of eternal love,
passion, delight and happiness. Many assume that such a view of
God is incompatible with the classical doctrines of perfection and
impassibility. Edwards was extremely well read in history, philosophy
and ecclesiastical history. Many of his leading ideas were nothing
more than an application of Augustine's theological insights. Given

---

34. Ibid. 5.20.

35. Jonathan Edwards, *Sermons and Discourses 1723–1729*, Works of Jonathan
    Edwards, 26 vols. (New Haven: Yale University Press, 1997), vol. 14,
    p. 147.

36. Jonathan Edwards, *Sermons and Discourses 1739–1742*, Works of Jonathan
    Edwards, 26 vols. (New Haven: Yale University Press, 2003), vol. 22,
    p. 289.

his knowledge of church history, it is unsurprising that Edwards wished to maintain what had been standard orthodox doctrine: 'Edwards is anxious to reaffirm the historic Christian doctrine of the perfection of God. Especially with regard to God's aseity or self-sufficiency . . . Edwards is resolute in refusing to make any compromises.'[37]

Nevertheless Lee thinks that Edwards's doctrine of God bursts the banks of the traditional views Edwards claimed to uphold:

> When it comes to classical theism's doctrine of God's immutability . . . the tradition cannot contain or restrain Edwards' dynamic reconception of the deity any longer. As long as the divine self-sufficiency is not questioned, Edwards forcefully asserts that God indeed can be added to.[38]

Unfortunately for Lee's argument, none of the subsequent pages of quotes from Edwards supports Lee's claim. Quite the opposite. They show that Edwards believed God's feelings and happiness are real, that they are perfect and appropriate to the nature of the divine being. They do not evidence a reconception of the classical doctrine of God, unless it is (wrongly) thought that Augustine, Anselm, Aquinas and Richard of St Victor thought God inert, unrelational and impassive. Lee claims that 'God's self-sufficiency, in Edwards' way of thinking, does not preclude addition to God's actuality.'[39] However, Lee proceeds to cite Edwards, not arguing for addition to God's actuality but rather for the perfection and immutability of God's genuine happiness:

> Many have wrong notions of God's happiness, as resulting from his absolute self-sufficiency, independence, and immutability. Though it be true that God's glory and happiness are in and of himself, are infinite and can't be added to, unchangeable for the whole and every part of which

---

37. S. Lee (ed.), *The Princeton Companion to Jonathan Edwards* (Princeton: Princeton University Press, 2005), p. 65.

38. Ibid., pp. 65–66.

39. Ibid., p. 66.

he is perfectly independent of the creature; yet it don't hence follow, nor
is it true, that God has no real and proper delight, pleasure or happiness,
in any of his acts or communications relative to the creature.[40]

So in the quotations claimed as evidence that Edwards recon-
ceived the classical doctrine of immutability, he actually affirms and
claims it is entirely consistent with the genuineness of God's
happiness and delight. This was the very position of Augustine and
other upholders of the traditional view. It appears to be a rejection
of the classical vision of God only to those who have accepted a
caricature of the classical God as incapable of feeling love.

When Edwards writes elsewhere that God's perfection is his love,
he is reflecting on something that is not at all original to him – it is
traditional, standard Augustinian theology:

> God's infinite beauty is his infinite mutual love of himself. Now God is
> the prime and original being, the first and last, and the pattern of all, and
> has the sum of all perfection. We may therefore doubtless conclude that
> all that is the perfection of spirits may be resolved into that which is
> God's perfection, which is love.[41]

It is almost an unchallengeable assumption in the modern church
that the God of Jonathan Edwards was different from the God of
Augustine, Aquinas and Anselm. Edwards would have been horrified
at such a misrepresentation of his teaching. Edwards's manner of
writing – not least his using English – makes it much easier for
contemporary readers to see the passionate love of God he wrote
of so beautifully. This should not obscure that Augustine describes
the same vision of God in the Latin of late antiquity; Aquinas and
Richard of St Victor did so in the scholastic Latin of the medieval
schools. Edwards stands as yet another figure of church history who
realized that God's unchangeableness and perfection were not at all

---

40. Jonathan Edwards, as cited by Lee in *Princeton Companion*, pp. 66–67.
41. Jonathan Edwards, *Scientific and Philosophical Writings*, Works of
    Jonathan Edwards, 26 vols. (New Haven: Yale University Press, 1980),
    vol. 6, p. 363.

opposed to his love: they were the guarantee of its perfection and infinity.[42]

Edwards opened his Discourse on the Trinity by describing God's perfection as an infinite enjoyment of his own being:

> When we speak of God's happiness, the account that we are wont to give of it is that God is infinitely happy in the enjoyment of himself, in perfectly beholding and infinitely loving, and rejoicing in, his own essence and perfections. And accordingly it must be supposed that God perpetually and eternally has a most perfect idea of himself, as it were an exact image and representation of himself ever before him and in actual view. And from hence arises a most pure and perfect energy in the Godhead, which is the divine love, complacence and joy.[43]

The perfection Edwards sees in God is one of love: an energetic, passionate joy. In a move strikingly similar to that made by Richard of St Victor, Edwards argues that this perfect vision God has of himself demands that he be not just a monad, but rather Father and Son:

> The Godhead being thus begotten by God's having an idea of himself and standing forth in a distinct subsistence or person in that idea, there proceeds a most pure act, and an infinitely holy and sweet energy arises between the Father and Son: for their love and joy is mutual, in mutually loving and delighting in each other.[44]

Edwards is reasoning that for God to be perfect love, he must have an image of himself that is infinitely worthy of his love. Thus the

---

42. Though upholding simplicity, Edwards did struggle to correlate aspects of this with his trinitarianism. The details of this can be followed up in Oliver Crisp, 'Jonathan Edwards on Divine Simplicity', *Religious Studies* 39 (2003), pp. 23–41.

43. Jonathan Edwards, *Writings on the Trinity, Grace, and Faith*, Works of Jonathan Edwards, 26 vols. (New Haven: Yale University Press, 2003), vol. 21, p. 113.

44. Ibid., p. 121.

Godhead must be more than oneness: there must be an image that is fully God, and so can be loved perfectly by God. That image is the Son.

The infinite love that is this God was never intended to be restricted selfishly within God's own being. If it did, it would not be love. Rather God's love desires and moves with passion towards others. This in no way implies that God is dependent upon those he loves: the love shared is a perfect love, free from dependency on creation and all the changes inherent in temporal creatures' love. The perfect love of God is shared. It is 'the office of the person that is God's love to communicate divine love to the creature'.[45]

The only way God's love can be shared with others is if love itself comes near. There must be a third member of the Trinity, one who is fully God and is love. This is the Spirit. It is often assumed that Augustine's view that the Spirit is God's love in some way depersonalizes the Spirit, or is a philosophical construct far removed from Scripture. Edwards thought the view biblical:

> The Scripture seems in many places to speak of love in Christians as if it were the same with the Spirit of God in them, or at least as the prime and most natural breathing and acting of the Spirit in the soul. *Philippians 2:1*, 'If there be therefore any consolation in Christ, any comfort of love, any fellowship of the Spirit, any bowels and mercies, fulfil ye my joy, that ye be like-minded, having the same love, being of one accord, of one mind.' *2 Corinthians 6:6*, 'By kindness, by the Holy Ghost, by love unfeigned.' *Romans 15:30*, 'Now I beseech you, brethren, for the Lord Jesus Christ's sake, and for the love of the Spirit.' *Colossians 1:8*, 'Who declared unto us your love in the Spirit.' *Romans 5:5*, having 'the love of God shed abroad in our hearts by the Holy Ghost which is given to us.' *Galatians 5:13–16*, 'Use not liberty for an occasion to the flesh, but by love serve one another. For all the law is fulfilled in one word, even in this: Thou shalt love thy neighbour as thyself. But if ye bite and devour one another, take heed that ye be not consumed one of another. This I say then, Walk in the Spirit, and ye shall not fulfil the lust of the flesh.' The Apostle argues that Christian liberty don't make way for fulfilling the

---

45. Ibid., p. 123.

lusts of the flesh, in biting and devouring one another and the like, because a principle of love, which was the fulfilling of the law, would prevent it; and in the *Galatians 5:16* he asserts the same thing in other words: 'This I say then, Walk in the Spirit, and ye shall not fulfil the lust of the flesh.'[46]

Edwards knew that this view of the Spirit as God's love was troubling to people. 'One of the principal objections that I can think of against what has been supposed is concerning the personality of the Holy Ghost, that this scheme of things don't seem well to consist with that, [that] a person is that which hath understanding and will.'[47] His response was to set his teaching of the Spirit as love in the context of Scripture's teaching about trinitarian relationships:

I would observe that divines have not been wont to suppose that these three had three distinct understandings, but all one and the same understanding. In order to clear up this matter, let it be considered, that the whole divine essence is supposed truly and properly to subsist in each of these three – viz. God, and his understanding, and love – and that there is such a wonderful union between them that they are after an ineffable and inconceivable manner one in another; so that one hath another, and they have communion in one another, and are as it were predicable one of another. As Christ said of himself and the Father, 'I am in the Father, and the Father in me' [*John 10:14*], so may it be said concerning all the persons of the Trinity: the Father is in the Son, and the Son in the Father; the Holy Ghost is in the Father, and the Father in the Holy Ghost; the Holy Ghost is in the Son, and the Son in the Holy Ghost. And the Father understands because the Son, who is the divine understanding, is in him. The Father loves because the Holy Ghost is in him. So the Son loves because the Holy Spirit is in him and proceeds from him. So the Holy Ghost, or the divine essence subsisting in divine love, understands because the Son, the divine idea, is in him. Understanding may be predicated of this love, because it is the love of the understanding both objectively and subjectively. God loves the

---

46. Ibid., pp. 125–126.
47. Ibid., pp. 132–133.

understanding and the understanding also flows out in love, so that
the divine understanding is in the Deity subsisting in love. It is not
a blind love.[48]

In other words, Edwards says the persons of the Trinity have will,
understanding and individuality, not as some kind of private possession, divorced from the other persons. Each has understanding
because he is in the other. As the Father loves because the Spirit is
in him, so the Spirit understands because he is in the Son. In this
way it can be seen that Augustine and Edwards held that the Spirit
is God's love, and has the particular role of communicating that love
to creatures. Further, they maintained that this in no way diminishes
the Spirit's relationality.

These insights Edwards shares with us help us grasp something
more of what it means for God to be love. They leave, indeed they
insist upon, mystery within God. As Edwards observed:

> I don't pretend fully to explain how these things are, and I am sensible
> a hundred other objections may be made, and puzzling doubts and
> questions raised, that I can't solve. I am far from pretending to
> explaining the Trinity so as to render it no longer a mystery. I think it
> to be the highest and deepest of all divine mysteries still, notwithstanding
> anything that I have said or conceived about it. I don't pretend to explain
> the Trinity.[49]

Nevertheless Edwards's doctrine of God was consonant with
classical doctrine. America's greatest theologian, renowned for
promoting a relational vision of God, did so in ways that Augustine
and Richard of St Victor would have been very much at home
with. Like them, Edwards realized that if God is a being of perfection, he must be the God who is perfect love. Such a God could
not be a monad. His oneness must include a threeness: only the
Father, Son and Spirit can be perfect love and share that love with
creatures.

---

48. Ibid., p. 133.
49. Ibid., p. 134.

Excessive and abundant love

We have seen that Augustine, Richard of St Victor and Edwards all taught that if God is a perfect God of love, there must be a threeness to his being. A God who is not a trinity of divine persons could not be perfect love, and could not share that love with creatures. The three persons of the Trinity each have a distinctiveness to them, which arises from their relations to one another. These relationships in no way undermine simplicity: they are immutably the God of love.

In this way we see that God's love is perfect. That is, the classical vision of God is as infinitely personal and loving as may be conceptualized. To say that God's love is infinite is to affirm its abundance, energy, excess and generosity. These claims for God are not alien to the classical doctrine of God; they are part of it. The traditional theological way for describing this constant abundance of God's love was to say that God is one perfect act. As Edwards put it, 'In God, there are no distinctions to be admitted of faculty, habit and act, between will, inclination and love: but that it is all one simple act.'[50]

The language of 'act' is technical language to sum up the unique timeless, perfect, exuberant generosity that is the love of God in Father, Son and Spirit. 'Act' contrasts with 'potentiality'. The former refers to that which is, potentiality to that which may yet be. To say with classical theologians that God is perfect act is to insist that his immutability is active. God has no potentiality because he is perfectly realized, infinitely in motion and as abundantly loving as possible. His immutability and the impossibility of his becoming any more perfect arises from his sheer perfection. That the language of 'act' has long been part of classical theology's terminology emphasizes that the tradition never saw God as unchangeable in an inert or unrelational sense. He is the God who is perfect act: one eternal, infinite act of love. God is perfect act. He is, unsurprisingly, of a different order to us. God is the infinite Creator, and we are his creatures. As a consequence:

---

50. Ibid., p. 113.

> God's love is by no means the same as ours . . . Unlike our love, which
> is awakened by the goodness perceived in the beloved, God's love is not
> caused by the goodness of its object. His love for himself is not caused
> by his own goodness since it is one with his goodness . . . Nor is his love
> for creatures caused by his love for his own creatures since it is by one
> and the same act that God wills both his own goodness as his proper
> object and the existence of creatures as ordered to his goodness.[51]

We find it difficult, even impossible, to conceptualize a God who
is perfectly loving. Perhaps this is part of the explanation for so
much resistance to the classical doctrine of God: it takes too much
effort to understand the teachings. Far easier to caricature it as
unrelational and unloving. Even when the classical doctrine of God
is understood, it is little more than the grammar and spiritual posture
requisite for creatures who wish to speak about their creator.
Much is mysterious, as it should be if God truly is our creator. All
this said, the language of 'act' preserves for us the idea that God's
perfection is of a kind that is an infinite motion of love, relationship
and intimacy. God's perfection demands he be a God of three
persons, each fully God. Such a God is immutable because in his
three persons he is as fully and actively divine love as is possible. In
his eternal act of love God predestined the elect, created the universe,
called Abraham, gave the Mosaic Law, spoke through the prophets,
became incarnate, redeemed humanity, exalted the Son, sent the
Spirit and glorified his people. God has always been who and what
he is and will be, for God is love.

Meditation: Father, Son and Spirit

O God, forgive me for the many occasions when I speak and think
of you in ways that suggest you are a vague conceptual entity. I
too easily forget your relationality: your threeness. The beautiful

---

51. Michael Dodds, *The Unchanging God of Love: Thomas Aquinas and
   Contemporary Theology on Divine Immutability* (New York: Catholic
   University of America Press, 2008), pp. 207–208.

lines of love that run between each of your persons: Father, Son and Spirit.

May I feel and know more intimately that I am loved by my heavenly Father. All the good things I enjoy in life are gifts that come from your providential care.

May I feel and know at my deepest points of sin that I am loved by Jesus Christ. His blood was poured out on the cross for my sins; every drop of blood and sweat was shed out of love.

May I feel and know all this love by the power of the Spirit. Come close to me God in the person of your Spirit. Keep me from wandering from your ways. Empower me to keep in step with your Spirit's holy ways.

When I feel distant, down or dismayed, may your love cheer me on my way, till that glorious day when I shall see your love in person, with all the other people upon whom you have poured out your rich and satisfying love.

Amen.

8. SWOPPING PLACES? A DOCTRINAL DEBATE

Those who uphold the classical doctrine of God have been accused of letting the simplicity of God swallow up his threeness. It is argued that the oneness of God is permitted to overwhelm the threeness. One of the most influential proponents of this claim was Jürgen Moltmann: 'Ever since Thomas Aquinas ... the doctrine of the Godhead's single substance has taken precedence in the West, logically and epistemologically, over the doctrine of the trinity.'[1]

Karl Barth did much to make this narrative almost the standard view in the theological academy. In Britain one of a previous generation's most gifted and influential theologians, Colin Gunton, gave the theory considerable rhetorical force and potency.

Exploring this debate is helpful as it serves as an example of what happens when we attempt to theologize about God apart from the classical grammar of simplicity. While outside the academy few are aware of the debate about threeness being occluded by oneness,

---

1. Jürgen Moltmann, *The Trinity and the Kingdom of God: The Doctrine of God*, tr. M. Kohl (London: SCM, 1981), pp. 16–17.

there are important parallels to widely known misunderstandings over issues such as the atonement. That being the case, familiarizing ourselves with Gunton's accusations against the classical doctrine of simplicity will help us surmount popular difficulties with the doctrine of the atonement.

The accusation of swopping

Colin Gunton's teaching on the doctrine of God had particular potency because not only did he contend that the classical tradition of theology allowed the distinctness and reality of the three persons to be subsumed under the oneness of substance, but he laid the blame for this firmly at the feet of Augustine. In a typical comment Gunton writes:

> Augustine either did not understand the trinitarian theology of his predecessors, both East and West, or looked at their work with spectacles so strongly tinted with neoplatonic assumptions that they have distorted his work. The tragedy is that Augustine's work is so brilliant that it blinded generations of theologians to its damaging weaknesses.[2]

Gunton thought 'there is in Augustine, and in Western theology after him, a tendency towards modalism'.[3] Gunton reasoned that Augustine had struggled to describe the persons of the Trinity in a way that let their relationships define them. Consequently, 'He is precluded from being able to make claims about the being of the particular persons, who, because they lack distinguishable identity tend to disappear into the all embracing oneness of God.'[4]

On Gunton's account, Augustine's preferring of God's oneness made the Father, Son and Spirit impersonal and interchangeable: an unrelational God. Gunton sought 'a relational concept of the

---

2. Colin Gunton, *The Promise of Trinitarian Theology* (Edinburgh: T. & T. Clark, 1991), pp. 38–39.

3. Ibid., p. 42.

4. Ibid.

persons in God which maintains their distinctness in a way that is
absent from Augustine'.[5] Gunton's narrative is significant not only
for the accusations it levels at Augustine, but also for the way in
which he linked theology with culture. Gunton was of the view that
much of the malaise in Western secular culture was actually the fault
of the poor theology Augustine had peddled. Other scholars such
as Charles Taylor have suggested that secularity is a philosophy that
falls short of Augustine's grand theological vision,[6] and Brad Green
has argued that Gunton's argument contains an ironically Pelagian
view of the human condition: we caused the problem by our wrong
understanding and we can fix it.[7] Nevertheless Gunton recognized
that secular culture struggles to relate the one and the many in a
flourishing manner. All too often either radical individualism
destroys community, or the masses trample on individual freedoms.
Gunton traced this back to Augustine, saying that 'the obscuring of
particularity begins in Augustine's theology'.[8] Gunton thought that
Augustine's concept of person was 'only used in order not to remain
silent'.[9] As we shall see, Augustine did say something along these
lines, but that does not mean he held that 'the divine attributes are
to be considered almost exclusively with respect to the doctrine of
the one God; all that is said of God's being is said of God as one,
leaving the particular persons to languish in a kind of limbo'.[10]

Ultimately Gunton thought that the classical theological approach
to the doctrine of God led to the intolerable view that the triune
persons could have swopped roles: 'Aquinas' view that the Father

---

5. Ibid., p. 95.

6. Charles Taylor, *Sources of the Self: The Making of the Modern Identity*
   (Cambridge: Cambridge University Press, 1989).

7. Bradley G. Green, 'Colin Gunton and the Theological Origin of
   Modernity', in Lincoln Harvey (ed.), *The Theology of Colin Gunton*
   (Edinburgh: T. & T. Clark, 2010), pp. 165–181.

8. Colin Gunton, *The One, the Three and the Many: God, Creation and the
   Culture of Modernity* (Cambridge: Cambridge University Press, 1993), p. 54.

9. Colin Gunton, *Act and Being: Towards a Theology of the Divine Attributes*
   (London: SCM, 2002), p. 134.

10. Ibid., p. 134.

or the Spirit could have been the one to become incarnate is the logical outcome of Augustine's trinitarian theology.'[11]

In other words, holding to a simple view of God leads to such a relativizing of the persons that God is conceived of as an unrelational being composed of three impersonal, interchangeable beings. These were serious charges to make of Augustine; however, they helpfully serve to make explicit fears and misunderstandings of relating simplicity to the persons that arise in other areas of theology.

Distinct persons

As scholars have evaluated the thesis Colin Gunton promoted, that Augustine elevated the oneness of God over the threeness, there have been noted demurrals to what has nevertheless been an influential charge.

So, for instance, John Webster commends the fact that

> Gunton was a major figure in retrieving the theology of the Trinity
> from the periphery and returning it to the centre of British theology.
> He did this by demonstrating across a wide spread of doctrinal loci the
> difference which could be made by an operative doctrine of the trinity.[12]

In further defence of Gunton's renewed focus on the three persons of the Trinity, we are reminded that 'Gunton's trinitarian theology has to be viewed against the background of the instinctive deism of the leading British theologians of the 1950s.'[13] Against the background of these genuine and well-deserved commendations John Webster critiques Gunton's polemical target as the

> somewhat monolithically conceived – Western theological tradition,
> whose fount is Augustine . . . In this tradition, the mutually determinative

---

11. Gunton, *Promise of Trinitarian Theology*, p. 102, n. 35.
12. John Webster, 'Systematic Theology after Barth', in David Ford (ed.), *Modern Theologians* (Oxford: Blackwell, 2005), p. 259.
13. Ibid., p. 261.

personal relations of the Father, Son and Spirit are not allowed to be constitutive of the being of God, which is thought to underlie God's triunity as its ontological ground. As a reading of Augustine and others, this is certainly sketchy.[14]

Rowan Williams opens a magisterial essay on the relationship between wisdom and the Trinity in Augustine by rejecting both the accusation that Augustine favoured oneness over personalness, and the charge that secular modernity is in some way related to such errors:

> Theologians have been inclined . . . to conclude that we have relatively little to learn from Augustine in the task of constructing a properly relational model of God's trinitarian life. Augustine's concern with the self-relatedness of the divine essence is seen as one of the primary sources of that pervasive Western European obsession with the individual's sense of him- or herself which has led, in the wake of Kant, to the fundamental illusion of modernity, the notion that the private self is the arbiter and source of value in the world. Augustine stands accused of collaborating in the construction of the modern consciousness that has wrought such havoc in the North Atlantic cultural world, and is busy exporting its sickness to the rest of the globe . . . I believe that the connection made between Augustine and the consciousness of 'modernity' is a serious error, resting on a superficial reading of his work.[15]

Another eminent Augustine scholar, Lewis Ayres, bemoaned that 'many textbooks [contain] accounts [that] frequently treat Augustine as the paradigm and origin of a distinct western tradition, over-emphasising the unity of God'.[16]

---

14. Ibid., p. 259.

15. Rowan Williams, 'Sapientia and The Trinity: Reflections on the De Trinitate', in M. T. J. Van Bavel (ed.), *Collectanea Augustiniana* (Leuven: Leuven University Press, 1990), pp. 317–318.

16. L. Ayres, 'Augustine on the Trinity', in Gilles Emery and Matthew Levering (eds.), *The Oxford Handbook of the Trinity* (Oxford: Oxford University Press, 2012), p. 123.

With such eminent rebuttals of Gunton's thesis it is only a matter of time before this particular caricature of Augustine is laid to rest. Even when that occurs, this debate will remain a useful case study in the need to hold together both oneness and threeness, both simplicity and relationality.

Popular evangelical theologian Wayne Grudem states that the three persons of the Trinity cannot be conceived of as swopping roles. 'These roles could not have been reversed or the Father would have ceased to be the Father and the Son would have ceased to be the Son.'[17] Given that this seems to be such an obvious point, how was Gunton able to suggest Augustine thought otherwise?

One of the points Gunton made was that Augustine expressed ambivalence about the very word 'person' in reference to the Trinity. So Augustine wrote, 'When you ask "Three what?" human speech labours under a great dearth of words. So we say three "persons", not in order to say that precisely, but in order to not be reduced to silence.'[18]

Gunton thought this demonstrated that Augustine struggled to understand the trinitarian legacy he worked with, and in the end thought distinguishing between the three persons a futile and unimportant task. The first book-length study on Gunton's treatment of Augustine offers a different explanation. Bradley Green concludes that Augustine was trying to say that the term 'person' serves a positive use in warding off heretical views of the Trinity. The hesitancy Augustine expressed was really a healthy warning against assuming we can understand God exhaustively: 'Augustine conceded that our best efforts are rather limited (although not useless), and that while personae serves a certain purpose, it does not really allow us to penetrate the mystery of the trinity in a thoroughgoing way.'[19]

---

17. Wayne Grudem, *Systematic Theology: An Introduction to Biblical Doctrine* (Leicester: Inter-Varsity Press, 1994), p. 250.

18. Augustine, *Trinity* 5.2.10. Cited in Gunton, *Promise of Trinitarian Theology*, p. 96.

19. Bradley G. Green, *Colin Gunton and the Failure of Augustine* (Eugene: Pickwick, 2011), p. 168.

When his theological humility is appreciated, it can be seen that Augustine regarded the term 'person' a satisfying, indeed important, part of trinitarian doctrine. Green further warns readers of Augustine's book *The Trinity* that many of the quotes taken from that work seeming to give undue preference to the oneness of God are found in the opening book. In that section Augustine's 'point is not really simply to affirm oneness of substance, but rather to affirm the full and complete unity and equality of the three persons'.[20] This is important since the background threat Augustine was responding to was Arianism, which denied the full equality of the Son with the Father. In a similar vein Ayres reminds those who too readily accept Gunton's reading of Augustine's book *The Trinity* that it assumed familiarity with other, more foundational, theologizing about the doctrine of God, found in places such as relevant sermons (52, 71 and 117), letters (120 and 238) and the commentary on John.[21] It is easy to misunderstand a writer if you take a polemical writing aimed at correcting a particular misunderstanding and mistake it for a foundational text.

Augustine was emphatic and clear in teaching that the three persons of the Trinity were distinct from each other, and could not swop places. This was something he understood early in his ministry. Only two years after his ordination the African bishops asked Augustine to present a theological paper at a synod. At a time when it was common for only bishops to preach in churches, one can imagine how unusual it was for a mere presbyter to teach bishops! The resulting paper, 'Faith and the Creed', taught, 'This trinity is one God only. Not that the Father is to be understood as identical with the Son and the Holy Spirit; rather the Father remains the Father, the Son remains the Son, and the Holy Spirit remains the Holy Spirit, yet this Trinity is one God.'[22]

From his earliest days of ministry Augustine was recognized by his peers and superiors as a man of exceptional ability. When

---

20. Ibid., p. 166.

21. Ayres, 'Augustine on the Trinity', p. 136.

22. Augustine, 'Faith and the Creed', in Boniface Ramsey (ed.), *On Christian Belief* (New York: New City, 1996), 9.16.

asked to teach his elders, he affirmed the very opposite of what modern theologians have castigated him for believing. He not only refused to countenance the idea that the three persons of the Trinity could swop roles, but rooted their distinctiveness in their relationships. The Son could not be the Spirit or Father, because then he would cease to be the Son. Far from exalting impersonal concepts of oneness or substance over the three persons, Augustine staked his defence of the persons' distinctiveness on the reality of their relationships. The fount of the classical tradition's conception of simplicity held a view of God that was most definitely relational.

The strangest thing about Gunton's attacks on Augustine is that one cannot help but think that Augustine ought to have been viewed by Gunton as his greatest ally and resource in expounding a relational view of the Trinity. Augustine's use of the grammar of simplicity meant that he viewed the persons as not only distinct, relational and non-interchangeable, but held that the one God who is three persons is perfect and so can never change or struggle. The tragic irony is not lost on Bradley Green, who writes wryly, 'Augustine need not be a foe of Gunton. Indeed, key Augustinian insights seem quite friendly to Gunton's theological project, and Gunton seems himself to be an Augustinian at key points in his own thinking, even if this indebtedness is not completely recognised.'[23]

Simplicity and relationality

The misrepresentation of Augustine we have been considering is a useful debate to acquaint ourselves with, since it would not have arisen if it had been realized that a correct doctrine of God must uphold both oneness and threeness, both simplicity and relationality. It is the assumption that one of these must be jettisoned to preserve the other that permits superficial readings of Augustine. If one cannot hold both simplicity and relationality, then one will examine a writer to see which he or she has lost sight of.

---

23. Green, *Colin Gunton and the Failure*, p. 205.

A full-orbed doctrine of God recognizes that nothing but instability is gained by trying to affirm the relationality of three persons, while rejecting simplicity.

Simplicity is the grammar that enables us to say that God is perfect. The simple God is three persons, who are perfectly God and perfectly relational.

For the sake of clarity, and due to their being so misremembered and misrepresented, we examined doctrines associated with God's oneness in the opening chapters of this book. Doctrines such as perfection, simplicity, eternality, omniscience and omnipotence were explored without detailed reference to the relational love of God and the three distinct persons. This was merely a necessary method of teaching, and there is no substantive reason why the persons could not have been studied first. That methodology aside, the burden of this book is to urge us all to realize that a healthy view of God requires we give full weight to both his oneness and his threeness. Simplicity is not opposed to relationality, but is the guarantee of perfect relationality.

Simplicity is without a doubt a difficult philosophical concept to understand. It is utterly astonishing, and deeply perplexing to us creatures, that the God who is simple is the God who is three persons. Still, it is taught in Scripture and affirmed by the historical church in its creeds and councils. As Rob Lister puts it in his well-titled book, *God Is Impassible and Impassioned*.[24] The classical doctrine of simplicity is precisely what makes it possible to affirm that God is perfectly impassible and impassioned: he is an unchangeable infinite act of perfect love in three persons. He is as fully emotional as it is possible to conceive.

The beautiful mystery of the simple trinitarian God is that we most fully believe that God is perfect love when we accept that God is simple, and the three persons are each fully God and eternally distinct in their unswoppable natures. If God were simple, but not trinitarian, he would not be perfect love. God would not be perfect love if the three persons were identical or interchangeable. Neither

---

24. R. Lister, *God Is Impassible and Impassioned: Toward a Theology of Divine Emotion* (Wheaton: Crossway; Nottingham: Apollos, 2012).

would he be perfect love if he were three persons but not simple. Such a 'God' could be very impressive: he would be more powerful than humans. He could be the subject of countless inspiring sermons and devotional evangelical books. Still, when all is said and done, he would not be perfect, infinite love. If we wish to defend God's relationality, we need to realize that we will not be doing that reliably if we merely talk about the three persons or repeat endlessly that God is relational. Classical trinitarianism requires an unattenuated commitment to God's oneness, or simplicity, and threeness. So Augustine argues that

> [w]e give a solid defence of the relationality that arises from the love which is God in Father, Son and Spirit only when we maintain an unreserved commitment to both God's simplicity and threeness. The God who is simple, is the God who is three persons. It is not possible to imagine a God of perfect love with any other kind of existence – least of all a monistic, solitary divine being.[25]

Simplicity and atonement

Attempting to understand any doctrine requires that it be considered on its own terms: since we are neither eternal nor omniscient we must take time to learn and understand one thing after another. We cannot do this perfectly, but the process of reading, understanding, rereading, talking with others and praying through what God has revealed is of necessity a time-bound task. Students will be lead through a curriculum of teachings, in an order and at a speed judged by teachers to be wise. Readers of books progress through chapters. A conversation with a more mature Christian has a shape and form to it. All of this is unavoidable, and since it is part of our creaturely natures, good. However, the act of trying to understand and learn something necessarily divorces it from its interconnected doctrines. Too often there has been a lack of sensitivity to the ecology of

---

25. Augustine, *City of God*, ed. H. Bettenson and G. R. Evans (London: Penguin, 1984), 11.10.

Christian doctrine, the way in which all doctrines are dependent upon each other, giving one another shape.

The ecology of doctrine is unbalanced when a doctrine such as simplicity is forgotten. Banished to philosophical and medieval texts, simplicity is a doctrine that ought to shape all our speech about God. When it does not, we find it difficult to give a faithful, coherent account of what God is like and what he does. We have seen how this is the case with regard to many of God's attributes. It is also the case with important doctrines such as the atonement.

When the death of Jesus is reflected upon, it understandably troubles us to think of the Father's punishing the Son for our sins. It seems to be a most unjust thing: punishing the innocent that the guilty may go free. Even if the Son meekly submits to the judgement, even if the goal is his people's redemption, it seems unrighteous.

Many people have pointed out this appearance of injustice in the atonement. The standard response is to explain that the Son and Father are not two separate beings, but are both God. Seen from that perspective, the traditional narrative of the atonement is not a case of the Father's punishing an innocent third party, but rather the one God's bearing his own wrath, in the person of the Son. Few have expressed this insight more graciously and carefully than John Stott:

> God through Christ substituted himself for us . . . We strongly reject, therefore, every explanation of the death of Christ which does not have at its centre the principle of 'satisfaction through substitution', indeed divine self-satisfaction through divine self-substitution.[26]

Stott's defence of penal substitution as the central (but not only) principle that shapes the atonement is based on the unity of Father and Son. This is indeed a crucial point to make, and one may, as Stott does, rightly ground this in Christology. Since Jesus is God, he is no mere bystander in the active side of the atonement: God is both wrathful and wrath-bearing. Correct though the Christological

---

26. John R. W. Stott, *The Essential John Stott: The Cross of Christ & The Contemporary Christian* (Nottingham: Inter-Varsity Press, 1999), p. 147.

basis of unity between Father and Son is, the reasonableness of this aspect of the atonement can be more persuasively articulated only by making appropriate use of the doctrine of simplicity.

The unity through Christology is externalized, while that which is obtained via simplicity is internal to the Trinity. Simplicity is the grammar that enables us to speak of God as creatures using analogical language. When we uphold the doctrine of simplicity, we necessarily reject any idea that there is disagreement, disunity, change or parts within God. As we have seen, the perfection of this simplicity does not mitigate against the three persons of the Trinity; rather their full personalness and divinity are necessary if God is indeed perfect. The will and desires of the Son are fully accounted for within the doctrine of simplicity – they flourish amid the perfection of God. Simplicity then grounds the unity of God more deeply than any other aspect of his being. As such it greatly strengthens the argument that a traditional view of the atonement, as articulated by writers such as Leon Morris, J. I. Packer and Stott, is just and righteous. When the atonement is seen as the action of the perfect, loving, simple God, the distinctive works of Father and Son are unreservedly affirmed as in no way conflicted or divided. Simplicity has for too long been forgotten by large swathes of the church. If it regained its place in the heart of God's people, we would find explaining other doctrines a lot easier. The ecological harmony of what God has revealed about himself would be somewhat restored.

Meditation: knowing God

O God, I long to enjoy knowing you better. Thank you that you have revealed yourself.

I praise you that you are so much more wondrous and beautiful than anything I have ever seen or heard of.

Help me to appreciate you more deeply as you truly are: one God who is three persons. Forgive me for the times I have been impersonal and unfaithful to you by thinking of you as a generic word: 'God'. Help me to sense more deeply that you truly are the Father, the Son and the Spirit. My Heavenly Father. The Son who died for me. The Spirit who dwells in me. Please would Father, Son and Spirit be God to me, for me, with me and over me. Draw me in my greatest need to the place where you showed your love in all its magnitude: the cross.

There is so much I do not understand about the death of Christ, so much I fail to see and appreciate. May I get to know you better at the foot of that cross – Father, Son and Spirit.

Amen.

9. ENGAGING WITH THE WORLD

> It is impossible to separate love, joy, peace, faith and hope from one
> another in practice. They lose their true nature when separated. Try
> imagining love without joy and peace, joy without love and peace,
> or peace without love and joy, or any combination of them without
> faith and hope. You will see that love, joy, and so on, without the
> others, would not be themselves or have the same essential
> character. The 'love' that the world takes as the height of human
> attainment, without joy and peace is a tawdry sham, because they
> complement it and make it whole and link it to its source in God.
>
> (Dallas Willard)[1]

It is the nature of creatures who have fallen away from God that we
try, individually and corporately, to grasp for good things in isolation
from the God who made them. We seek love, but are unable to see
that since God is the Creator and is love, there is no true love apart
from him. The history of Western civilization is little more than a
series of experiments proving the truth of this from countless
perspectives.

We have been considering the God who created all things, the
God who is love. Catching the vision of God as other than us, both
simple and relational, both one and many, should drive us to worship,
prayer, Scripture and increased desire for God. Many books on the
doctrine of God or the Trinity rightly and understandably explore
such implications. However, my concluding focus will be rather
different. Instead I shall lay down some pointers suggesting the value

---

1. Dallas Willard, *The Renovation of the Heart* (Nottingham: Inter-Varsity
   Press, 2002), pp. 103–104.

this classical doctrine of God has for some aspects of contemporary life, which are in various ways contested. These include entertainment, work, freedoms and mission.

My goal cannot be any more than to show that a recovery of the classical vision of God as simple and relational would help Christians speak intelligently into debates with a perspective and experience that would be wise, and could increase the credibility of our witness to God in these days.

Our culture struggles to distinguish the temporal from the eternal, the significant from the insignificant. Our world does not know how to relate the individuality of particular people to the homogeneity of the masses. Our generation is frightened by the implications of people changing deeply held beliefs in general, and seeking to persuade others to do so in particular. All these problems are deep-seated in the hearts and experiences of those around us. Reflection upon the God who is one and many, and who draws people to love him, would offer ways of handling these aspects of living together. Since God is so different from anything we encounter in creation, getting to know him challenges our preconceptions and experiences. As Colin Gunton so helpfully observed:

> Christian theology [has] a genuine contribution to make to the
> understanding and shaping of the modern world and [can] enable us
> to probe some of the mysteries of what it means to be a human being
> living on earth before God and in varying structures of relations with
> our neighbour and with the universe in which we are set.[2]

Entertainment

In the mid-1980s sociologist Neil Postman realized that television was an entertainment medium that would transform the way our culture understood itself:

---

2. Colin Gunton, *The One, the Three and the Many: God, Creation and the Culture of Modernity* (Cambridge: Cambridge University Press, 1993), p. 154.

> [It] is not that television is entertaining but that it has made
> entertainment itself the natural format for the representation of all
> experience . . . The problem is not that television presents us with
> entertaining subject matter but that all subject matter is presented
> as entertaining . . . Television is our culture's principal mode of
> knowing about itself.[3]

Postman's seminal book still repays reading today. The totalizing power of television has resulted in entertainment culture dominating all fields of human endeavour and communality. The implications of television's cultural victory are still being worked out – in the lives of people who feel stressed because they have not got time to watch all seven seasons of a television programme they have purchased. In the lives of people who feel they are more artistic because of the brand of mobile phone they own. In the lives of children starving themselves to achieve an unreal body image they saw on television. In the lives of men who spend hours eating unhealthy food in front of a screen as they watch the team they obsess over. In the lives of young people who think relationships can be fixed and arranged on a similar schedule to the cliffhanger ending of their favourite television show. Reality blends into fantasy in our modern entertainment culture. We struggle to sift the trivial from the significant.

One study of the entertainment culture of London between 1890 and 1918 observed that people rose to prominence in the public eye for achievement in some arena that was admired, such as boxing, singing or dancing. During this period more and more such people tried their hand in the grand entertainment halls of the day, where music, jokes, dance and satire reigned. Those who made a living found the need to change and update their performances rapidly. The crowds demanded something new and fresh at regular intervals. This led to the rise of 'celebrities' who were famous and popular for performances that ranged far beyond their original areas of expertise:

---

3. Neil Postman, *Amusing Ourselves to Death: Public Discourse in the Age of Show Business* (London: Penguin, 1985), pp. 87, 92.

The new Londoners soon found that up-to-date culture was dynamic and transitory . . . mastering up-to-dateness required a sophisticated understanding of just how to dazzle audiences with sensational performances. Though a steady stream of cyclists, boxers, footballers and pilots tried their skills on the halls, only the most tenacious performers remained in the public consciousness for long. Up-to-dateness and professionalisation in popular culture led to the emergence of modern celebrities who starred simultaneously in several different activities.[4]

Today the entertainment culture is dominated by celebrities: people known for being known. As we follow their exploits on the Internet and various media outlets, our lives are shaped by the entertainment culture's values. Those who are seeking to live as disciples of Jesus feel stressed and anxious because the values he commends have little room in the entertainment culture. Those who do not know God feel stressed because there is so much going on in the entertainment world that it is impossible to keep up with all of it. In any case, no matter what 'news' is gleaned, it feels transitory and rootless. The anxiety, stress and dissatisfaction are only going to increase as the entertainment industry leverages digital resources to become even more global, targeted and effective. 'Entertainment culture is the central feature of contemporary globalisation.'[5]

One of the most important features of the entertainment culture is the loss of a traditional understanding of time. In modern cultures 'entertainment time' was what could be enjoyed after a day's work ended. Today 'entertainment' is something watched on a phone on the way to work, and thought about during work. The entertainment is often consumed online, where other users may be commenting from the other side of the globe. As a result, traditional time concepts do not share the interaction. It may be evening for

4. A. Horrall, *Popular Culture in London 1890–1918: The Transformation of Entertainment* (Manchester: Manchester University Press, 2001), pp. 237, 243.

5. K. Hafez and A. Skinner, *The Myth of Media Globalization* (Oxford: Polity, 2007), p. 82. See also T. Mirrlees, *Global Entertainment Media: Between Cultural Imperialism and Cultural Globalization* (Abingdon: Routledge, 2013).

you, but it is morning for her. As a result of all this the entertainment culture is permanently on:

> Modernity's clock, or concept of time, is devalued. At best it grants awareness of time outside the on-line universe: when we logged on, how long we have been on-line, and what time it is when we complete our on-line journeys. But while we are on-line, modernity's time tools have absolutely no use. We enter a world where time and space mean something else. In the on-line universe, there is no need for traditional senses of time and space because we are, in a sense, in a new dimension of both.[6]

The triumph of the entertainment culture represents humanity's loss of its creaturely sense of being in time. We cannot return to a previous age where entertainment is not dominant – nor should we want to. That would be the way of romanticism. However, we can reconnect with the God who is eternal. This will give us awareness of a fresh perspective on our status, which will help us handle the pressure to immerse ourselves in a timeless flow of entertainment. Gunton reflects on this approach:

> If the denial of God leads to the idolatrous confusion of time and eternity, the finite and the infinite, we must ask what theological proposals will allow for their appropriate integration, according to which their due order, eternity first and then time, may be asserted without the overwhelming of the latter by the former.[7]

The frenzied pressure we feel from the entertainment culture around us is the consequence of facing life without appreciation of the distinction between the time-bound and eternal. Until we develop a healthy sense of our own temporal limitations, we will be unable to live in time. Recovery of that begins when we behold the God who is other than us, the eternal God who gives us the gift of time

---

6. B. Taylor, R. Johnston and W. Dyrness, *Entertainment Theology: New-Edge Spirituality in a Digital Democracy*, Cultural Exegesis (Grand Rapids: Baker Academic, 2008), p. 33.

7. Gunton, *One, the Three*, p. 157.

to live in for him. When our lives are viewed as temporary gifts to be lived before God's face, we are able to enjoy parts of the entertainment culture, without losing ourselves in the timeless stream of trivia and entertainment that overwhelms so many.

Work and ministry

In both secular work and Christian ministry people labour under immense burdens of stress. There is strong pressure to achieve, and providing for family can be difficult. We have expectations from parents and friends – even from ourselves. Many jobs have an endless list of things that could be done; mobile technology means the work can, indeed often must, be brought home.

With financial obligations, long working hours, the fear (or experience) of unemployment and the frenetic pace of life, is it any wonder that so many people find their work or ministry a cause of stress?

Much of this difficulty arises from the curse God laid on our earth when Adam refused to trust God's words. In that sense the problems will remain till Jesus returns. However, more can be said. We are responsible for how we respond to living in a fallen world. There are particular patterns of sin, and tendencies towards accepting sin that we should be cognizant of.

Christians, as those who feel the need for God's grace, should be particularly sensitive to the seductive power of money and possessions. Since we know that our hearts long for something or somebody to worship, we are aware that work can be an arena where those desires often latch on to something other than God.

> The anthropology of grace considers human beings to be extremely vulnerable to the lure of possessions. If there is one thing certain about human nature, it is its disposition to be dazzled and attracted to things. Things become idols, substitutes for God . . . Things possess inexhaustible appeal for human beings, and enough is never enough. We all know this.[8]

---

8. Paul Zahl, *Grace in Practice: A Theology of Everyday Life* (Grand Rapids: Eerdmans, 2007), p. 219.

We live in a culture that encourages us to pursue ever-increasing affluence:

> Every person can choose their own unique way to self-fulfilment, empowered by family, market and society. That is the promise of liberal societies. By creating conditions for the pursuit of wealth, markets and government enlarge the range and quality of choice for every individual. That vision underpins the 'free society' and 'free markets' hailed by politicians and business people as priorities for society.[9]

Stress and pressure in such a context inevitably arise in the secular workplace. Even secular philosophers have realized not only that our constant labouring to get things and achieve what we want in life does not bring happiness, but also that the root of the problem lies in our turning away from God. So Pascal Bruckner wrote:

> When man substitutes himself for God as the foundation of law, and religion withdraws from the public sphere to become a private matter, time gains a certain autonomy. It is no longer solely a path toward the eternal, and whether it goes somewhere depends on us alone. It becomes an environment in which the individual can blossom and construct himself, but it also becomes a mire in which he can get bogged down; he is both a creator and a driveller. That is the modern discovery: life is not as repetitive as people say it is; new things can be invented, but life also repeats itself dreadfully . . . the withdrawal of the divine provides . . . human independence with a chance to develop itself freely, but the burden of everyday life has somehow to be borne alone.[10]

Knowing God should reshape the way we bear the curse of the fall in our workplaces. It is not surprising that the resources that flow from loving the God of Scripture are not relied on by people

---

9. A. Offer, *The Challenge of Affluence: Self-Control and Well-Being in the United States and Britain Since 1950* (Oxford: Oxford University Press, 2006), p. 357.

10. Pascal Bruckner, *Perpetual Euphoria: On the Duty to Be Happy*, tr. S. Rendall (Princeton: Princeton University Press, 2011), pp. 70–71.

in the secular workplace. Sadly places of Christian ministry are all too often a religious image of the secular workplace. At the end of a book that considers many aspects of the problems of stress, burn out, depression and overwork in ministry Peter Brain comments, 'It is often difficult for us to rest, because we are involved in too many ministries. This can arise from others' expectations, having a Messiah complex, a desire to be noticed and appreciated, or any combination of the three.'[11]

Adam's sin may make stress, pressure and failure in ministry unavoidable, but our responses and approach to ministry often exacerbate the problems. Many young people are encouraged into ministry by older leaders who had hugely positive impacts on their Christian growth, perhaps even having been the one to lead them to trust in Jesus for the first time. That is one of the reasons so many Christian ministers live their lives under the burden of trying to please and impress an older Christian leader. We would deny it strenuously, but far too many of us find ministry stressful because in the final analysis we are seeking to serve a Christian leader we have placed on a pedestal. We need to be warned against this:

> There are no super-Christians, and if you think you have found one, you have diminished yourself. It gets worse. When you have demeaned yourself that way, you will find yourself in a prison of shame, guilt, and impossible expectations. The false idol of super-Christians has destroyed the freedom of those who aren't! . . . When we worship at the altar of another human being, we chain ourselves to false expectations about our idol and about ourselves. Our freedom to risk, to be who God created us to be and to think, feel, and act in freedom, dissipates in the face of the idol.[12]

There are a number of vital areas of theological reflection that the church down the ages has realized help us in this area of work

---

11. Peter Brain, *Going the Distance: How to Stay Fit for a Lifetime of Ministry* (Kingsford: Matthias Media, 2004), p. 231.

12. Steve Brown, *A Scandalous Freedom: The Radical Nature of the Gospel* (West Monroe, La.: Howard, 2004), pp. 122–123.

Davis set down the hood and redialed the number of the last incoming call on the satellite phone. Hodges answered on the first ring.

"We're outside the facility," Davis said.

"Were you able to find everything?"

"I think so. What are we supposed to do now?"

He heard the clatter of a palm covering the microphone and muffled voices on the other end.

"The chopper will be there in fifteen minutes. Be ready."

CULLEN STRUGGLED BACK TO CONSCIOUSNESS. His thoughts were watery and sluggish. He was peripherally aware of the warmth of blood on his face and the sensation of something pinned under his chest, something sharp and penetrating. The pain hit him a heartbeat later, agony beyond anything he'd experienced in his lifetime. He gingerly touched his torn eyelid, even that slight pressure sending an electric bolt through his head.

The needle.

He recalled the woman stabbing it right into his eye. Blinding him. He roared in anguish and forced himself to sit up. The tranquilizer syringe rested on the floor in his blood, broken off at the hub. He pried the needle from his chest and flung it aside.

Where were Middleton and the cowardly little pusbag who'd shot him? The last thing Cullen remembered was gripping the man's head like a melon and forcing it to the ground, feeling the pressure building and the bones about to break and then—

Crack.

The sound still reverberated in his skull, along with the impact of the butt of the rifle against the back of his head. Clots of blood and hair surrounded the tattered flesh, which was already curling away from the wound. It took all of his strength to rise to his feet. He leaned against the wall until the pain relented enough for him to stand on his own. His reflection stared back at him from the window of the security station, his lone remaining eye the only part of his face not covered with blood.

He'd make them suffer for what they'd done to him.

Cullen pushed away from the wall, grabbed the rifle from the ground at his feet, and staggered toward the observation room to his right. He opened the airlock and stared down at Edgerton, who lay on the floor, as fragile and pathetic as a fledgling fallen from its nest.

"You can't die yet." He propped Edgerton against the wall and slapped him across the face. The anthropologist's eyes opened the smallest crack and his face crinkled as though he were about to cry. "I'm not finished with you."

Cullen dragged Edgerton down the hallway by his collar, his legs sliding limply behind him, through pools of blood, past bodies left to rot where they'd fallen and creatures that had served their violent purpose. Footprints appeared every so often before the blood transferred off once more. Two sets: the larger tracks featured the telltale tread of the isolation suits; the smaller impressions were bare, just like Middleton's feet. He followed them through the facility and into the earthen substructure. A gentle air current caressed his features, drawing him toward the source. The footprints led in that direction, fading with each step until they vanished altogether. There was only one reason his prey would have gone outside on foot, especially when one of them didn't even have shoes. They were waiting for extraction.

A wicked grin filled with teeth slashed Cullen's face.

EDGERTON WATCHED the granite ceiling pass overhead, the irregularities in the rock creating shadows that seemed to come to life before his very eyes. He'd seen true darkness, sensed it flowing through his veins, lurking inside of him. He'd experienced its thoughts as his own, relived its memories, felt its emotions. And when it had left him, he'd been certain that death had come for him at last and welcomed it with open arms. Anything was preferable to being trapped in the hell that was his mind, drowning in the evil that grew stronger with every passing second.

"Kill me," he whispered.

Laughter echoed all around him, a sound he recognized from inside his head. He'd heard it countless times before, while his grad students had been tearing each other apart with their bare hands and teeth, while his filthy and disheveled tribe had chosen starvation over salvation, while watching the scientists in their white suits prancing around as though they'd ever had any control over the situation, and while the last of the infected had slowly died inside his tomb, but even then he'd known that his only prison was time.

Acid rippled up from his stomach, burning the back of his throat until he retched it up. He was too weak to struggle, too exhausted to even keep his eyes open.

Freezing air raised the goosebumps on his arms. A thrumming sensation passed through the ground. He heard a distant pulsing sound, like the heartbeat of some great mechanical beast, and recognized it for what it was.

"Get up," Cullen said, twisting his collar and lifting him from the ground.

Edgerton felt the cold concrete beneath his bare feet. His legs tried to fold underneath him, but another twist on his collar summoned strength he didn't realize he possessed, spurring him toward an orifice through which he saw only darkness and towering evergreens. He gasped for air and felt the pressure in his chest lessen, if only enough to draw a single breath. Red and green lights materialized from the night, intermittently appearing and disappearing through the branches.

Cullen ducked behind Edgerton, as though using him like a human shield, and together they stepped out into the open.

RILEY WATCHED the flashing lights of the helicopter approaching from the deep canyon, the wind battering it with each wailing gust, the thupping of rotors echoing from the sheer granite escarpments. Were the cloud cover any denser, there would have been no light at all. As it was, the diffuse aura of moonlight was barely enough to limn the pine needles in the upper canopy, stranding the two of them in the complete darkness clinging to the trunks.

Davis waved his arms over his head to get the pilot's attention. They'd found a small clearing near the invisible dirt road, one offering them an unobstructed view of a narrow sliver of sky.

Riley checked and double checked that the semiautomatic rifle's safety was off. The weapon was so heavy that she wouldn't be able to trust her aim. She prayed to God she wouldn't have to use it, but her nerves crackled with galvanic potential. Something was wrong; she could feel it in the air, like static electricity building before a lightning strike. It was *him*, she knew. The sentience she'd seen behind Edgerton's eyes through the campfire and felt inside the cave where she'd hidden. He was coming. She could almost hear the whispering of voices from the trees.

"Over here!" Davis shouted.

Riley took a few steps uphill, dead pine needles prodding the soles of her bare feet, and tried to get a better view of the trench where the road disappeared into the mountain. She crouched to see through the brush and detected movement within the shadows.

"Davis!"

He turned and looked at her—

A clap of thunder and wooden shrapnel burst from the trunk of the tree beside his head. He dove to the ground and scurried toward her, bullets tearing up the detritus all around him.

Riley saw the flicker of discharge and fired at the source. The stock kicked and the barrel rose, releasing a fusillade into the lower canopy. Worse, the errant shots betrayed her location.

She stepped to the side, pressed her back against a tree, and felt bullets hammer the other side of the trunk.

Davis ducked behind a boulder just downhill from her. She could barely see his wide eyes and pale face.

The helicopter raced toward them, the wind of its passage tossing the tree-tops as though before a hurricane. She caught a glimpse of an armature projecting from its open side door, lowering a gondola-like basket through the branches, aiming for the gap where Davis had been mere seconds ago.

"No . . . " she whispered.

The hood containing the tablet and everything they'd collected from the lab lay on the ground, the fabric flaring on the rotor wash. They needed to get it on that chopper—

Another flicker from the corner of her eye and bullets stitched up the tree beside her head. She ducked back and tried to steady her grip on the rifle.

The basket twirled down through the canopy and settled to the earth. Shadows emerged from the dense shrubbery and stepped out into the open.

Riley drew a deep breath, raised the rifle, and leaned out—

Dale stood at the edge of the small clearing, his trembling hands raised at his sides. Cullen hid behind him, his lone good eye barely visible over Dale's shoulder. He aimed his weapon and fired—

Riley rolled onto her side as bullets pounded the ground where she'd just been.

The ferocious wind filled the air with dirt and debris, forcing her to shield her eyes as she rose to her knees and sighted the rifle on Dale's chest. Behind him, Cullen dropped his weapon and grabbed the hood. He pulled Dale backward by his scrub top, urging him closer to the basket. Riley could barely see Cullen and lacked the skill to hit him without shooting her colleague in the process.

Cullen lowered himself into the basket and pulled Dale down on top of him. The cable tightened and they slowly ascended.

Davis shouted something she couldn't make out over the roar of the rotors and darted out from behind the boulder. Riley ran downhill toward the clearing as the basket crashed through the branches overhead. The moment it cleared the treetops, the chopper banked out over the canyon and veered away from them.

Riley dropped the rifle and stared helplessly at the horizon, where the helicopter vanished into the darkness once more.

35

Kansas City, Missouri

Duvall pulled up against the guardrail on top of the overpass and killed the Explorer's headlights to better see the men on the highway below him, maybe a quarter of a mile away. Their old pickup was parked on the shoulder, shining its high beams onto a billboard advertising a diner some number of miles up the road. It was old and faded, the kind of sign some farmer had likely made a quick grand to let some fast-talking salesman prop up on his land, much like the one Duvall had passed outside of Columbia. It hadn't been the gas station on the advertisement that had caught his attention, but rather the symbols painted over it, symbols that few outside of himself could recognize, let alone decipher. He'd painted similar characters, only of a dramatically different nature, on the walls of the greenhouse in the abandoned building where he'd hidden for the last few months, sensing that the time to step from the shadows was drawing near.

The moment had finally arrived, and, despite what the old man ducking under the barbed wire fence would have people believe, no one was going to survive, regardless of which direction they fled.

Duvall was curious, though. Who was this ancient bag of bones and what had possessed him to spread his message in the middle of nowhere? There was something familiar about him, something he hadn't seen in so many years that even the memories had turned to dust. He supposed there was no harm in getting a closer look. Perhaps he could even draw out the old man and learn what he was up to, not that it would make any difference in the end, for this old Indian, like all of his kind, would soon be a feast for the carrion birds.

The ravens perched on the guard rail took flight when Duvall hit his lights, squawking and squalling and filling the sky. He made a U-turn and accelerated down the offramp.

SAKEVA TURNED at the sound of tires on the gravel shoulder. He shielded his eyes from the headlights and struck off through the weeds toward the road. The newcomer climbed from the driver's seat of his SUV and closed the door.

"You want me to stop?" Billy asked.

"Just finish as quickly as you can."

Sakeva felt a flutter in his stomach, a nervousness he hadn't experienced in years. It was more than the fact that this was the first car that had stopped in all of the times they'd painted their message; there was something unnerving about the small man with the thinning hair who walked around from behind the car and stopped at the fence line. Moonlight reflected from his glasses in such a way that Sakeva couldn't see his eyes, although he could feel them crawling all over his skin.

The man raised his hand in greeting.

"How are you all doing tonight?"

Sakeva grunted and stood on the other side of the barbed-wire barrier, his heart hammering in his chest. His hands trembled so badly that he had to shove them into the pockets of his dusty jeans so the other man wouldn't notice. He licked his dry lips to wet his mouth.

"I came across one of those signs of yours a ways back," the man said. "I was wondering what it meant."

The way he spoke made Sakeva uncomfortable. Not his cadence or the sound of his voice, but rather the way it didn't seem to match the movement of his lips or the expression on his face.

"Just extending a helping hand to those who might need it," Sakeva said.

"That's awfully generous of you. These are trying times, after all, but I've got to say that it seems you'd be able to reach a lot more people if you used words they were able to understand."

"The message will reach those who need to see it."

The man nodded and looked up into the dark sky, where black birds wheeled as though waiting for one of them to die. He smiled and Sakeva recognized him for who — or, rather, *what* — he was.

"Hustle on up, child," Sakeva called. "Time to get back on the road."

"I didn't mean to frighten you off."

"You do not frighten me," Sakeva said.

The man's smile grew even wider. He took off his glasses and rubbed his eyes. Sakeva caught the flicker of flames from the man's irises before he once more hid them behind the reflections on his lenses.

Billy stomped the lid back onto the bucket and shushed through the tall weeds behind Sakeva, who didn't take his eyes off the small man.

"I suppose I'd best be getting back on the road, too," the man said. "I just thought it might be nice to introduce myself, but I have a feeling you already know who I am, don't you?"

Billy made a move to duck underneath the barbed wire. Sakeva reached out and stopped him.

"I know your kind," he said.

"Then you must have a pretty good idea of how this all ends." The small man smiled. "Anyway, I'm sure we'll meet again, somewhere down that crooked path."

"Count on it," Sakeva said.

The man nodded and walked around to the other side of his SUV. He opened his door and stared at Sakeva through the windows for several interminable seconds before climbing inside and revving the engine. He peeled onto the highway, showering them with gravel. His taillights, as red as arterial blood, vanished into the distance.

Sakeva clutched his chest. He couldn't seem to make himself breathe. He'd spent his entire life preparing to face his adversary, and yet in the countless times he'd imagined this confrontation, he'd never walked away so shaken. He'd been paralyzed by fear, while that man had merely seemed amused, taunting him for no other reason than he could. When they met again, Sakeva was afraid he wouldn't have the strength to do what needed to be done.

"Come on," he said. "We still have a long way left to go."

BILLY DROVE ON AUTOPILOT, the trees lining the road gliding past in the darkness. They'd decided to detour around Kansas City on Highway 50. The last thing they wanted was another experience like the one they'd had in St. Louis. Leaving that man on the side of the road still didn't sit right with him, but he could tell that wasn't what was bothering his great-grandfather, who hadn't spoken a word since their encounter with the man in the Explorer. He just sat there, alternately staring out the cracked windshield and the open side window, the long gray hairs that had come loose from his braid flowing on the breeze.

"What was that back there?" Billy finally asked.

His great-grandfather appeared to have aged a decade in the last twenty minutes alone. The bones in his wrinkled face were more pronounced, the creases around his eyes deeper.

"Are you familiar with *yee naaldlooshii*?" Sakeva said, his eyes settling upon a car on the side of the road, its bumper down in a ditch, its rear window shattered.

Billy shook his head.

"The name comes from the Diné. It means 'with it, he goes on all fours.' There is no comparable word in the Hopi language, for our ancestors believed that to speak it would only invite evil into our midst. It is because of *yee naaldlooshii* that our people avoid going out alone at night, why we do not directly touch the bodies of our dead, and why we do not wear the pelts of predatory animals like the wolf and the bear."

"You're talking about skinwalkers."

"I am talking about witchcraft. Not of the kind you associate with the Christian traditions of the Bahanna, but simply another aspect of our own spirituality, another way of being. The Diné call it the Witchery Way. It is a path that leads to great power; however, not just any man can walk it."

"I thought only women could be witches," Billy said.

Sakeva's eyes became unfocused and distant.

"There is so much I should have taught you," he said. "And now, I fear, it is too late."

He said nothing more for several minutes as the world rushed past, the wind whistling through the cab. Billy waited the old man out.

"There have always been those among us who are more closely attuned to the ways of the spiritual world. We call them shamans, medicine men responsible for our physical and spiritual wellbeing. They use plants and herbs to treat sickness and disease, but it is not only the body that suffers. The infection must also be cleansed from the soul, which requires the help of someone capable of passing between our world and the next, someone who can bend both to his will. It is a terrible burden, one that cannot be shouldered lightly, for with it comes extraordinary power beyond the ability of most to comprehend. And that power can be seductive. Imagine having the ability to prolong life and cheat death, to inflict harm upon those who have wronged you without anyone ever knowing. To become a god among men. It is simply a matter of exhaling the light and inhaling the darkness."

"And how does he do that?"

"It is said that to be initiated in the Witchery Way, to become *yee naaldlooshii*, a man must kill a member of his family and defile the corpse, whether by rite or by dark magic. In doing so, he becomes a being of pure evil, one capable of transforming into other forms of life. It is said that by wearing the pelt of an animal he can physically change into that animal, that by donning its skull he's capable of adding its power to his own."

Billy merged onto I-470, the first of many highways that would eventually lead them back to I-70, just outside of Topeka.

"My grandfather believed differently," Sakeva continued. "He said *yee naaldlooshii* wore not the skins of animals, but rather those of other human beings, that they could enter another man's body merely by looking into his eyes. According to stories passed down through the generations, they were shamans who'd consumed the flesh of the dead, and by doing so were cursed to walk the earth until the end of time. They became creatures of darkness capable of reading the minds and manipulating the thoughts and behaviors of the bodies they inhabit. It is said they can control animals, call up the spirits of the dead, and even reanimate corpses. They envy our mortality, despise our humanity, and eagerly await our extinction."

"And you buy all of this?" Billy said.

"I freely admit that I found such stories as unbelievable as you do," he said. "Until tonight, when I looked into that man's eyes and saw the ancient evil looking back at me."

"You think that guy in the Explorer was a skinwalker?"

"It doesn't matter what he is," his great-grandfather said. He sighed and closed his eyes. "The only thing that matters now is preparing ourselves for the battle to come. He wanted us to see him tonight, to recognize him for what he truly is. He wanted to scare us. Because he knows that the next time we face him, the Fourth World will be at an end."

36

Snoqualmie, Washington

Banks hung up her cellphone and dropped it in the cup holder. It had taken twenty minutes to get through to the local FBI office and another fifteen waiting on hold before she finally talked to someone who could help her. With all of the bridges across Lake Washington closed and I-5 barricaded at both ends of Seattle, authorities were rerouting all military and law-enforcement personnel to a staging ground at Joint Base Lewis-McChord, a sprawling military complex southeast of Tacoma on Nisqually Reach.

She glanced into the rearview mirror and found seven pale faces looking back at her, each of them exhibiting the telltale symptoms of shock, save for one. Wes held her stare for several moments before averting his eyes, the moonlight passing through the trees momentarily framing his head with shadows resembling antlers. She tried to tell herself that there was something wrong with the way he was reacting to the situation, not that there was something wrong with him, but she'd sensed it the first time she saw him, and she trusted her instincts. The moment she could separate him from the other children, she would do just that.

Beside him, the little girl with the stuffed dog sucked her thumb. A boy of maybe ten or eleven leaned his head against the shoulder of a girl roughly his own age, who patted his back and made shushing sounds, like waves rolling to shore. The three in the far back were little more than silhouettes against the rear window, across which the wiper flapped every few seconds like the wing of some majestic bird.

Ciara squeezed Banks's shoulder. She turned toward the passenger's seat and found the young girl looking back, a question in her eyes. Banks wasn't used to having to justify, or even explain, her actions to anyone.

"We're going to a military base," she said. "We'll be safe there."

"You're not going to leave us, are you?" the little girl asked around the thumb plugged between her lips.

"No." Banks saw genuine terror in the child's eyes and couldn't help but wonder what kind of abandonment the poor girl had already endured. "I'll stay with you the whole time. You have my word."

"Yeah, right," Wes said. "You'll be gone the moment you can dump us on someone else."

One of the girls in the far back started to cry.

"I guess you'll just have to trust me."

Wes scoffed and resumed staring out the window into the dense trees ascending the hills to either side. The state forest was so thick that Banks imagined a person could get lost straying more than a hundred yards from the highway. They didn't pass a single car until the two-lane became four and they left the forest behind. Houses materialized from the trees, little more than dark shapes squatting in the deep valleys. Were it not for the subtle smell of smoke and the faint orange glow on the horizon, she might have been able to convince herself that none of the images she'd seen on TV had been real.

The closer they got to the outskirts of Seattle, the more reality bled through. Emergency lights flashed through the distant streets, tires squealing, sirens blaring. Once she even thought she'd heard the prattle of automatic gunfire but chalked it up to the grinding sound of the wipers on the windshield between spats of rain.

Fortunately, their route took them wide of the population centers. She didn't know what she'd do with these kids if they encountered a roadblock or were forced to abandon the vehicle. When it came right down to it, she had zero experience dealing with children. She'd been an only child and hadn't reached the point in her life when she'd begun to think about settling down, but she meant what she'd said. Until she knew they'd be safe, she wasn't leaving their side.

The thought was simultaneously comforting and surprising. She didn't know them, and she didn't owe them a thing, but she could see the fragile hope in their eyes and realized that right now she was their entire world.

Ciara drew her bare feet up onto the seat and wrapped her arms around her legs. The blood on her skin looked like mud. Leading the other children out of that place had taken serious courage. It broke Banks's heart to think that this poor girl had gone through a similar nightmare only a few days prior, one that had traumatized her so badly that she'd been rendered mute and started drawing such horrifying pictures, and yet here she sat, staring dry-eyed through the windshield. She reminded Banks of herself when she was that age, constantly telling herself that tears flowed on the outside because they were meant for others, people who were just waiting for her to expose her vulnerabilities. Looking at this poor girl now, she realized how wrong she'd been. So much pain had never been meant to be borne alone.

Before Banks even knew what she was going to do, she held out her hand. Ciara didn't even hesitate. She took it and drew it right up against her cheek. Only then did the tears start to fall.

Banks left it there until civilization encroached upon the highway. Cars screamed past in the opposite direction, speeding toward the mountains and away from the city, where smoke rose from the horizon, stained in artificial shades of red and blue by fire trucks and ambulances. Lights burned in the windows of houses spread out to either side of the highway, where families had been awakened from a dead slumber to learn that the world had gone to hell while they were sleeping. She imagined them gathered around their televisions, watching the chaos unfold in horror and listening to voices telling them to stay where they were, lock their doors, and pray.

A shadow ran down the hill toward their car and quickly vanished into their wake. The front end of a truck burst through the chain-link barrier of the overpass ahead, its front tires spinning uselessly. The rear end of a sedan stood from a ditch, the body of its driver lying on the shoulder in a pool of blood.

"Don't look," Banks said.

The crying started anew behind her.

Banks took the I-5 South toward Portland and followed the signs for McChord Field. Convoys of military vehicles leaving the base indirectly guided her to the secured entrance. She opened her badge jacket and showed it to one of the guards, while the others walked a circuit around the car with undercarriage mirrors and German shepherds.

She sought the eyes of the children behind her in the rearview mirror and tried to think of something reassuring to say.

"Everything's going to be all right."

"No, it's not," Wes said. "This is only the beginning."

Banks's heart stalled in her chest at the repetition of The Executioner's last words.

And for a second, she could have sworn she'd seen the boy smile.

———

EVERYTHING AFTER PASSING through the outer gates was a blur. Ciara vaguely remembered following a procession of cars around a bunch of low-lying industrial buildings to a massive parking lot, where a bus had been waiting to transport them to a series of hangars. After standing in line for their temperatures to be taken and their biographical data to be processed, they'd been led out the side door, across the tarmac, and into another hangar that had been divided into hundreds of individual rooms with collapsible walls on three sides and a curtain in the front.

Banks had arranged for several other beds and sleeping bags to be brought to their assigned quarters so they could all stay together, despite the initial protests of the National Guardsmen, who'd never stood a chance against the federal agent. She might have been small, but she was ferocious. Ciara could hear her on the other side of the curtain, trying to gather information about what was going on outside, although it didn't sound like anyone had the slightest idea. At least they were all safe, for the time being anyway, which was just going to have to be enough for now.

She stared up into the exposed rafters, where deep shadows lurked beneath the corrugated aluminum roof. The hangar had been darkened to allow people to sleep, the only illumination provided by the lights shining through the windows of the elevated office spanning the width of the building. An undercurrent of whispered voices and soft crying hung in the air. The place smelled of gasoline and fuel oil. Try as she might, she couldn't make herself sleep. Something prevented her from doing so, a familiar nagging sensation, like an itch beneath her skin that she needed to find a way to scratch.

Ciara slid out from underneath the children who'd fallen asleep on top of her, stepped over the boys cocooned in sleeping bags on the floor, and parted the curtains just in time to see Banks follow a man in camouflage fatigues up the staircase at the end of the narrow walkway. Ciara hurried to catch up, blended into the shadows of the dark anteroom, and stared through the doorway into a brightly lit office stuffed with uniformed men and women, all crowded around a wall adorned with video monitors. The aura of fear radiating from them was palpable, causing the goosebumps to rise on the backs of her arms and scaring her worse than any of the images playing on the screens. They knew what they were going to have to do, just as she did.

A howling sound drew her eye to the window. A coyote sat on its haunches in the tall weeds behind the hangar, its eyes reflecting the moonlight. It howled again and vanished into the night.

Ciara walked straight to the reception desk in the corner. There was a legal pad sitting by the phone, in front of the computer, just as she'd known it would be. She grabbed it, plucked a pencil from the cup beside it, and hurried back to the cubicle where the other kids were sleeping.

Her spot on the narrow gurney had disappeared, so she found a little space on the bare concrete and leaned against the wall. There was barely enough light to see the lined yellow page, but it didn't matter. Everything went dark the moment she touched the sharpened graphite to the paper.

———

BANKS WATCHED the monitors with a growing sense of dread. How had everything fallen apart so quickly? That was the question etched on the faces of the men and women surrounding her, soldiers from the Air Force's 62nd Airlift Wing, the Army's I-Corps, and the National Guard's Western Air Defense Sector. Worst-case scenarios were being enacted everywhere she looked. Fighter jets screamed across the dark screens, city lights blurring behind them. Explosions overwhelmed the cameras, which struggled to rationalize the blinding flashes of missile strikes and the resultant scenes of bridges falling into Lake Union and Lake Washington, effectively cutting off Seattle from the land masses to the north and east. The same thing happened simultaneously down the coastline, where the Golden Gate and Bay Bridges fell, and across the country, as Manhattan was similarly isolated from the mainland.

A sensation of numbness settled over her as she descended the stairs to the maze of tentlike partitions. The lack of sleep over the past few days finally caught up with her, bringing with it a soul-deep exhaustion that threatened to overwhelm her before she even reached her room. She drew back the curtain and found kids lying everywhere, on the gurneys that served as beds and in sleeping bags on the floor. There was even a little girl curled up like a cat in the lone chair.

Banks took a moment to make sure that each and every one of them looked comfortable enough, watching their chests rise and fall and listening to the whispering sounds of their exhalations passing their lips. There was no mistaking the enormity of the responsibility she'd willingly accepted, and yet she felt strangely comforted by it, as though perhaps she needed these kids as much as they needed her.

She leaned against the back wall and slid to the ground beside Ciara in one of the few gaps between sleeping bodies large enough to accommodate her. The young girl had fallen asleep sitting up, her forehead resting against her knees. Banks eased Ciara to the ground so she wouldn't wake up with a crick in her neck, a pad of paper falling from between her thighs and her chest in the process. The girl had folded back the top few pages and drawn a picture on the first blank one.

Banks quickly looked away when she recognized the subject.

Ciara whimpered and rolled over, wrapping her arm around Banks, who watched the young girl sleep, stroking her hair and wishing she could take those horrible images from her mind. She thought about the drawings of The

Executioner's victims and the one of Hannah Serviess, who'd been spared the fate that Ciara had imagined, proving that the young girl's visions weren't carved in stone.

Banks tore off the page, folded it up, and slid it into her back pocket, careful not to wake the sleeping girl. Hopefully Ciara didn't remember drawing this one any more than she did the others. With any luck, she'd just finished it and fallen asleep without getting a better look at it than Banks had.

After all, there were some things that one simply didn't want to know.

Banks had seen her own face. That was more than enough.

The last thing in the world she wanted to know was how she died.

37

The old man's words were still ringing in Milana's ears when her cellphone's battery died and the flashlight extinguished.

Only next time you won't recognize me until I'm bathing in your blood!

Her heart was pounding so hard she could feel it in her throat. The walls seemed to narrow with every step, as though she were being swallowed by a giant python. The ground, which had only minutes prior been level enough that she hadn't felt the need to watch her footing, now conspired to trip her with every step she took, the rails willing her to stumble and fall. It was so dark she couldn't tell if her eyes were open or closed and she was certain she heard the squeaking of rats at the very edge of hearing range, stalking her.

She felt the weight of a hundred and fifty vertical feet of bedrock and water, suffocating her in the darkness. The desire to run was unbearable, an instinctive response to terror as real as any she'd ever experienced. There could be someone standing mere inches away from her, just waiting for the right moment to move in for the kill, her heavy breathing and echoing footsteps masking his stealthy approach. She needed to get out of here, get out of this infernal—

The tunnel brightened ahead of her, so subtly that at first she hadn't noticed it. Slowly, the arched contours of the walls and faint reflections from the twin tracks materialized from the darkness. She heard a faint rumbling sound and stopped dead in her tracks.

Milana held her breath and listened. The sound resolved into distant voices, too far away to make out what they were saying. They guided her the rest of the way to the station, where the columns lining the platform cast slanted shadows across the vacant tracks.

She crept closer, keeping to the wall, trying to get a good look so she could figure out what was going on. The voices originated from just around the corner. She risked a peek and was surprised to find the platform packed with people, none of whom spoke above a whisper. They stood with their backs to her, waiting for the train to arrive on the far track. Many wore nightgowns and cradled sleeping children to their chests. Others were older and appeared to have thrown on whatever clothes were within reach, including bathrobes and slippers. Still others wore camouflage fatigues with insignias on their breasts and sleeves.

There was something somber about the gathering, as though none of them wanted to discuss the reason they were all here so early in the morning or why a haze of smoke clung to the top of the staircase leading up into the terminal.

Milana waited until she was certain no one was looking before climbing onto the platform and merging into the crowd. An incoming train announced itself with a clatter and a squeal of brakes. She caught snippets of conversation, enough to piece together what was happening. These people had been awakened by family members in various branches of the military and civil service and told to get to the PATH terminal as quickly as possible for emergency evacuation. None of them had the slightest idea where they were going or what to expect when they got there. They were all frightened and nervous. And none of them had tickets.

She worked her way into the press of bodies, shouldered past people, and—

—*finds herself alone, snow falling from above as though she stands beneath the open sky. The flakes alighting on her shoulders and hair are the color of ashes. She rubs them between her fingertips, which she draws away greasy. Distant cries shatter the unnatural silence. She hears someone approaching, a dark form moving through the shadows, and knows she can't allow it to find her. Panic rises inside her and a scream builds behind her lips. She turns and—*

—secured a spot near the middle of the pack as the train rumbled to a stop. She waited for a woman with a toddler under one arm and a backpack slung over the other to board before helping an elderly woman roll her suitcase across the gap. People crowded past her and staked their claim to the seats and handrails. She caught a glimpse of a man climbing up onto the platform from the other track and running for the next car in line. He ducked through the closing doors and stood in the aisle, looking across the sea of faces first in his car, and then through the aligned windows between cars and into hers, as though searching for someone.

Milana felt an acute sense of unease wash over her and stepped out of sight, blending into the crowd. She grabbed a rail, held on as the train started to roll, and released a breath it felt like she'd been holding since she first crawled under the gate on the other side of the river.

EVERYONE HAD DISEMBARKED at Newark Penn Station, where they'd been herded onto another train bound for Liberty International Station and the Air Train that took them the rest of the way to the airport. Exhaustion had set in with a vengeance and Milana had allowed herself to be carried along as though in a dream. She tried not to think about her mother's lifeless body hanging halfway out of her bedroom window, Mrs. Lovato attacking her husband while he slept, or the old man in the tunnel, crawling with rats. Her entire world had gone to hell and there was nothing she could do about it. She couldn't even see five minutes into the future, let alone what she was supposed to do from here. At least she was safe, for the moment anyway.

The airport grounds had been lit up with freestanding lights on the runways and perimeter fences, and the spotlights of helicopters sweeping the surrounding highways and streams. There were soldiers and military vehicles everywhere. Emergency personnel took their temperatures, drew their blood, and provided them with surgical masks.

Milana had left the house without her ID and wasn't on their list of expected arrivals, but she'd been able to access her student account at NYU, which contained all of the information they could have ever wanted. There'd been lots of questions about how she'd come to be here, and she'd answered them truthfully. She'd omitted the parts about her visions and her grandmother's dying words, as she figured it was better to be viewed as an opportunist than a nutjob, especially considering they were discreetly separating those exhibiting symptoms from the crowd and loading them onto buses bound for the hotel at the heart of the roundabout, beneath the air traffic control tower.

She ended up in Terminal B with hundreds of other people, although there wasn't a familiar face among them. Not that she'd expected any with the entirety of her life having been lived in Manhattan, which was intermittently visible against the horizon through smoke flashing with the running lights of choppers. The diffuse glow of flames silhouetted the skyscrapers downtown.

All of the restaurants and stores were closed, and the gates were crowded. People huddled in the seats and curled up on the floor, either sleeping or staring at their phones or watching the TVs mounted to the ceiling. It'd been days since she'd last slept and with the adrenaline that had sustained her waning, all she wanted to do now was find a corner she could call her own, close her eyes, and escape this nightmare for just a few precious hours.

She propped herself against the wall, drew her legs to her chest, and closed her eyes.

" . . . *live footage of the civilian quarantine center in Federal Plaza, where flames can be seen through the windows of the upper floors . . . "*

Milana's eyes snapped open. A humming sound filled her head and drowned out the noise around her as she watched the live feed from a helicopter high above the plaza, imagery she'd seen yesterday through the window of a restaurant. She recognized the Jacob K. Javits Federal Building by its unique configuration of windows, despite the black smoke gushing from the higher levels, a haze of which had settled over the military trucks, emergency vehicles, semi-trailers, and FEMA RVs in Foley Square. The sandbag barricade surrounding them appeared to have fallen, flooding the street with figures flickering in the strobe of automatic gunfire.

She rose from the floor, her heart beating so loudly in her ears that she could hear nothing else, and walked over to the window overlooking the runways. She nudged her way right up against the glass beside a man wearing jeans and cowboy boots and stared across the distant Hudson toward the Manhattan skyline, where she could see the fire rising from the rooftop of the federal building like a flame from a struck match.

" . . . *believed to be several thousand people inside . . . "*

She thought of the men and women from the bus, fiery debris raining down on them, their hair catching fire, their skin blistering and beginning to burn. They were dead. All of them. She'd saved herself and left them to die. She felt the warmth of tears on her cheeks, heard herself crying as though from miles away, and collapsed to the floor.

Lucas knelt beside the woman and wrapped his arms around her. She grabbed fistfuls of the shirt on his back, her nails raking his skin.

"It's going to be all right," he whispered, but he knew that wasn't the case.

The Fourth World was ending and there was nothing anyone could do to stop it.

38

Santa Maria, California

Crawford tasted blood in his mouth, felt it dripping onto his thigh. He opened his eyes and immediately regretted it. The pain overwhelmed him. A car horn blared from somewhere far away. He raised his face from the steering wheel and the sound ceased, leaving behind the rumble of the engine. Blood dribbled from his broken nose onto the casing housing the airbag, which had failed to deploy, keeping his current run of luck intact. On the positive side, his headache had passed, or maybe just faded into the background behind the other pains, but at least when he looked out the cracked windshield, the world was no longer tilting from side to side.

A gentle breeze riffled the tall yellow weeds stretching away from the road into the valley, the movement like a golden wave rolling toward a stand of dwarf pine trees. He caught the reflection of moonlight from hundreds of tiny, polished spheres, which revealed themselves to be the eyes of so many ravens when their bodies took form from the shadows. He felt the weight of their stares. They were watching him. A glance in the opposite direction confirmed that the trees across the highway were burdened with them, too. As were the wires strung from the telephone poles.

One of the black birds alighted on the hood of his truck. Its talons clattered on the slick metal. He felt the sudden urge to shoo it away before it scratched the paint, but one look at the front end of his truck, crumpled against the hillside, and he burst out laughing.

The raven shrieked and flapped off into the weeds, where he could see it through the tall grass, perched upon what looked like a rock.

Crawford opened the door, unlatched his seatbelt, and fell to the ground, which was a lot farther down than he'd expected. His front tires were wedged in a narrow gully, canted at odd angles on the rocks lining it. His hand hurt like a mother when he pushed himself up, the skin on the back red and blistered. He headed around to the bed of his truck, but the only thing in there was a scattering of dirt and debris.

His briefcase was gone.

The lone raven in front of his truck made a grunting sound. He walked around the passenger side and headed toward it. The blades of grass shushed against his torn, bloodstained khakis. He felt a cold sentience behind the creature's eyes, summoning him like a moth to a flame.

"What do you have there?" he asked.

The bird waited until he was nearly upon it before shrieking and taking flight, its massive wings beating the air. It had been perched on top of his briefcase, which must have been thrown from the bed on impact.

Crawford picked it up, knocked off the dirt, and carried it back to his truck beneath the eyes of hundreds of ravens. He tossed it over the tailgate and turned in a full circle. There was no doubt in his mind that he had the full attention of each and every one of those carrion birds. If he looked half as bad as he suspected, they were probably just waiting for him to keel over so they could have their way with him. The image his mind conjured was like something out of a cartoon and struck him as hilarious. He laughed out loud, only this time he didn't laugh alone.

A chorus of grunting noises filled the night.

The ravens were in on the joke, too. Laughing with him, not at him. And it made him feel good.

He pumped his fist as he climbed back into the truck. The transmission went into reverse easily enough, but it sounded like the entire undercarriage ripped off when he started backing up. With a rattling sound, the engine shuddered and died.

Crawford didn't care in the slightest.

The world had taken its best shot at him — twice actually: first with the stroke and then with the car crash — and yet he was more than just standing. He felt better than he had in a long time. Broken nose and radiation-burned hand aside, anyway.

Whistling to himself, he grabbed his briefcase, climbed from the truck, and struck off toward the highway.

LETICIA ROLLED over onto her back and stretched her arms above her head. The nausea, the headache, the fever . . . all gone. She felt like her old self again. In fact, she felt somehow lighter, as though she hadn't noticed there'd been a weight on her chest until it was gone. She sat up and let her legs hang over the side of the bed, surrounded by the comforting scent of the man to whom it belonged. The room was only vaguely familiar to her, and yet she felt completely at home. Or perhaps it was merely the darkness that set her at ease.

Crack.

She stood and approached the window, already knowing what she would find. A raven perched on the sill, its feathers limned by the crimson glow of her Camry's taillights. Several more materialized from the night sky and alighted on the eaves of the porch, which rested on the roof of her car. Their eyes all fixed upon her.

It was time to go.

Bits of broken glass crunched underfoot as Leticia strode down the dark hallway and exited through the garage. A scream erupted from the house across the street, but she paid it no mind. For the first time in her life, she felt as though she knew exactly what she was doing and wasn't about to let anyone or anything slow her down.

The driver-side door of her car stood open, the interior light spilling onto the concrete porch. It took several attempts to close it, as the frame must have bent in the collision, but the engine still ran and, with a little finagling, she was able to jiggle the gear stick into reverse. She revved the engine a couple times for good measure and backed away from the porch, urging the ravens to flight. The roof slid down her windshield and across her hood with a screeching sound loud enough to wake the dead. She caught a glimpse of the overturned pineapple upside-down cake in her lone functional headlight before the rubble collapsed onto it. She'd have a little chat with Mr. Crawford about his casual disregard of her gift when she found him.

And, make no mistake, she would find him. The pull of destiny was almost more than she could bear.

Leticia backed over the curb and onto the road. Something underneath her car scraped on the asphalt as she weaved through the maze of residential streets. Houses with broken windows and open front doors passed in her peripheral vision, the occasional figure streaking through the shadows or emerging from the back alleys. A Lexus ran the red light on Johnson and nearly T-boned her Camry. She stopped in the middle of the intersection, her heart threatening to hammer straight through her ribcage.

Sirens wailed in the distance. She could have sworn she heard gunshots from off to her left, where the faint glow of emergency lights stained the horizon. Something was happening downtown. The last thing she wanted to do was run into the police, so she turned in the opposite direction and headed away from the city. If she hoped to find Mr. Crawford, she was going to have to find someplace to turn around, but there was an accident on westbound Orcutt and the wrecked cars had been abandoned right there in the middle of the road, forcing her to detour to the southeast, into the countryside.

The occasional raven watched her pass from its perch on the telephone wires running alongside the two-lane road. She took that as a sign she was heading in the right direction and just kept on going, passing vineyards and pastures, the city lights falling away in her rearview mirror. All was dark, save for the reflection of her headlight from the eyes of the otherwise invisible birds. She didn't encounter another vehicle until she entered the rolling hills above the town of Verde, although subsequent cars passed with increasing frequency as her course led her back toward the coast. By the time she reached Arroyo Grande, it had become obvious that whatever was happening out there wasn't confined to San Luis Obispo.

Taillights lined the 101 North toward Pismo Beach, beyond which helicopters streaked across the sky, heading straight toward distant Diablo. She could have sworn she saw chaos on the highway below — people climbing over the hoods of their cars and fighting on the shoulders — as she crossed the overpass and turned onto the southbound onramp. Ravens appeared in the treetops on either side of the road as fancy homesteads gave way to interminable grasslands. She didn't have the slightest idea where she was going and was on the verge of turning around when she saw the sign for Exit 175, Maricopa-Bakersfield, looming over the highway. There were so many ravens perched on top of it that she was surprised it didn't collapse beneath their weight.

They took to the air as she passed underneath it and descended the offramp. She watched them flock to the east, barely distinguishable from the night sky. A woman appeared as if from nowhere and struck the rear windshield, but Leticia paid her no mind as she passed below the highway and sped onto Highway 166. The ravens guided her higher into the mountains, around tighter and tighter turns, until she saw the scarlet glow of taillights off the side of the road.

She passed the abandoned truck without slowing and felt a growing sense of anticipation rise within her. More and more birds joined the flock, their shrieks growing louder with every passing mile until they abruptly descended onto the telephone wires on one side of the road and the bushes on the other. A silhouette materialized at the very edge of her headlight's reach, walking right down the middle of the lane. Her heart beat faster and faster as she approached. She slowed when she recognized the man.

Leticia rolled down the passenger-side window as she pulled up beside Mr. Crawford. He ducked his head and peeked into the dark vehicle. His face looked like it had been raked with a cheese grater, but his smile was unmistakable, as was the flutter in her stomach when he aimed it at her.

"Well, if it isn't my favorite Golden Bear," he said.

"Climb in, Mr. Crawford," Leticia said, her voice filled with a confidence she hadn't known she possessed.

"Call me Nick," he said.

"Nick," she whispered, savoring the taste of his name in her mouth.

Leticia reached across the console and pulled the handle on the door, which miraculously opened and flooded the interior with light.

"Where should we go?" Leticia asked.

Crawford smiled and settled back in his seat. The truth was that he simply didn't care. All that mattered was finding a place where he could hide out for a while, away from prying eyes, a place where he could set up a lab and harvest the residual plutonium from the briefcase in this wonderful woman's trunk and contemplate how best to utilize the end product of his life's work. If he rigged his homemade device to the reactors at Diablo just right, he could drop the entire coastline of California into the Pacific, crack it right off at the San Andreas Fault and wipe out every last one of the people who'd used, abused, and cast him aside when he'd needed them most. Or maybe there was a better way to use his talents. Who knew? With the world spread out before him, he could go anywhere and do anything he wanted.

Leticia's car idled in the middle of the road while they contemplated their destination. The decision seemed to be of monumental importance, a choice that required careful thought. Or maybe that was the problem. Too much thinking always seemed to get him into trouble.

The ravens erupted from their perches and swirled silently overhead.

"Perhaps we should let the birds decide," he finally said.

Leticia looked at him curiously for a moment, and then offered a smile that made his heart skip a beat.

The night filled with avian screams as the flock veered uphill, away from the ocean and into the mountains.

"East it is," he said.

And, together, they accelerated toward their destiny.

39

Riverton, Wyoming

Davis stared across the canyon toward the point where the helicopter had vanished, praying to hear the whupping of rotors from beneath the screaming wind. Every passing second brought him closer to facing the grim reality of the situation . . .

The chopper wasn't coming back.

What were they supposed to do now? He'd stuffed the satellite phone into the hood and now it was gone, along with the trial dose of the therapeutic and the technical details about the antibodies. All of that information was now in the hands of the man who'd massacred the staff and nearly killed them, too.

Riley squeezed his shoulder and spoke so quietly that he could barely hear her.

"We need to warn Hodges."

He nodded. She was right, but the last thing in the world he wanted to do was go back inside that charnel house.

They hurried through the underground structure and entered the subterranean facility. The scent of freshly spilled blood was overwhelming. Davis did his best not to look at any of the bodies for fear they would rob him of his resolve, like they had so many years ago, when the paramedic had wrapped him in a blanket and guided him out of the school, whispering for him to just keep his eyes focused straight ahead as he navigated the remains of his fallen classmates.

The door to Rankin's office was open. There had to be another phone or some other means of contacting the outside world in there. He found several more satellite phones on a charger in the conference room and returned to the office, where Riley had taken a seat at the desktop computer. There was a sticky note affixed to the monitor. Written in black marker was a number that started with the same 617 area code from which Hodges had called earlier. Maybe they'd finally caught a break.

Riley opened a live feed on a cable news network site. The light from the screen lent her face an ethereal glow.

"Oh my God," she gasped. "What are we supposed to do now?"

Davis glanced at the broadcast and felt as though the earth fell out from underneath him. He watched the madness unfold as he dialed the number on the satellite phone.

THE ARMY NATIONAL GUARD BLACK HAWK thundered through the canyon, heading east toward the distant flatlands, which appeared as intermittent slivers between the granite escarpments. Cullen could barely keep his eyes open against the raging wind, which shook the rescue basket on its cranelike armature as two men in camouflage fatigues hauled it through the open side door and into the chopper. The moment it was all the way inside, one of the men closed the door and rounded on him. His name tape identified him as Bradley. He wore tactical isolation gear with a full-face respirator mask, through which he had to shout to be heard.

"Tell me you have what we need."

Cullen figured whatever they wanted was among the items in the hood of the isolation suit. He grabbed it as he climbed out and handed it to the man, who rushed to one of the seats in the back, opened his laptop, and connected it to the tablet from inside the hood. Cullen took a seat across from him and donned the cans hanging from the headrest. He heard the voices of the pilots coordinating with someone on the ground, although it didn't sound as though they had any intention of landing, at least not anytime soon.

"Where are we going?" he asked, speaking into the attached microphone.

"Depends on what we find on this tablet," Bradley said. He glanced up and recoiled. "The hell happened to you?"

"The infected," Cullen said. "We barely got out of there alive."

The soldier nodded as though that were explanation enough.

Edgerton collapsed into the seat beside him, his face pale and expressionless, his eyes focused on something only he could see. He was obviously going into shock, but he wasn't the priority. The second soldier buckled him into his harness and took the seat beside his partner.

"This was in there, too," he said, holding up a vial of clear liquid.

"We have the therapeutic," Bradley said into the microphone he wore beneath his mask. "And it looks like this tablet contains everything else we need. Transmitting data now."

"You might have just saved us all," the second soldier said. He leaned across the aisle and clapped Cullen on the shoulder. "Why don't we see if there's something we can do about that eye?"

He grabbed the emergency first aid kit and took a seat on the other side of Cullen, who steeled himself against the impending sting of the topical antiseptic and the injection of a local anesthetic.

"So you're Davis?" Bradley said, as his partner scrubbed the dried blood from Cullen's eye.

"I'm Cullen." He inclined his chin toward Edgerton. "He's Davis."

"What happened to everyone else? We saw gunfire on our approach."

"We did what we had to do. You have no idea what these people are capable of doing once the virus takes hold."

"No idea? Hell, man. It's all over the news. Why do you think we're in such a hurry to get you there?"

"Get us where?"

"Cheyenne Mountain." Bradley closed his laptop and disconnected the tablet. "USNORTHCOM's transferring operational command to NORAD. We're taking this stuff you saved straight to the people who know what to do with it. I'm sure the President will want to personally thank you."

"We need verification that you retrieved everything of importance from inside the facility," the pilot said through the headset.

"As far as I know," Cullen said.

"And we need confirmation that there are no other survivors."

Cullen understood exactly what the pilot was saying. Events had spiraled out of control, and both NeXgen and the federal government needed to maintain plausible deniability, which meant erasing the evidence of everything that had transpired at Riverton.

He thought of Middleton and the kid who'd somehow mustered the courage to shoot him with the tranquilizer gun.

"No, sir," he said, suppressing a grin. "We're the only ones left."

"Confirmed," the pilot said. "Close the facility."

A fighter jet screamed past, so close that the wind of its passage made the chopper lurch. Cullen glanced through the window in time to see a flash of light in the distance, followed by a concussive explosion that made the air shiver. The entire face of the mountain collapsed behind them, swallowing Riverton whole.

He closed his eyes and allowed the faint hint of a smile to trace his lips. Everything was working out perfectly. There was no better place to end the world than where it began.

In the darkness beneath the earth.

A THUNDEROUS BOOM and the ground bucked violently. Riley fell from the chair and landed on her side, near where Davis had been driven to his knees. A section of the ceiling collapsed and smashed the computer.

"What was that?" he asked, pushing himself up from the floor.

"I don't know. It almost sounded like . . . " Her words trailed off as she realized what had happened. It had sounded like an explosion because that's exactly what it had been. "Oh, no."

She stumbled out into the hallway, where broken acoustic tiles and chunks of concrete and granite had fallen onto the bodies. A haze of dust hung in the air, one so thick she had to pull her scrub top over her mouth and nose to keep from coughing. Several of the wall panels had separated, revealing the cracked bedrock behind them. The door leading to the docks had buckled outward, the frame warped. She ducked through and ran toward the garage.

They never should have gone back into the facility. She should have known . . .

Riley burst from the outer door and into the cavernous substructure. Boulders had fallen from the earthen roof, cratering the asphalt where they'd landed. Pebbles rained from the cracks where they'd once been. A cloud of dust, stained red by the emergency lights, hung in the stagnant air, confirming her worst fears.

She ran up the ramp toward the guard shack, already knowing what she'd find. Carbon scoring blackened the walls, which still radiated the heat of the blast. The tunnel was completely sealed by what had to be a solid fifty feet of fallen rocks. A rumbling sensation passed through the earth, forcing her to retreat as even more of the ceiling collapsed, sending stones tumbling toward her.

"There has to be another way out!"

She ran back toward the underground facility, where she saw Davis through the dust, holding the satellite phone over his head, trying to get a better signal. The outgoing call crackled with static as it rang from the speaker.

"Hodges will answer," he said. "He'll find a way to get us out of here."

Riley detected the slightest movement of air and followed the gentle current across the cavern. A dark maw emerged from the dust. She stepped into the mouth of a manmade tunnel that extended well beyond her range of sight, the sound of the ringing phone echoing away from her into the depths of the mountain.

40

National Airborne Operations Center

Hodges held the ringing phone in his trembling hands. He couldn't bring himself to answer it. The caller ID identified the number as one of the satellite phones assigned to the Riverton biolab. The pilot of the evacuation chopper had confirmed there were no other survivors, so the President had ordered the lab to be sanitized, a decision Hodges had blessed with his silence. And now here was a call ringing through from a facility that was supposed to contain nothing more than dead bodies, a facility buried beneath thousands of tons of rock.

Time slowed around him. Frantic voices faded to a tinny hum. His blood made rushing sounds in his ears.

The woman seated across the aisle from him leaned against the window, her eyes closed and her face dripping with sweat, which soaked into her discolored surgical mask. A tear squeezed from between her lashes and rolled down her cheek.

He glanced at Bergstrom, who gestured toward one of the televisions at the front of the room, his lips framing words that dissociated into the chaos. Hodges could only stare at the sweeping aerial view of Boston Common on the screen. The helicopter capturing the live imagery banked out over the Charles River to get a clear shot of the flames rising from the rooftops of Back Bay. His home was concealed beneath the smoke. His wife and son . . .

Hodges rose on unsteady legs, the floor tilting underneath him.

"Severn?" Bergstrom said. His voice sounded as though it came from the bottom of a deep well. "Are you okay?"

Hodges couldn't breathe. Needed air. One thought cut through the dawning panic: He had to call his wife to make sure she was — *still alive* — all right. And he needed to do so right this very second.

He stumbled down the aisle and shouldered his way through the narrow corridor behind the conference room, from which he heard voices raised in frustration and desperation. They blamed him. Every single one of them. But that didn't matter anymore; all that mattered was getting through to his wife. He had to warn her that this virus was deadlier than he'd initially thought, and he needed to tell her that he loved her and that he was sorry, for all of the long hours and missed dinners, for choosing his work over his family, time and time again. And for this. More than anything, he needed her to know that was sorry for the role he'd played in killing them all.

The phone continued to ring in his hand. He pressed the button to connect and then immediately disconnected. He needed an open line to dial out, and he needed fingers that weren't shaking so badly he couldn't press the right blasted numbers. It took several tries, but finally the call rang through.

Hodges pressed his free hand to his opposite ear. Between the roar of the engines and the racket of voices, he couldn't hear a blasted thing. He pushed through the service station, startling the flight attendant, and rounded the corner. A spiral staircase led upward into what had once been the first-class section of the renovated aircraft, the ruckus diminishing with every step. He realized the call was no longer ringing.

"Sharon?" he said, sobbing aloud when her voice came through the earpiece.

He stepped into the main aisle. To his right was the cockpit; to his left, an aisle with seats and tables on one side and recessed bunks on the other, where the relief crew slept behind drawn curtains. It was a million times quieter up here than it was down below, despite the men seated at the tables barking orders into their headsets.

His wife said something, but he couldn't hear her well enough to make out her words.

"I just need you to listen, okay?" he said. "And do exactly as I tell you. Lock the doors and move whatever you can find in front of them. Couches, chairs, tables. Anything, as long as it's heavy. Wake up Henry and have him help you. Slide bookcases in front of windows. Lock yourselves in our bedroom — Stop talking. Please, Sharon. For the love of God, just this once, will you please listen to me? Call Steven and Ryan and make sure they do the same thing. Tell them not to leave their apartments under any circumstances."

Someone moaned from the back of the cabin.

Hodges glanced in that direction as a hand flopped out from beneath the curtain concealing the upper bunk in the second row and dangled over the aisle. One of the crewmembers rose from his seat and peered curiously up at where the relief pilot slept. The title stitched into his headrest identified him as the crew chief.

"You're going to hear a lot of stories about how all of this happened," Hodges said. "There'll be plenty of finger-pointing. I need you to remember that everything I've done — everything I've always done — has been for you and the kids. It might not always seem like it, but you guys are my world."

"Are you all right up there?" the crew chief called.

The curtains rustled in response and the hand vanished, leaving behind a crimson stain on the fabric.

"Please do as I ask, Sharon. Don't go anywhere and don't let anyone in the house. Stay inside. Keep safe. I'll catch up with you in a few days. The virus will run its course in seventy-two hours. All we have to do is wait it out—"

The relief pilot burst from behind the curtain. Tumbled to the floor. Sprung back up and sprinted down the aisle. The crew chief jumped aside at the last possible second, leaving no one standing between the charging man and Hodges, who turned and ran in the opposite direction, right as the cockpit door opened and the navigator emerged.

The man's eyes widened in surprise as Hodges slammed into him, driving him back through the open door and into the cockpit. They tumbled to the ground in a tangle of limbs, slid across the floor and hammered the back of the pilot's seat.

The phone fell from Hodges's hand and skittered beyond his reach. He could hear his wife screaming his name through the receiver.

"Close the door!" the co-pilot shouted.

The relief pilot shouldered through the door before the flight engineer could close it and lunged for the men trying to rise from the floor.

Hodges raised his arms and deflected the impact. The pilot screamed, and a rush of warmth flooded onto Hodges's face. He wiped the pilot's blood out of his eyes and tried to squirm out from under the relief pilot, but he couldn't gain traction on the navigator, who was pinned beneath him, simultaneously struggling to push him off. Hodges caught a glimpse of blood draining down the inside of the windshield and the co-pilot trying to wrestle the infected man away from the pilot, whose screams abruptly became a gurgle.

The co-pilot drew his sidearm and pressed it to the temple of the relief pilot, who ducked underneath the weapon and went straight for the co-pilot's throat.

A clap of gunfire and the side window shattered, sucking the pressurized air through the hole. Everything that wasn't physically bolted to the frame flew toward it.

Hodges reached underneath the dead pilot's seat for his phone. It slid away from him, trailing his wife's cries.

The relief pilot's fingers knotted into his hair. Wrenched his head back. He felt pain in his neck, a bib of wet heat on his chest.

Hodges saw flashing lights on the console, the ground rising too fast through the windshield—

41

Big Springs, Kansas

Sakeva finished the final symbol and dropped the brush into the empty bucket. The confrontation with *yee naaldlooshii* had rattled him. He'd barely found the courage to get out of the truck to paint the billboard beside the road and had found himself looking over his shoulder the entire time, especially when the ravens began wheeling overhead. They'd eventually settled into the cottonwoods, from which they'd watched him through cold black eyes. He feared he lacked the strength to stand against the darkness, which he could feel growing more powerful by the minute.

Bringing Billy had been a mistake. He'd exposed his great-grandson to forces beyond his comprehension and in doing so had invited danger into the boy's life. Billy should have been at home with his grandmother, but Sakeva feared that even Third Mesa wouldn't be saved from what was to come.

He heard a distant screaming sound and saw a light appear above the horizon, brighter than any of the stars fading into the coming dawn. As the shrill noise grew louder, small green and red lights separated from the blinding white glow.

Sakeva dropped the bucket and charged through the waist-high weeds toward the truck, where Billy waited with the engine running. The boy saw his great-grandfather coming and climbed from the driver's seat, his stare rising to the sky, where the scream of wind shear metamorphosed into the roar of turbines.

The airplane tossed the treetops and rocked the truck on its suspension as it crossed the highway, so low they could have reached up and touched it.

Sakeva barely managed to stay on his feet as he jumped over the ditch and climbed into the truck.

The plane vanished over the hill on the opposite side of the road and crashed with a flash of light and a thunderous boom that shook the earth and filled the heavens with dust and smoke. An orange glow stained the churning cloud as flames rose from the wreckage.

"Go!" Sakeva shouted.

"Did you see that?" Billy asked, pinning the gas.

"Focus on the road." Sakeva had seen it, all right, and he knew exactly what it was. "Take the next exit."

The truck raced up the offramp and crossed the overpass. The growing fire flickered through the trees as it spread into the surrounding grasslands, above which a black pall hung.

You will hear of a dwelling place in the heavens, above the earth, that shall fall with a great crash.

They sped toward the blaze, navigating the winding road until the asphalt gave way to gravel and the wreckage spread out before them. There was burning debris everywhere: seats and luggage, electrical components and body parts.

It will appear as a blue star.

The fuselage had broken apart on impact, leaving the tail standing over the dirt trench like a tombstone. Painted upon it was an Air Force roundel: a blue star bracketed by red, white, and blue bars.

Very soon after this, the ceremonies of my people will cease.

"The ninth sign," Sakeva said. "The Blue Star Kachina."

Billy pulled to the side of the road, right up against the barbed-wire fence. The heat radiating from the blaze was palpable, even inside the truck. Smoke gushed from the shattered windows of the cockpit, blackening the roof. Flames burned from the spilled fuel soaking into the harvested field.

Sirens wailed and helicopters whupped in the distance.

"There is nothing we can do for these people," Sakeva said.

Billy nodded, turned the truck around, and headed back toward the highway.

It was time to go home.

The Day of Purification was at hand.

AUTHOR'S NOTE

Flashback: July, 2019 . . .

I'm in New York City for ThrillerFest, so I meet my editor from St. Martin's Press for a drink at Pershing Square, across the street from Grand Central Station. He suggests that I write an apocalyptic story like Stephen King's *The Stand* or Robert McCammon's *Swan Song,* but as only I can write it (i.e., full of history, science, and violence). So I head home a few days later and get to work.

Now, an epic like that involves a ton of research and even more labor, especially if you're hoping to create something worthy of even being mentioned in the same breath as the aforementioned classics, so I invested everything I had into developing some fun characters and building a realistic doomsday virus. Everything was coming along just as I'd envisioned . . . and then COVID hit.

Needless to say, my editor didn't really think people would be in the mood to read about the end of the world while they were actively living it, so that left me with an orphaned, half-written book. I debated setting aside the work, but ultimately decided that I was simply having too much fun with this cast and in this world to walk away, so I doubled down instead and expanded the storyline.

You hold the end result in your hands. Or at least the first part of it. . .

I hope you enjoyed CONTAGION, Book One of the Viral Apocalypse Series, and take a chance on the sequels and some of the other books from my catalog, where you'll find more adventure, science, history, and nightmarish creatures.

ACKNOWLEDGMENTS

Special thanks to Alex Slater at Trident Media Group; Pete Wolverton; Jeff Strand; Joe Hempel; Andi and Kimmy; Jennie Levesque; Douglas Preston; James Rollins; Stephen King; Robert McCammon; Kim, Jovana, and Milo at Deranged Doctor Design; my family; and all of my loyal readers, without whom this book wouldn't exist.

ABOUT THE AUTHOR

MICHAEL McBRIDE was born in Colorado Springs, Colorado to an engineer and a teacher, who kindled his passions for science and history. He studied biology and creative writing at the University of Colorado and holds multiple advanced certifications in medical imaging. Before becoming a full-time author, he worked as an x-ray/CT/MRI technologist and clinical instructor. He lives in suburban Denver with his wife, kids, and a couple of crazy Labrador Retrievers.

and ministry pressures. These include a theology of work,[13] and a theology of vocation.[14] Both are essential areas for prayerful study of the Scriptures in the light of historical teaching. There is plenty of room for alternative ways of expressing the conclusions, and some may be more or less helpful for different settings. Nevertheless there is a long tradition in the church of giving due regard to theologies of work and vocation, and that needs to be done afresh for our present day.

A theme that has risen to prominence in secular and Christian circles recently is that of being human: anthropology. Christian writers have drawn to our attention the fact that underlying our problems with work and ministry lies a failure to appreciate what it truly means to be human. Some of the first modern Christian authors to do this were Ranald Macaulay and Jerram Barrs.[15] In their classic study *Christianity with a Human Face* they write, 'Humanness, being made in the image of God, is like a key which unlocks all the doors in the house of the Christian life.'[16]

Losing our grip on what it means to be a human certainly damages our theological view of work, and hinders a healthy sense of what it might mean to live out a vocation. In a very real sense those writers seeking to help us recover our humanity are aiming at a root of the malaise in the work and ministry environments. With reference to Christian ministers and his own experience, Zach Eswine counsels, 'Trying to be an exception to the human race encourages arrogance among most of us and burnout among many of us – the two invasive fruits of having to prove that we are not flawed, that we do not need Jesus the way our neighbours do.'[17]

---

13. Leland Ryken, *Work and Leisure in Christian Perspective* (Leicester: Inter-Varsity Press, 1987).

14. D. Schuurman, *Vocation: Discerning Our Callings in Life* (Grand Rapids: Eerdmans, 2004).

15. They were, as they would both admit, very indebted to Francis Schaeffer.

16. Ranald Macaulay and Jerram Barrs, *Christianity with a Human Face* (Leicester: Inter-Varsity Press, 1978), p. 28.

17. Z. Eswine, *Sensing Jesus: Life and Ministry as a Human Being* (Wheaton: Crossway, 2012), p. 22.

We cannot avoid the curse of the fall at work or in ministry. However, failure to live as if we are human beings – fallen creatures made in God's image – condemns us to multiplying the burdens of sin in our lives. Recovering our sense of being limited human beings is surely wise counsel to those who feel harried by the pressures of work.

Regaining a clear vision of what it means to be human cannot be done in isolation from getting to know God better. As Calvin realized, 'Nearly all the wisdom we possess, that is to say, true and sound wisdom, consists of two parts: the knowledge of God and of ourselves. But while joined by many bonds, which one precedes and brings forth the other is not easy to discern.'[18]

The most sure, indeed the only, way to recover a sense of what it means to be a human in the workplace is to develop a sense of who God is. Only by knowing God can we know what it means to be his image. Only in the process of humbling ourselves before his gracious glory can we accept we are limited creatures. As Eswine writes:

> We . . . need a dose of God's incommunicable attributes. These show how little of a resemblance to God we have. We are not infinite, everywhere at once, all-powerful, or all-knowing. We are not meant to try to be or expect this of others. And this is my concern. Forgetting our place as only human, we grasp for incommunicable attributes and try to make them our own as we live and minister with others. Our worldly and church cultures often applaud this and urge us on. You can be like God! This makes us prone, especially in ministry, to try to do what only God is meant to do. The paradox is this: only by surrender to our proper human place can we glorify and enjoy God the way we say we want to and the way he requires.[19]

There is no route of theological reflection more calculated to help us 'surrender to our proper human place' than that which takes

---

18. John Calvin, *Institutes of the Christian Religion*, tr. Ford Lewis Battles, ed. John T. McNeill, 2 vols. (Philadelphia: Westminster, 2001), 1.1.1.

19. Eswine, *Sensing Jesus*, p. 24.

seriously the Creator–creature distinction. When we understand that God is unlike us, that due to his simplicity he is perfect and infinite, we realize that we are limited creatures. If the church forgets the classical doctrine of God, it will forget with it the nature of humanity. The doctrines of God and humanity stand or fall together, for we are other than God, yet made in his image.

Religious freedoms

Secular nations are struggling to find ways to integrate waves of economic migration that bring challenges of finance, languages and community cohesion. Even the most ardent supporters of a policy of promoting multiculturalism admit a 'disillusionment and anxiety about multiculturalism'.[20] Evidence abounds that governments across the globe are struggling to know how to govern and legislate in a way that encourages communality, generosity and peace.

Christians have little cause to be smug when it comes to matters of community cohesion. Even looking at Christian groups such as churches and seminaries, we have a catalogue of failures to mourn. Bonhoeffer reflected on his experience of theological college:

> Those who love their dream of Christian community more than the Christian community itself become destroyers of that Christian community even though their personal intentions may be ever so honest, earnest, and sacrificial. God hates this wishful dreaming because it makes the dreamer proud and pretentious. Those who dream of this idealised community demand that it be fulfilled by God, by others and by themselves. They enter the community of Christians with their demands, set up their own law, and judge one another and even God accordingly . . . Whatever does not go their way, they call a failure.[21]

20. T. Modood, *Multiculturalism* (Hoboken, N.J.: Wiley, 2013), location 1891.
21. D. Bonhoeffer, *Life Together and Prayerbook of the Bible: Dietrich Bonhoeffer Works*, ed. G. Kelly, D. Bloesch and J. Burtness, 16 vols. (Minneapolis: Fortress, 2004), vol. 5, p. 36.

Not only in colleges but also in churches Bonhoeffer knew that loving community was often elusive. He warned:

> Pastors should not complain about their congregation, certainly never to other people, but also not to God. Congregations have not been entrusted to them in order that they should become accusers of their congregations before God and their fellow human beings.[22]

Given that both believers and non-believers find community so difficult to maintain, it is no surprise that there are tensions in public life between Christians and non-Christians. Roger Scruton expresses frustration at some of the developments in England that have contributed to this:

> English society is no longer explicitly Christian, and our Parliament is no longer sovereign. The unique position of the Church of England depended on the belief that England was an autonomous, largely Christian, nation, regulating its affairs through the Parliament of Westminster. Parliament was supposed to represent a united kingdom, in which due account would be taken of Scotland, Wales and Northern Ireland, but in which the English settlement would provide the central source of political authority. The Church of England depended on that settlement as it depended on the Crown. However, the English settlement has now disappeared . . . To single out Christianity for any kind of protection or preferential treatment is to offend the ruling ideology of 'non-discrimination'. Legislation expressive of Christian values is repeatedly condemned by the European Court of Human Rights . . . The new ideology is less ferocious than the sectarian religious that fought each other to a standstill in the seventeenth century. But it is just as determined to triumph. Christianity must be removed from the public sphere, and deprived of its historical privileges in the settlement of Europe. This is particularly evident when it comes to sexual relations. If you adopt a traditional Christian position with regard to homosexual unions, for example, then you must keep

---

22. Ibid., p. 37.

quiet about it, or lose all chance of advancement in the institutions of secular government.[23]

Commentators point out that in the majority of legal rulings that go against public expressions of religious convictions, the defendants are Christians. Various reasons are noted for this, including for example the fear of challenging other groups. However, one reason that is not often commented on is that, at least in Europe and the Americas, the relationship between Christianity and secular convictions is problematic due to the fact that historically it was Christianity itself that provided the framework within which community cohesion and disagreements were negotiated. The problem of how secular cultures can relate to Christian groups may have distinctive features depending on the historical particularities of the nation under consideration. Nevertheless the deep contribution Christianity made to the formation of Western sensibilities about ethical values, intergenerational duties, neighbourliness and intellectual endeavour means it is singled out as a special case of aberrance by the powers determined to impose their conception of equality and fraternity upon people. MacIntyre notes this link between Christian beliefs and communal judgment:

> The question of what it is in virtue of which a particular moral
> judgement is true or false has come to lack any clear answer. That this
> should be so is perfectly intelligible if the historical hypothesis which I
> have sketched is true: that moral judgements are linguistic survivals from
> the practices of classical theism which have lost the context provided by
> these practices.[24]

The classical doctrine of God provided humanity with a vision of an ultimate being who commended values consistent with his character. There were limits imposed on humanity by our creatureliness. There was a due respect for the order of society, which could

---

23. Roger Scruton, *Our Church: A Personal History of the Church of England* (London: Atlantic, 2012), pp. 188–189.

24. A. MacIntyre, *After Virtue* (London: Bloomsbury, 2013), p. 60.

not be inherently evil since there was an order to the trinitarian relationships within God's perfect being. The loss of belief in this perfect God not only cuts down a culture that has flourished in its soil; it drives people to rail against that which enabled their flourishing in the first place.

Underneath the modern unpicking of traditional community lurks a belief that everyone can, or should, possess the power within their own individual will to be whatever they want. This radical individualism instructs people that they are self-created. In terms of how people choose to live their lives and arrange their relationships, there may in the self-empowered, individualistic life be a shadow-like image of earlier Christian ways of living. Foucault predicted this:

> As the arts of living and the care of the self are refined, some precepts emerge that seem to be rather similar to those that will be formulated in the later moral systems. But one should not be misled by the analogy. These moral systems will define other modalities of the relation to self: a characterisation of the ethical substance based on finitude, the Fall, and evil; a mode of subjection in the form of obedience to a general law that is at the same time the will of a personal god; a type of work on oneself that implies a decipherment of the soul and a purificatory hermeneutic of the desires; and a mode of ethical fulfilment that tends toward self-renunciation. The code elements that concern the economy of pleasures, conjugal fidelity, and relations between men may well remain analogous, but they will derive from a profoundly altered ethics and from a different way of constituting oneself as the ethical subject of one's sexual behaviour.[25]

So today our culture may use words like 'faith', 'male', 'female', 'marriage', 'integrity', 'sorry' and 'humility', but each means something rather different in daily life than when the speakers were in touch with a classical vision of God.

The modern culture, which has been cut off from the vision of God that enabled its flourishing, has lost its ability to relate the one

---

25. Michel Foucault, *The Care of the Self: The History of Sexuality*, 3 vols. (London: Penguin, 1990), vol. 3, pp. 239–240.

to the many. We teeter between seemingly opposed poles of totalitarian conformity and radical individuality. Conformity is imposed sometimes by the force of unjust laws, sometimes by the legalized power of marketing. Radical individualism breaches the bonds of trust and sacrifice that make community possible; yet those who most loudly demand their individual freedoms are first to protest when others will not sacrifice their freedoms on the altar of values they oppose.

There are no easy solutions to the conundrum – human rights legislation has no more succeeded to manage unity in diversity than did the Spanish Inquisition. Gunton recognized this problem as the key challenge for society; one that could be resolved only in the context of God, who is one and many:

> Central dimensions of the thought and practice of antiquity and modernity share a common failure in conceiving and practising relationality. The many can find their true being and be understood only as they are related to each other and to the One, but the main streams of neither antiquity nor modernity have been able to conceive the patterns of relation adequately.[26]

Living together in community, with diversity as well as individuality is something that has eluded the greatest politicians and philosophers through history. The classical vision of God is a unique instance of unity in diversity, since the one God is three persons, each of whom is divine. People who know such a God, and take time to familiarize themselves with the traditions of reflection on him that form the classical theological heritage, are uniquely placed to foster creaturely communities that reflect something of his generosity, love, unity and diversity. There is no other instance of oneness and threeness so able to inspire love, sacrifice, trust and devotion to other people. Left merely to human resources, a society is doomed to frame legal and social relations in a manner that gnaws away at the very freedoms it claims to uphold. Such a culture loses its hold on not only God but also created reality. As Oliver O'Donovan writes:

---

26. Gunton, *One, the Three*, p. 37.

Secular social reality, we may say, is constantly subverted by a conspiracy of nature and grace. The community-building love that the Creator has set in all human hearts, and that makes even Hell a city, will always need redemptive love if it is to realise its own capacities. Secular community has no ground of its own on which it may simply exist apart. It is either opened up to its fulfilment in God's love, or it is shut down, as its purchase on reality drains relentlessly away.[27]

Mission

When Christians engage in mission, they seek to 'make disciples of all nations' (Matt. 28:19). When people become disciples of Jesus, they make the most fundamental and radical changes to their lives. To 'repent' (Matt. 4:17) means changing direction in life: reorienting one's values, desires and plans away from sinful ones, towards God's kingdom. Being 'baptized' (Matt. 28:19) draws people into the life of a local church, where they live as countercultural agents of grace in a world that Jesus warned would 'hate' (John 15:18) his followers.

There are features of our present culture that make helping people make such a radical shift, challenging. Our culture is resistant to people making major, life-altering changes, whenever these flow from convictions that do not conform to the majority view. At least two features of our societies contribute to this in no small measure. First, our generation is very apathetic about the possibilities of change generally. This is seen in low voting and involvement in political parties: the preference is now for low-commitment, single-issue movements. By definition these are utopian and irresponsible in that they refuse to examine the wider implications of their narrow demands. Research has shown that many people in Western societies have retreated in their interests to care only for a narrow circle of friends and family, while wider concerns such as future generations, people of a different class or those located elsewhere in the country are ignored. One study observed the following:

27. Oliver O'Donovan, *Common Objects of Love: Moral Reflection and the Shaping of Community* (Grand Rapids: Eerdmans, 2002), p. 24.

Citizens' circles of concern shrank when they spoke in public contexts . . . Broad political concerns surfaced and then mysteriously vanished behind very personal-sounding concerns: 'my house,' 'my children,' 'close to home.' . . . We need to understand how so many Americans manage to make the realm of politics seem irrelevant to so many everyday enterprises. We often assume that political activism requires an explanation, while inactivity is the normal state of affairs. But it can be as difficult to ignore a problem as to try and solve it; to curtail feelings of empathy as to extend them; to feel powerless and out of control as to exert an influence; to stop thinking as to think.[28]

Apathy is as common in Britain as America. Major political parties have so few members that they fear to release their membership numbers. David Willetts has detailed how the baby-boomer generation as a whole received immense wealth and advantages from the post-war generation, but is failing to pass that inherited wealth on to their children. He notes that the baby-boomer generation pride themselves on their great political achievements, wrought for the betterment of society. However, when these are examined more closely, it is found that they were actually rather partisan and self-interested:

The boomers' civil rights campaigns and cultural wars divided people by age and attitudes whereas the soldiers of the Second World War had fought on behalf of whole nations and united different generations. So the boomers' battles, however justified, were more destructive of social capital. Indeed, one of their deliberate aims was to open up institutions to greater diversity: they wanted less conformity and for institutions to be more porous. This made it easier to join them and also to leave, but at the price of generating less trust.[29]

---

28. N. Eliasoph, *Avoiding Politics: How Americans Produce Apathy in Everyday Life* (Cambridge: Cambridge University Press, 1998), p. 6.
29. David Willetts, *The Pinch: How the Baby Boomers Took Their Children's Future – and Why They Should Give It Back* (London: Atlantic, 2010), Kindle ed.

Even the activism of the boomer generation obscured a deep apathy about genuine engagement and change on a wide and deep scale. The real focus was a narrower, more inward one that made them resistant to anything that challenged their priorities.

In addition to apathy our culture finds it difficult to hear challenges to change values and priorities, because debate about matters of import is incessant and irresolvable. As our culture has privatized its values and interests it has lost any external authority and so finds it impossible to resolve disagreements. So Alasdair MacIntyre observed:

> The most striking feature of contemporary moral utterance is that so much of it is used to express disagreements; and the most striking feature of the debates in which these disagreements are expressed is their interminable character. I do not mean by this just that such debates go on and on – although they do – but also that they apparently can find no terminus. There seems to be no rational way of securing moral agreement in our culture.[30]

Having wearied of endless debates that seem to have profited little, many in our culture are reluctant to get drawn into discussion about matters that demand huge changes in belief and behaviour. People feel the pain of secularism's relational and cultural failures, but are fearful of trying something new. Such a contrary attitude is not new. Speaking of England just before the First World War, one historian noted, 'Perversely and illogically, the Edwardian citizen tended more and more to call in a new kind of secularism to cure the hell which secularism had made.'[31]

The cumulative effect of widespread apathy and the wreckage of failed programmes for human flourishing is that there is genuine fear and hostility to any group that urges people to change their beliefs on matters of fundamental importance. This most certainly is the case for followers of Christ, who call on people to repent and be baptized as disciples of Jesus.

---

30. MacIntyre, *After Virtue*, p. 6.
31. Roger Lloyd, *The Church of England 1900–1965* (London: SCM, 1966), pp. 143–144.

The church faces stiff opposition to its message of spiritual change, in a climate that is apathetic and weary. How can recovery of the classical doctrine of God help? At least three points may be made.

First, the vision of God in all his perfection and simplicity is one that fills us with awe at his power, wisdom and glory. This is great encouragement not to give up in seeking to share the message about his salvation we have heard. The God who strengthens and aids us is not just another political leader calling for change; he is not just a more powerful version of us. Being changed by God does not just involve following yet more practical life guidance – it is an encounter with the one true God who is radically different from anything else in all creation. Realizing how immense and perfect God is gives considerable fortitude and strength to those who feel intimidated by the vast challenge of mission today.

Secondly, we take encouragement from the fact that mission is, in the most basic sense, a work of God. God sends his people out, that he may do his work of gathering people through them. To be sure, Christians do real work and labour in mission, but it is empowered by the awareness that it is Jesus who builds his church (Matt. 16:18), and in mission we are 'struggling with all his energy that he powerfully works within' (Col. 1:29). When we recall that the God who is building his church is the simple, perfect, omnipotent God, we gain great confidence. When we remember that this perfect God is three persons with distinct roles and a shared love that is infinite, we can rest assured that his plans for mission are loving and kind. We can trust him.

Thirdly, Christians know that the one God, who is simple yet three persons, is an ultimate arbiter and reference point for resolving debates that are otherwise endless. We can share our culture's frustration with interminable debates, but point them to the God who made all things and therefore rises above our weaknesses to speak truth, clarity and peace into our world. We do not need to be apathetic, clinging to our little privatized world for fear it will be taken from us. The God who is there is perfectly loving. His plans for us are good. We do not have to work things out on our own, for the God who is infinite, omniscient and perfect has revealed to us all we need. Mission can proceed with joyful confidence so long as it is based on drawing people's attention to what God has said and done. That way lies an exit from the dead end our culture finds itself in.

No doubt mission in our day will be costly, and will involve many disappointments. Still we shall find ourselves sufficiently resourced if we stop putting our trust in programmes, human leaders, techniques and marketing, and instead re-envision ourselves with the classical doctrine of a God who is perfect and relational, one and many.

Church

Membership of a church is not optional for a Christian. Being a part of the family of people who meet to hear from God and encourage each other to follow Jesus is an essential part of living in God's kingdom.

Given the reality of cultural opposition to the God revealed in Scripture, it is no surprise that many would like to reframe being a Christian as a merely private activity, which can be kept relatively isolated from matters of politics, employment, family life and finances. However, 'Christian faith in the New Testament, though doubtless highly personal, was never merely private. Inevitably, the larger culture was going to be confronted – and this included the state.'[32] And yet even if the error of privatized religion is eschewed, there is much disagreement about what it means for Christians to be involved in a church that confronts the culture.

For many there is a focus on social transformation and cultural works that commend good things such as art, sport or music. For others there is an emphasis on works that express love and care for outsiders: perhaps the homeless, unwell, housebound or children. For many the emphasis falls on teaching and training Christians so that they can explain the Christian message to their friends, colleagues and family. All of these options naturally combine in

---

32. D. A. Carson, *Christ and Culture Revisited* (Nottingham: Apollos, 2008), p. 171.

various churches; rarely would any church have exclusively one stream of involvement. The picture is complicated by para-church organizations that may campaign, educate and promote various social programmes or single-issue agendas.

How might the classical doctrine of God help a church to be engaging with the world, when so many confusing alternative approaches are available?

First, the infinite creator God has decreed that the church be at the centre of his plans for the universe. Every local church is central to God's plans for the universe:

> Paul consistently refers to *the* church which meets in a particular place. Even when there are several gatherings in a single city (e.g. at Corinth) the individual assemblies are not understood as *part* of the church in that place, but as *one* of 'the churches' that meet there. This suggests that each of the various local churches are manifestations of that heavenly church, tangible expressions in time and space of what is heavenly and eternal.[33]

Weak and irrelevant it may appear, but 'through the church the manifold wisdom of God might now be made known to the rulers and authorities in the heavenly places' (Eph. 3:10). When we are thrilled by the immensity of God's power and knowledge, or are overwhelmed by the Spirit and Son's love for us, we should find that moves us to be excited about church. The 'church of God [was] obtained with his own blood' (Acts 20:28). How could we not be enthusiastic to be involved in something that is so precious to the infinite, perfect God of love? Learning what it means for God to be one and many should increase our love of the church.

Secondly, as the church worships God, teaches about him and helps people learn how to help each other know God better, people are formed spiritually. Church is the arena in which people are healed and restored from the ravages of Adam's sin. Church is the place where thieves learn to be generous (Eph. 4:28) and the liar

---

33. P. T. O' Brien, *Colossians and Philemon*, Word Biblical Commentary 44 (Waco: Word, 1982), p. 61 (italics original).

learns to speak truth (Eph. 4:24). The bitter person becomes kind (Eph. 4:31–32) and we all learn to 'walk in love' (Eph. 5:2). All of this happens as we have our creaturely desires refined and refocused on the infinite God who has loved and given himself for us. The church that preaches and shares the vision of God revealed in Scripture forms people into flourishing creatures able to help others become disciples. This has genuine, but limited, potential to impact a culture. We need to be both hopeful and realistic about cultural transformation. Confronting a culture that resists God may lead to transformation – it will certainly lead to suffering and rejection. The call to sober action, with due awareness of our creaturely limitations, is well captured by Josh Hordern:

> Local churches should be at the heart of building a trust which is subtle enough to support and critique governmental authority amidst the scepticism and alienation of the twenty-first-century West. Churches' fragile and patchy attempts to live a life worthy of this calling is no argument against the reality of the calling itself. Rather, the good news of Christ is a gracious summons to bear witness to the passing away of multiple political loyalties, occluded finally by the descent of the new Jerusalem, the city where God dwells in everlasting light as both king and temple.[34]

A focus on God as revealed in classical theology cannot but elevate people's views of him. This has a formative impact, shaping people into the kinds of people able to affirm and resist other powers, as and when appropriate.

Finally the classical vision of God grants such an exalted view of him and his ways, that we shall not make the mistake of thinking that our church involvement can ever be a kind of humanly managed strategy for achieving our plans. We keep the immensity of God's power and plans at the forefront of our thoughts. If this is done, we remember that God's plans for the church extend to the heavenly rulers and powers (Eph. 3:10). We cannot understand

---

34. J. Hordern, *Political Affections: Civic Participation and Moral Theology* (Oxford: Oxford University Press, 2012), p. 293.

how that is achieved, so a bit of creaturely humility is wise. Since God has such overarching plans to accomplish through his church, we engage in various ministries and enterprises, but entrust the outcomes and eternal significance to his knowing wisdom. We cannot possibly, with our limited powers, know what the result of any venture will be. What appeared to be a social-renovation programme might lead to immense evangelistic opportunity. What began as a door-knocking exercise to explain the message of Jesus might alert a church to financial needs that could be relieved. A ministry focused mainly on a political injustice related to health care might save the life of a person who goes on to teach the gospel to thousands. We do not know how God will use the ministries of our church, but we can be sure his plans are bigger than our strategies. Those who have begun to appreciate the immense love and power of God as outlined by the classical vision of the God who is one and many are content to heed his divine wisdom:

> Trust in the LORD with all your heart,
>   and do not lean on your own understanding.
> In all your ways acknowledge him,
>   and he will make straight your paths.
> Be not wise in your own eyes;
>   fear the LORD, and turn away from evil.
> (Prov. 3:5–7)

Those who have a high view of God have an appropriately humble view of their own strategies:

> Many are the plans in the mind of a man,
>   But it is the purpose of the LORD that will stand.
> (Prov. 19:21)

The classical doctrine of God humbles us, and liberates us to be involved in church in such a way that God transforms and uses us in his world. The precise details of this are in his hand, and beyond our control.

Meditation: God's power

O God, forgive me for trying to change the world, when it is me who must first be changed.

Give me a vast vision of yourself, such that I am changed into the creature you want me to be.

Help me to humble myself under your mighty hand.

May my discipleship not be in my strength, but by your mighty power.

Guide me to works of service that you have prepared for me to do, and give me the humility to accept the help of your church in doing them.

Help me to not concern myself with matters that are beyond me: may I leave the outcomes of my witness and ministry in your hands. Return to your world that you may fulfil, heal and restore all that remains incomplete and broken. At that point, may all see and wonder at the immense power and love that have brought all things to be as they are.

Amen.

CONCLUSION

Like all cultures, our generation struggles to relate unity and difference. Torn between the desire for relationships and independence,
we veer from one extreme to another. As Pascal Bruckner comments:

> There is a twofold will to embrace the world and to free ourselves from
> it: dependency devastates and humiliates us, but total independence
> distresses us just as much because it isolates us. On the one hand,
> we need communion, and on the other, self-affirmation, and modern
> consciousness, halfway between its dream of mastery and its dream
> of harmony, cannot choose between the two.[1]

The angst all sensitive people feel over what it means to live a flourishing life that is wisely related to self and others is a consequence
of having forgotten the God who is one and many. If God is the
most perfect being who can possibly be conceived to exist, then he

---

1. Pascal Bruckner, *Perpetual Euphoria: On the Duty to Be Happy*, tr.
S. Rendall (Princeton: Princeton University Press, 2011), p. 98.

must be as Scripture reveals him: perfect, simple and unchangeable. As Augustine reflected, 'God exists in the supreme sense, and the original sense, of the word. He is altogether unchangeable, and it is he who could say with full authority, "I am who I am."'[2]

When we are no longer animated by the vision of a God who is both perfect love and perfectly one, we are condemned to run after idols that can portray only caricatures of either extreme: uncommitted individualism or crushing conformity. The church is the community called to hold forth to a harassed world the good news that the perfect God exists, and has come to earth in Jesus Christ to die for us. The church makes this task all the more difficult if it forgets or ignores its heritage of classical theological reflection. Such doctrinal grammar enables us to proclaim faithfully all God has revealed of himself in Scripture, and drives us to admit in humility that the God who is there is far more than a slightly larger version of his creatures. God truly is God, and there is no other (Isa. 45:5).

---

2. Augustine, *De Doctrina Christiana*, tr. R. P. H. Green, Oxford Early Christian Texts (Oxford: Oxford University Press, 1995), 1.32.

BIBLIOGRAPHY

Angelici, R., *Richard of Saint Victor, On the Trinity: English Translation and Commentary* (Eugene: Cascade, 2011).

Anselm, *Monologion and Proslogion, with the Replies of Gaunilo and Anselm*, ed. T. Williams (Indianapolis: Hackett, 1996).

Aquinas, Thomas, *The Academic Sermons*, ed. C. P. Mark-Robin Hoogland, The Fathers of the Church, Mediaeval Continuation (Washington: Catholic University of America Press, 2010).

————, 'Commentary on the Gospel of John, Lecture 3', Magi Books, http://dhspriory.org/thomas/english/John3.htm (accessed 10 Nov. 2013).

————, *Scriptum Super Libros Sententiarum*, ed. S. E. Fretté and P. Maré, Opera Omnia, 57 vols. (Paris: Vivè, 1882–9), vols. 7–11.

————, *Summa Theologica*, 5 vols. (Notre Dame: Ave Maria, 1948).

Arendt, Hannah, *Love and Saint Augustine* (London: University of Chicago Press, 1996).

Augustine, *City of God*, ed. H. Bettenson and G. R. Evans (London: Penguin, 1984).

————, *The Confessions*, tr. Maria Boulding, ed. John Rotelle, The Works of Saint Augustine, a Translation for the 21st Century, 11 vols. (New York: New City, 1997), 1.1.

————, *The Confessions*, tr. R. S. Pine-Coffin (London: Penguin, 1961).

————, *De Doctrina Christiana*, tr. R. P. H. Green, Oxford Early Christian
     Texts (Oxford: Oxford University Press, 1995).

————, 'Enchiridion on Faith, Hope and Charity', in Boniface Ramsey
     (ed.), *On Christian Belief* (New York: New City, 1996), pp. 265–344.

————, 'Faith and the Creed', in Boniface Ramsey (ed.), *On Christian Belief*
     (New York: New City, 1996), pp. 151–176.

————, *Homilies on the First Epistle of John*, tr. Boniface Ramsey, ed. John
     Rotelle, 11 vols., The Works of Saint Augustine, a Translation for the
     21st Century (New York: New City, 2008), 3.14.

————, *Homilies on the Gospel of John 1–40*, tr. Edmund Hill, ed. Allan
     Fitzgerald, The Works of Saint Augustine, a Translation for the 21st
     Century (New York: New City, 2009), 3.12.

————, *Sermons*, tr. Edmund Hill, ed. John Rotelle, The Works of Saint
     Augustine, a Translation for the 21st Century, 11 vols. (New York: New
     City, 1991), 3.4.

————, *Teaching Christianity*, tr. Edmund Hill, ed. John Rotelle, The Works
     of Saint Augustine, a Translation for the 21st Century, 11 vols. (New
     York: New City, 1996), 1.11.

————, *The Trinity*, tr. Edmund Hill, ed. John Rotelle, The Works of Saint
     Augustine, a Translation for the 21st Century, 11 vols. (New York: New
     City, 1991), 1.5.

Ayres, L., 'Augustine on the Trinity', in Gilles Emery and Matthew Levering
     (eds.), *The Oxford Handbook of the Trinity* (Oxford: Oxford University
     Press, 2012), pp. 123–137.

Barnett, P., *Jesus and the Logic of History* (Leicester: Apollos, 1997).

Beeke, Joel, and Mark Jones, *A Puritan Theology: Doctrine for Life* (Grand
     Rapids: Reformation Heritage, 2012), Kindle ed.

Boethius, *The Consolation of Philosophy*, ed. V. E. Watts (London: Penguin,
     1969).

Bonhoeffer, D., *Life Together and Prayerbook of the Bible: Dietrich Bonhoeffer
     Works*, ed. G. Kelly, D. Bloesch and J. Burtness, 16 vols. (Minneapolis:
     Fortress, 2004), vol. 5.

The Book of Common Prayer (Cambridge: Cambridge University Press, 2005).

Borg, M., and N. T. Wright, *The Meaning of Jesus: Two Visions* (London: SPCK,
     1999).

Bradley, James, and Richard Muller, *Church History: An Introduction of Research,
     Reference Works, and Methods* (Grand Rapids: Eerdmans, 1995).

Brain, Peter, *Going the Distance: How to Stay Fit for a Lifetime of Ministry* (Kingsford: Matthias Media, 2004).

Bray, Gerald, *Creeds, Councils & Christ* (Leicester: Inter-Varsity Press, 1984).

———, 'Does God Have Feelings?', in Michael Jensen (ed.), *True Feelings: Perspectives on Emotions in Christian Life and Ministry* (Nottingham: Apollos, 2012), pp. 95–112.

———, *God Is Love: A Biblical and Systematic Theology* (Wheaton: Crossway, 2012).

———, *The Personal God: Is the Classical Understanding of God Tenable?* (Carlisle: Paternoster, 1998).

Brower, Jeffrey, 'Simplicity and Aseity', in T. P. Flint and M. Rea (eds.), *The Oxford Handbook of Philosophical Theology* (Oxford: Oxford University Press, 2009), pp. 105–128.

Brown, Peter, *Augustine of Hippo* (London: Faber & Faber, 2000).

Brown, Steve, *A Scandalous Freedom: The Radical Nature of the Gospel* (West Monroe, La.: Howard, 2004).

Bruckner, Pascal, *Perpetual Euphoria: On the Duty to Be Happy*, tr. S. Rendall (Princeton: Princeton University Press, 2011).

Burrell, D. B., *Aquinas: God and Action* (Chicago: University of Scranton Press, 2008).

Calvin, John, *Acts 14–28 & Romans*, Calvin's Commentaries, 22 vols. (Grand Rapids: Baker, 2005), vol. 19.

———, *Concerning the Eternal Predestination of God*, ed. J. K. S. Reid (Cambridge: James Clarke, 2000).

———, *Institutes of the Christian Religion*, tr. Ford Lewis Battles, ed. John T. McNeill, 2 vols. (Philadelphia: Westminster, 2001).

Carr, E. H., *What Is History?* (London: Penguin, 2008).

Carson, D. A., *Christ and Culture Revisited* (Nottingham: Apollos, 2008).

———, *The Difficult Doctrine of the Love of God* (Leicester: Inter-Varsity Press, 2000).

———, *How Long, O Lord? Reflections on Suffering and Evil* (Grand Rapids: Baker; Leicester: Inter-Varsity Press, 2006).

———, 'New Testament Theology', in R. Martin and P. Davids (eds.), *Dictionary of the Later New Testament & Its Developments: A Compendium of Contemporary Biblical Scholarship* (Downers Grove: InterVarsity Press; Leicester: Inter-Varsity Press, 1997), pp. 796–814.

Charnock, Stephen, *Discourses upon the Existence and Attributes of God* (London: T. Tegg, 1840).

Connerton, P., *How Societies Remember* (Cambridge: Cambridge University Press, 1989).

Craig, William Lane, *God, Time, and Eternity: The Coherence of Theism*, 2 vols. (Houten, Netherlands: Springer, 2001), vol. 2.

———, 'The Tensed Versus the Tenseless Theory of Time: A Watershed for the Conceptions of Divine Eternity', in Robin Le Poidevin (ed.), *Questions of Time and Tense* (Oxford: Oxford University Press, 1998), pp. 221–250.

Crisp, Oliver, 'Jonathan Edwards on Divine Simplicity', *Religious Studies* 39 (2003), pp. 23–41.

Dickson, John, *Humilitas: A Lost Key to Life, Love, and Leadership* (Grand Rapids: Zondervan, 2011).

Dodds, Michael, *The Unchanging God of Love: Thomas Aquinas and Contemporary Theology on Divine Immutability* (New York: Catholic University of America Press, 2008).

Dolezal, James, *God Without Parts: Divine Simplicity and the Metaphysics of God's Absoluteness* (Eugene: Wipf & Stock, 2011).

Edwards, Jonathan, *Scientific and Philosophical Writings*, Works of Jonathan Edwards, 26 vols. (New Haven: Yale University Press, 1980), vol. 6.

———, *Sermons and Discourses 1723–1729*, Works of Jonathan Edwards, 26 vols. (New Haven: Yale University Press, 1997), vol. 14.

———, *Sermons and Discourses 1734–1738*, Works of Jonathan Edwards, 26 vols. (New Haven: Yale University Press, 2001), vol. 19.

———, *Sermons and Discourses 1739–1742*, Works of Jonathan Edwards, 26 vols. (New Haven: Yale University Press, 2003), vol. 22.

———, *Writings on the Trinity, Grace, and Faith*, Works of Jonathan Edwards, 26 vols. (New Haven: Yale University Press, 2003), vol. 21.

Eliasoph, N., *Avoiding Politics: How Americans Produce Apathy in Everyday Life* (Cambridge: Cambridge University Press, 1998).

Eswine, Z., *Sensing Jesus: Life and Ministry as a Human Being* (Wheaton: Crossway, 2012).

Feiss, H., *On Love: A Selection of Works of Hugh, Adam, Achard, Richard, and Godfrey of St. Victor* (New York: New City, 2012).

Flint, T. P., and M. Rea (eds.), *The Oxford Handbook of Philosophical Theology* (Oxford: Oxford University Press, 2009).

Ford, David, *The Shape of Living: Spiritual Directions for Everyday Life* (Grand Rapids: Zondervan, 2002).

Foucault, Michel, *The Care of the Self: The History of Sexuality*, 3 vols. (London: Penguin, 1990), vol. 3.

Frame, John, *The Doctrine of God: A Theology of Lordship* (Phillipsburg: P. & R., 2002).

――――, *No Other God: A Response to Open Theism* (Phillipsburg: P. & R., 2001).

Gatiss, Lee, *For Us and for Our Salvation: 'Limited Atonement' in the Bible, Doctrine, History, and Ministry*, Latimer Studies 78 (London: Latimer, 2012).

Gibson, David, *Reading the Decree: Exegesis, Election and Christology in Calvin and Barth* (Edinburgh: T. & T. Clark, 2009).

Goldsworthy, G., *According to Plan* (Nottingham: Inter-Varsity Press, 1991).

Green, Bradley G., *Colin Gunton and the Failure of Augustine* (Eugene: Pickwick, 2011).

――――, 'Colin Gunton and the Theological Origin of Modernity', in Lincoln Harvey (ed.), *The Theology of Colin Gunton* (Edinburgh: T. & T. Clark, 2010), pp. 165–181.

Grudem, Wayne, *Systematic Theology: An Introduction to Biblical Doctrine* (Leicester: Inter-Varsity Press, 1994).

Gunton, Colin, *Act and Being: Towards a Theology of the Divine Attributes* (London: SCM, 2002).

――――, 'Historical and Systematic Theology', in Colin Gunton (ed.), *The Cambridge Companion to Christian Doctrine* (Cambridge: Cambridge University Press, 1997), pp. 3–20.

――――, *The One, the Three and the Many: God, Creation and the Culture of Modernity* (Cambridge: Cambridge University Press, 1993).

――――, *The Promise of Trinitarian Theology* (Edinburgh: T. & T. Clark, 1991).

Hafez, K., and A. Skinner, *The Myth of Media Globalization* (Oxford: Polity, 2007).

Helm, Paul, *Calvin: A Guide for the Perplexed* (London: T. & T. Clark, 2008).

――――, *Calvin and the Calvinists* (Edinburgh: Banner of Truth, 1982).

――――, 'Calvin, Indefinite Language, and Definite Atonement', in David Gibson and Jonathan Gibson (eds.), *From Heaven He Came and Sought Her: Definite Atonement in Historical, Biblical, Theological and Pastoral Perspective* (Wheaton: Crossway, 2013), pp. 97–120.

――――, *Eternal God: A Study of God Without Time*, 2nd ed. (Oxford: Oxford University Press, 2010).

――――, *The Providence of God* (Leicester: Inter-Varsity Press, 1993).

Heppe, Heinrich, *Reformed Dogmatics* (London: Wakeman, 2010).

Hodge, A. A., *The Confession of Faith* (Edinburgh: Banner of Truth, 1992).

Holmes, Stephen, 'The Attributes of God', in John Webster, Kathryn
    Tanner and Iain Torrance (eds.), *Oxford Handbook to Systematic Theology*
    (Oxford: Oxford University Press, 2007), pp. 54–71.

———, *The Holy Trinity* (Milton Keynes: Paternoster, 2012).

———, *Listening to the Past: The Place of Tradition in Theology* (Carlisle:
    Paternoster, 2002).

———, '"Something Much Too Plain to Say": Towards a Defence of the
    Doctrine of Divine Simplicity', in *Listening to the Past: The Place of Tradition
    in Theology* (Carlisle: Paternoster, 2002), pp. 50–67.

Hordern, J., *Political Affections: Civic Participation and Moral Theology* (Oxford:
    Oxford University Press, 2012).

Horrall, A., *Popular Culture in London 1890–1918: The Transformation of
    Entertainment* (Manchester: Manchester University Press, 2001).

Irenaeus, *Against Heresies* 2.13.3, http://www.newadvent.org/fathers/
    0103213.htm (accessed 10 Nov. 2013).

Jeanrond, W. G., *A Theology of Love* (London: Bloomsbury, 2010).

Kahneman, D., *Thinking, Fast and Slow* (London: Penguin, 2012).

Keller, Tim, *The Meaning of Marriage: Facing the Complexities of Commitment
    with the Wisdom of God* (London: Penguin, 2013).

Kendall, R. T., *Calvin and English Calvinism to 1649* (Eugene: Wipf & Stock,
    2011).

Lee, S. (ed.), *The Princeton Companion to Jonathan Edwards* (Princeton:
    Princeton University Press, 2005).

Leftow, Brian, 'Eternity', in C. Taliaferro, P. Draper and P. Quinn, *A
    Companion to Philosophy of Religion* (Oxford: Wiley, 2010), pp. 278–284.

Lewis, C. S., 'God in the Dock', in Lesley Walmsley (ed.), *Essay Collection and
    Other Short Pieces* (London: HarperCollins, 2000), pp. 33–37.

Lister, R., *God Is Impassible and Impassioned: Toward a Theology of Divine Emotion*
    (Wheaton: Crossway; Nottingham: Apollos, 2012).

Litton, E. A., *Introduction to Dogmatic Theology: On the Basis of the 39 Articles of
    the Church of England* (London: James Clarke, 1960).

Lloyd, Roger, *The Church of England 1900–1965* (London: SCM, 1966).

Luther, Martin, 'Heidelberg Disputation', in *Luther's Works*, 55 vols.
    (Philadelphia: Fortress, 1957), vol. 31, pp. 35–70.

———, *Luther's Works*, 55 vols. (St. Louis: Concordia, 1958), vol. 14.

Macaulay, Ranald, and Jerram Barrs, *Christianity with a Human Face* (Leicester:
    Inter-Varsity Press, 1978).

Machen, G., *The Virgin Birth of Christ* (London: James Clarke, 1958).

MacIntyre, A., *After Virtue* (London: Bloomsbury, 2013).

McNamara, M. A., *Friends and Friendship for Saint Augustine* (New York: Alba House, 1957).

Martin, R., and P. Davids, *Dictionary of the Later New Testament & Its Developments: A Compendium of Contemporary Biblical Scholarship* (Downers Grove: InterVarsity Press; Leicester: Inter-Varsity Press, 1997).

Martyr, Justin, *The First and Second Apologies of Justin Martyr*, tr. L. W. Barnard (Mahwah, N.J.: Paulist Press, 1997).

Mirrlees, T., *Global Entertainment Media: Between Cultural Imperialism and Cultural Globalization* (Abingdon: Routledge, 2013).

Modood, T., *Multiculturalism* (Hoboken, N.J.: Wiley, 2013).

Mohler, James A., *Late Have I Loved You: An Interpretation of Saint Augustine on Human and Divine Relationships* (New York: New City, 1991).

Moltmann, Jürgen, *The Trinity and the Kingdom of God: The Doctrine of God*, tr. M. Kohl (London: SCM, 1981).

Muller, Richard, *Post-Reformation Reformed Dogmatics*, 4 vols. (Grand Rapids: Baker, 2006).

Murray, A., *Humility and Absolute Surrender* (Peabody: Hendrickson, 2005).

Nazianzus, Gregory, *Select Orations*, ed. M. Vinson (Washington: Catholic University of America Press, 2010).

Nicholls, D., *One Day* (London: Hodder & Stoughton, 2009).

O'Brien, P. T., *Colossians and Philemon*, Word Biblical Commentary 44 (Waco: Word, 1982).

O'Donovan, Oliver, *Common Objects of Love: Moral Reflection and the Shaping of Community* (Grand Rapids: Eerdmans, 2002).

———, *The Problem of Self-Love in St. Augustine* (New Haven: Yale University Press, 1980).

Offer, A., *The Challenge of Affluence: Self-Control and Well-Being in the United States and Britain Since 1950* (Oxford: Oxford University Press, 2006).

Olson, R., *Arminian Theology: Myths and Realities* (Downers Grove: InterVarsity Press, 2009).

Packer, J. I., *Evangelism and the Sovereignty of God* (London: Inter-Varsity Fellowship, 1966).

Phillips, J. B., *Your God Is Too Small* (London: Epworth, 1952).

Pieper, F., *Christian Dogmatics*, 4 vols. (St. Louis: Concordia, 1957).

Pink, Arthur, *The Attributes of God* (Grand Rapids: Baker, 1975).

Pinnock, Clark, *Most Moved Mover* (Grand Rapids: Baker Academic, 2001).

————— (ed.), *The Openness of God: A Biblical Challenge to the Traditional Understanding of God* (Downers Grove: InterVarsity Press, 1994).

Piper, John (ed.), *Beyond the Bounds: Open Theism and the Undermining of Biblical Christianity* (Wheaton: Crossway, 2003).

Postman, Neil, *Amusing Ourselves to Death: Public Discourse in the Age of Show Business* (London: Penguin, 1985).

Rice, R., *The Openness of God: The Relationship of Divine Foreknowledge and Human Free Will* (Hagerstown: Review & Herald, 1980).

Rogers, Katherin, *Perfect Being Theology* (Edinburgh: Edinburgh University Press, 2000).

Ryken, Leland, *Work and Leisure in Christian Perspective* (Leicester: Inter-Varsity Press, 1987).

Sanders, Fred, *Embracing the Trinity: Life with God in the Gospel* (Nottingham: Inter-Varsity Press, 2010).

—————, 'The Trinity', in John Webster, Kathryn Tanner and Iain Torrance (eds.), *Oxford Handbook to Systematic Theology* (Oxford: Oxford University Press, 2007), pp. 35–53.

Sarot, Marcel, 'Trinity and Church: Trinitarian Perspectives on the Identity of the Christian Community', *International Journal of Systematic Theology* 12.1 (2010), pp. 33–45.

Schuurman, D., *Vocation: Discerning Our Callings in Life* (Grand Rapids: Eerdmans, 2004).

Scruton, Roger, *Our Church: A Personal History of the Church of England* (London: Atlantic, 2012).

Shedd, W. G. T., *Dogmatic Theology*, 3 vols. (New York: Scribner, 1888), vol. 1.

Shults, F. LeRon, *Reforming the Doctrine of God* (Grand Rapids: Eerdmans, 2005).

Sigward, E. H. (ed.), *The Articles of Cornelius Van Til* (New York: Labels Army, 1997), electronic ed.

Sölle, Dorothee, *Thinking About God: An Introduction to Theology* (London: SCM, 1990).

Soskice, J., *Metaphor and Religious Language* (Oxford: Clarendon, 1987).

Stanglin, K., and T. McCall, *Jacob Arminius: Theologian of Grace* (New York: Oxford University Press, 2012).

Stewart, Kenneth, *Ten Myths About Calvinism: Recovering the Breadth of the Reformed Tradition* (Downers Grove: InterVarsity Press; Nottingham: Apollos, 2011).

Stott, John R. W., *Between Two Worlds: The Art of Preaching in the Twentieth Century* (Grand Rapids: Eerdmans, 1982).

———, *The Essential John Stott: The Cross of Christ & The Contemporary Christian* (Nottingham: Inter-Varsity Press, 1999).

Swinburne, R., *The Coherence of Theism* (Oxford: Clarendon, 1993).

Taliaferro, C., P. Draper and P. Quinn, *A Companion to Philosophy of Religion* (Oxford: Wiley, 2010).

Taylor, B., R. Johnston and W. Dyrness, *Entertainment Theology: New-Edge Spirituality in a Digital Democracy*, Cultural Exegesis (Grand Rapids: Baker Academic, 2008).

Taylor, Charles, *Sources of the Self: The Making of the Modern Identity* (Cambridge: Cambridge University Press, 1989).

Thielicke, Helmut, *The Evangelical Faith*, 3 vols. (Grand Rapids: Eerdmans, 1974), vol. 1.

Trueman, Carl, *The Creedal Imperative* (Wheaton: Crossway, 2012).

———, *Histories and Fallacies: Problems Faced in the Writing of History* (Wheaton: Crossway, 2010).

———, 'Reason and Rhetoric: Stephen Charnock on the Existence of God', in *Faith, History and Philosophy: Philosophical Essays for Paul Helm* (Aldershot: Ashgate, 2008), pp. 29–46.

Turretin, Francis, *Institutes of Elenctic Theology*, 3 vols. (Phillipsburg: P. & R., 1992), vol. 1.

Ussher, James, *A Body of Divinity* (London: Church Society, 2007).

Van Til, Cornelius, *A Christian Theory of Knowledge* (Phillipsburg: P. & R., 1969).

———, *Collected Articles and Reviews* (New York: Logos Electronic Edition).

———, *An Introduction to Systematic Theology* (Phillipsburg: P. & R., 2007).

Vos, Gerhard, 'The Scriptural Doctrine of the Love of God', *Presbyterian and Reformed Review* 49 (1902), pp. 1–37.

Walsh, J., *The Pursuit of Wisdom and Other Works*, Classics of Western Spirituality (Mahwah: Paulist Press, 1988).

Warfield, B. B., *Calvin and Augustine* (Philadelphia: P. & R., 1956).

Webster, John, 'Systematic Theology after Barth', in David Ford (ed.), *Modern Theologians* (Oxford: Blackwell, 2005), pp. 249–264.

Weinandy, Thomas G., *Does God Suffer?* (Edinburgh: T. & T. Clark, 2000).

Wells, David, *God in the Wasteland: The Reality of Truth in a World of Fading Dreams* (Leicester: Inter-Varsity Press; Grand Rapids: Eerdmans, 1995).

Wenham, John, *Christ and the Bible* (London: Tyndale, 1972).

Willard, Dallas, *The Renovation of the Heart* (Nottingham: Inter-Varsity Press, 2002).

Willetts, David, *The Pinch: How the Baby Boomers Took Their Children's Future – and Why They Should Give It Back* (London: Atlantic, 2010), Kindle ed.

Williams, Anna, 'What Is Systematic Theology?', *International Journal of Systematic Theology* 11.1 (2009), pp. 40–55.

Williams, Rowan, 'Sapientia and the Trinity: Reflections on the De Trinitate', in M. T. J. Van Bavel (ed.), *Collectanea Augustiniana* (Leuven: Leuven University Press, 1990), pp. 317–332.

———, *Tokens of Trust: An Introduction to Christian Belief* (London: Canterbury, 2007).

Wright, N. T., *The Challenge of Jesus* (London: SPCK, 2000).

———, *Jesus and the Victory of God* (London: SPCK, 2001).

———, *The Last Word: Scripture and the Authority of God: Getting Beyond the Bible Wars* (New York: HarperCollins, 2005).

———, *Simply Christian: Why Christianity Makes Sense* (London: HarperCollins, 2009).

Zahl, Paul, *Grace in Practice: A Theology of Everyday Life* (Grand Rapids: Eerdmans, 2007).

Zinn, G. A., *The Twelve Patriarchs; the Mystical Ark; Book Three of The Trinity*, Classics of Western Spirituality (Mahwah, N.J.: Paulist Press, 1979).

INDEX OF SCRIPTURE REFERENCES